The Thrills of 1924:
Dorothy Day Encounters the "Underworld Denizens" of New Orleans

Frontis-Jackson Square, overlooking the St. Louis Cathedral, New Orleans. From a photochrom postcard published by the Detroit Photographic Company (circa 1897-1924). Beinecke Rare Book and Manuscript Library, Yale University.

The Thrills of 1924:
Dorothy Day Encounters the "Underworld Denizens" of New Orleans

Robert P. Russo

EPIPHANY
PRESS
LTD

Epiphany Press, Ltd.
2019

First Printing: 2019

ISBN 978-0-692-13458-0

Library of Congress Control Number: 2018906587

Epiphany Press, Ltd.
1010 Valley Bluff Road, #9
Perrysburg, Ohio 43551

www.epiphanypressltd.wordpress.com
E-mail: epiphanypressltd@gmail.com

Dedication

This work is lovingly dedicated to my wife, Patricia M. Russo, who introduced me to Dorothy Day, in her own way, many years ago.

Thank you. Without your support and patience, I would have never achieved my dream.

Contents

ACKNOWLEDGEMENTS

The author would like to thank the following individuals for help on this and other works: Jim Allaire, Richard P. Becker, Sean C. Benjamin (Louisiana Research Collection-Tulane University), Germain J. Bienvenu (Louisiana State University Libraries), Sr. Nancy Brousseau, OP, Casey Cook, Elias Crim (Solidarity Hall), Robert B. Ellis, Robert Ellsberg, Emma Florio (The Newberry), Mark Giglio, Rev. Anthony Grasso, CSC (Kings's College), Pat Jordan, Anne Klejment, Mira E. Kohl (Tulane University), Jeffry Odell Korgen, Fr. Thomas Leyland, Br. Mickey O'Neill McGrath, OSFS, Sr. Brigid O'Shea Merriman (Lourdes University), Fr. Jack Podsiadlo, S.J., Lance B. Richey (University of Saint Francis), Rosalie G. Riegle, Phil Runkel (Raynor Memorial Libraries-Marquette University), Christopher M. Tkaczyk, and Derek R. Wood (Tulane University).

ILLUSTRATIONS

Cover and Frontis-Jackson Square, overlooking the St. Louis Cathedral, New Orleans. From a photochrom postcard published by the Detroit Photographic Company (circa 1897-1924). Beinecke Rare Book and Manuscript Library, Yale University.

Figure 1-Apartment rental advertisement, *The Times-Picayune*, November 28, 1923.

Figure 2-Map of New Orleans, from the *New Orleans Tourist Guide*, circa 1920s. Day and company lived on St. Peter Street, near the Spanish Cabildo and St. Louis Cathedral.

Figure 3-View in City Park, New Orleans, LA, circa 1920s.

Figure 4-Saint Roch Chapel Altar, 1920. Photograph courtesy of John Tibule Mendes.

Figure 5-Jerusalem Temple, A. A. O. N. M. S., New Orleans, LA, circa 1920s.

Figure 6-The new Roosevelt Hotel, fronting Baronne Street, near Canal and extending to University Place, New Orleans, LA, circa 1920s.

Figure 7-Eleonora Duse, *The Shreveport Times*, November 14, 1900.

Figure 8-Mrs. Henry Fuqua, *The New Orleans Item*, January 27, 1924.

Figure 9-The Fuqua family home on Napoleon Street, Baton Rouge, LA, *The New Orleans Item*, January 27, 1924.

Figure 10-Mrs. Walter M. Scott, *The New Orleans Item*, January 27, 1924.

Figure 11-Henry L. Fuqua, Jr., *The New Orleans Item*, January 27, 1924.

Figure 12-Henry L. Fuqua, *The New Orleans Item*, January 27, 1924.

Figure 13-Campanile, Louisiana State University, Baton Rouge, LA. Photograph by Francis Fuller, circa 1920s.

Figure 14-Kitchen, State Penitentiary at Baton Rouge, circa 1900. Henry L. Fuqua, Jr. Lytle Photograph Collection and Papers, Mss. 1898, Louisiana and Lower Mississippi Valley Collections, LSU Libraries, Baton Rouge, LA.

Figure 15-Inside view of hospital, Angola State Farm, circa 1900-1901. Henry L. Fuqua, Jr. Lytle Photograph Collection and Papers, Mss. 1898, Louisiana and Lower Mississippi Valley Collections, LSU Libraries, Baton Rouge, LA.

Figure 16-Bakery, State Penitentiary at Baton Rouge, circa 1900. Henry L. Fuqua, Jr. Lytle Photograph Collection and Papers, Mss. 1898, Louisiana and Lower Mississippi Valley Collections, LSU Libraries, Baton Rouge, LA.

Figure 17-Floor of the Arcadia Dance Hall, *The Times-Picayune*, August 13, 1922.

Figure 18-Arcadia Dance Hall, Dauphine and Canal Street, circa 1921. Gift of Buzzy Williams, June 18, 1980. Tulane University Digital Library.

Figure 19-"Doc" Kearns and Champion Jack Dempsey, photograph by William Sadlier, *The New Orleans Item*, February 11, 1924.

Figure 20-Morning Call cafe, French Market, New Orleans. Interior view, 1930s. Unnamed WPA photographer-Works Project Administration photograph.

Figure 21-City Park-New Orleans Race Track, circa 1913, *The Times-Picayune* archive.

Figure 22-"Religious goods store," where Day possibly purchased her manual of prayers. *The Times-Picayune*, December 16, 1923.

All images known to be in the public domain.

TIMELINE OF EVENTS

- December 3, 1923: Dorothy Day arrives in New Orleans with her sister, Della, and friend from Chicago, Mary Gordon; they rent a room for one night at the Y.W.C.A., at 929 Gravier Street.
- December 4, 1923: Day and company rent an apartment (two rooms and bath) in Jackson Square, at 520 St. Peter Street; their apartment overlooks the Spanish Cabildo and the St. Louis Cathedral.
- December 5, 1923 to March 18, 1924: During this span, Day is hired to write local pieces for *The New Orleans Item*; her articles, approximately forty-nine in number, are part of a column ("All Around New Orleans") written by an unnamed gentleman for the previous fifteen years. Sometime in the middle of January, Day is temporarily removed from the column when the man threatens to resign for unknown reasons; Day's articles are unsigned, and are sporadically published through the third week of March of 1924.
- December, 1923: Day is given a rosary as a Christmas gift from Mary Gordon. Day attends Benediction services at the Cathedral.
- January 2, 1924: Day visits the Arcadia (Burgundy Street) and Roseland (Canal Street) dance halls. She is hired as a taxi-dancer, but since it is the day after New Year's and business is slow, she officially starts the following evening. The results of this evening are published on February 3, 1924.
- January 3, 1924: Day describes in detail her first night of taxi-dancing at the Arcadia Dance Hall. She reports on the rampant usage of both alcohol (during Prohibition) and marijuana, and jealous encounters between the drunken men and the "steadies" of the dancers. Day also describes the jealousy encountered amongst her fellow flappers, who dislike any popular dancer. The results of this evening are published on February 4, 1924. A mention of a drunken sailor in the article is more than likely the cause of Day's upbraiding by naval representatives at the offices of *The New Orleans Item*, in early February of 1924.
- January 4, 1924: Day relates the events of her second evening of employment at the Arcadia, including the sordid details of being stranded at City Park at one-thirty in the morning by a dance hall patron who had offered her a ride home. The patron tried to ply Day with alcohol and marijuana; Day refused the man's advances, and was forced to walk an estimated four miles to reach her apartment. The results of this evening are published on February 5, 1924.
- January 5, 1924: On her third evening of employment, Day moves over to the Danceland. She describes the coarse sense of humor some of the taxi-dancers employ, the cheapness of the evening's patrons (referring to them as "pikers"), and the eccentricities of certain band members. The results of this evening are published on February 6, 1924.
- January 6, 1924: On her fourth evening as a taxi-dancer, Day moves over to the Roseland Dance Hall. Amidst a drastic drop in temperature, she describes the inane antics of a drunkard named Mert. The results of this evening are published on February 7, 1924.
- January 6, 1924: Day's first signed article, entitled "Here and There About New Orleans," is published in *The New Orleans Item* (P. 11, Special Edition).
- January 7, 1924: On Day's fifth evening of employment, she relates the harrowing tale told by a fellow taxi-dancer, who was chased down Royal Street by a woman brandishing a knife. The results of this evening are published on February 8, 1924.

- January 8, 1924: On her sixth evening of employment, Day relates the amorous designs some taxi-dancers have on their fellow females; lesbianism is hinted at, as an older female is constantly badgering a younger dancer as to her "living arrangements." The results of this evening are published on February 9, 1924.

- January 9, 1924: During her final night of employment at the three dance halls, Day relates the story of an unidentified taxi-dancer, who was so plied with liquor that she woke up in a strange room in a hotel on Baronne Street. The results of this final evening are published on February 10, 1924.

- January 13, 1924: Italian tragedienne Eleonora Duse arrives in New Orleans, for a week of rest, and to perform at the Jerusalem Temple. Duse stays in a suite on the sixth floor of the Roosevelt Hotel. Day unsuccessfully tries to interview Duse, but writes an article based on information from Duse's traveling companion, Katherine Onslow.

- January 15, 1924: Day's article, "Mme. Duse Here as Recluse; Even Sleuth Tactics Fail to Break Actress' Privacy" is published in *The New Orleans Item* (P. 17).

- After January 15, 1924: Day travels to Baton Rouge in order to interview the family of Henry L. Fuqua; three subsequent articles are published in *The New Orleans Item*.

- January 22, 1924: Eleonora Duse and company perform in Marco Praga's "La Porta Chiusa" at the Jerusalem Temple on St. Charles Avenue.

- January 27, 1924: Day's article, "Mrs. Fuqua Gives First Interview" is published in *The New Orleans Item* (Pp. 1, 3; Section 2).

- January 29, 1924: Day's article, "Henry Fuqua's Friends in Baton Rouge Recall Deeds of Life of Achievement" is published in *The New Orleans Item* (P. 4).

- January 31, 1924: Day's article, "Fuqua Liked by Convicts for Making Prison Comfortable as Possible" is published in *The New Orleans Item* (P. 14).

- February 3, 1924: Day's article, "Dance Hall Life of City is Revealed" is published in *The New Orleans Item* (Pp. 1-2).

- February 4, 1924: Day's article, "Dance Halls Flooded by Drink, Dope" is published in *The New Orleans Item* (Pp. 1, 3).

- February 5, 1924: Day's article, "Hangers-On Scramble to Gain Dance Hall Girls, Then Offer Them Whisky, Dope Smokes" is published in *The New Orleans Item* (Pp.1, 4).

- February 6, 1924: Day's article, "Danceland Girls Make Only 4 Cents But Manager Explains That it 'Isn't a Rough Joint'" is published in *The New Orleans Item* (Pp. 1, 4).

- February 7, 1924: Day's article, "Too Drunk to Dance, Some Swagger, Boast and Quarrel During Dance Hall Orgies" is published in *The New Orleans Item* (Pp. 1, 4).

- February 8, 1924: Day's article, "Woman With Knife Chases Dance Hall Girl Through Streets After Café Clash" is published in *The New Orleans Item* (Pp.1, 5).

- February 9, 1924: Day's article, "Girl Supplements Wages as Store Clerk by Work at Dance Hall at Night" is published in *The New Orleans Item* (P. 2).

- February 10, 1924: Day's article, "Dance Hall Girl Wakes Up in Strange Room After Night of Carousing in Cabarets" is published in *The New Orleans Item* (P. 1).

- February 10, 1924: Jack Dempsey arrives in New Orleans by train; Day briefly interviews Dempsey at Union Station; Dempsey playfully calls Day "Little Girl." Day's interview is published on February 11, 1924.

- February 11, 1924: Day's article, "Dempsey Scores Another Knockout When He Calls Dorothy Day 'Little Girl,'" is published in *The New Orleans Item* (P. 10).

- February 11, 1924: Heavyweight boxing champion Jack Dempsey boxes three, two-round exhibitions at the Coliseum Arena in New Orleans as part of an evening of sanctioned and unsanctioned contests. Day arrives late for the first contest and, as a result of not securing a program, inadvertently records the names of several boxers incorrectly.
- February 12, 1924: Day's article, "Boxers Seem Fine Fellows by Comparison After Sleek Sheiks Mincing at Cabarets" is published in *The New Orleans Item* (P. 10).
- February 24, 1924: Day's article, "Women Crowd Fashionable Gambling Halls" is published by *The New Orleans Item* (Pp. 1, 4). The article describes Day and a relative of Aaron Burr's review of the dice game better known as "craps."
- February 25, 1924: Day's article, "The Thrills of 1924" is published in *The New Orleans Item* (P. 5). The article describes Day's humorous attempt to "make a killing" while playing roulette.
- February 26, 1924: Day's article, "The Thrills of 1924" is published in *The New Orleans Item* (P. 13). The article is not about gambling, and is seemingly a leftover from Day's "All Around New Orleans" column.
- February 27, 1924: Day's article (unsigned), "The Thrills of 1924" is published in *The New Orleans Item* (P. 5). The article is not about gambling, and is seemingly a leftover from Day's "All Around New Orleans" column.
- February 28, 1924: Day's article (unsigned), "The Thrills of 1924" is published in *The New Orleans Item* (P. 12). The article explores the rise of "Women's Only" poker clubs in the New Orleans area.
- February 29, 1924: Day's article, "The Thrills of 1924" is published in *The New Orleans Item* (P. 3). The article exposes the segregation that women gamblers experienced in the horse racing industry.
- March 1, 1924: Day's final signed article, "The Thrills of 1924," is published in *The New Orleans Item* (P. 3). The article relates the harrowing details of how gambling addictions affect the health of women.
- Day's articles continue to be published in "All Around New Orleans." Her final article appears on March 18, 1924.
- Spring of 1924: Sometime during March or April of 1924, Day returns to New York in anticipation of the publishing of her first novel, *The Eleventh Virgin* (New York, NY: Albert and Charles Boni, 1924).

Introduction

On December 3, 1923, Dorothy Day, her younger sister Grace Delafield "Della" Day, and their friend Mary Gordon arrived in New Orleans from Chicago. The elder Day had varying reasons for leaving the Windy City behind. She was tired of northern winters, which had left her physically ill by springtime, and trying to avoid the consumption of alcohol, which she had sometimes used in order to keep warm. Day would later confide to her friend Llewellyn Jones, literary editor of the *Chicago Evening Post*, that "…I never needed much excuse when the liquor flowed free as it generally did in Chicago. Fortunately we know of no place to get it here and there is no one to drink with, so we never think of it."[1]

Day's notions that she could avoid cold winters, and the presence of alcohol in New Orleans were ironic, given that a record cold wave would permeate the area in early January of 1924, and Prohibition was rarely, if ever, enforced.

Having no connections in the Crescent City, the women decided to stay the night at the Y. W. C. A., which was then located at 929 Gravier Street. With very little money between them, the women decided to look for a two-bedroom apartment the next morning.[2]

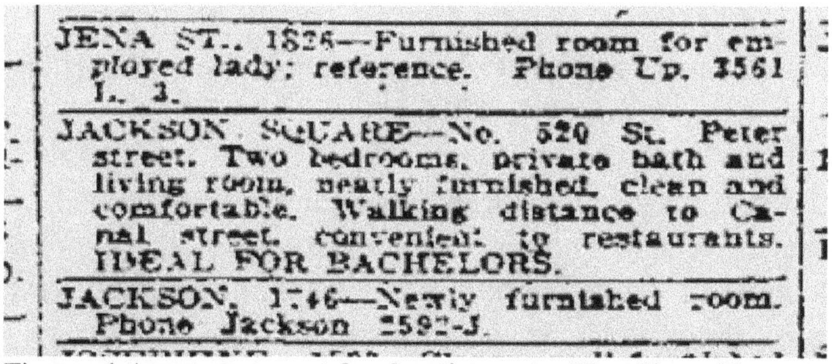
JENA ST., 1826—Furnished room for employed lady; reference. Phone Up. 3561 L. 3.

JACKSON SQUARE—No. 520 St. Peter street. Two bedrooms, private bath and living room, neatly furnished, clean and comfortable. Walking distance to Canal street, convenient to restaurants. IDEAL FOR BACHELORS.

JACKSON, 1746—Newly furnished room. Phone Jackson 2592-J.

Figure 1-Apartment rental advertisement, *The Times-Picayune*, November 28, 1923.

During the previous month, a rental advertisement had appeared in the pages of *The Times-Picayune*, which read as follows, "JACKSON SQUARE—No. 520 St. Peter street. Two bedrooms, private bath and living room, neatly furnished, clean and comfortable. Walking distance to Canal street, convenient to restaurants. IDEAL FOR BACHELORS."[3]

The three women found an apartment on December 4, after an all-day search. The apartment, which Day later described as "a large room with a balcony," was located in the French Quarter, overlooking the Spanish Cabildo, and St. Louis Cathedral.[4] She further explained to Jones that they were living in a house run by a French landlady, who had a daughter. Day had enjoyed reading French to the daughter, adding playfully that, "I'll learn lots from her."[5]

---

[1] Dorothy Day, "To Llewellyn Jones (undated, 1923)," in *All the Way to Heaven: The Selected Letters of Dorothy Day*, edited by Robert Ellsberg (New York, NY: Image Books, 2010), 5.

[2] Day, "To Llewellyn Jones (December 4, 1923)," in *All the Way to Heaven*, 4.

[3] The advertisement ran on three separate days, during the last week of November. See "Jackson Square," *The Times-Picayune*, November 28, 1923.

[4] Dorothy Day, *The Long Loneliness* (1952; repr., San Francisco, CA: Harper, 1997), 108. Day had affirmed that she had lived on St. Peter Street in numerous sources. See Dorothy Day, *From Union Square to Rome* (1938; repr., Maryknoll, NY: Orbis Books, 2006), 112; Dorothy Day, "About Mary," *Commonweal* 39, (November 5, 1943): 62-63.

[5] Day, "To Llewellyn Jones (undated, 1923)," in *All the Way to Heaven*, 5. The 1920 U.S. Census showed that an Elizabeth Thompson, a French woman who ran a boarding house, resided at 520 St. Peter Street. Her married

Money would soon become an issue for the women, as the rent for their apartment was eight dollars a week, and they had put down five of their combined seven dollars as a deposit. With only two dollars remaining, and no immediate job on the horizon, Day had had to borrow money from Jones in order to survive on fare other than bananas.[6]

After Day had received the much-needed funds from Jones, she described life in New Orleans in December of 1923:

> We weren't quite driven to bananas for the milkman delivers two quarts of milk a day and we had bought lots of rice and oranges—the latter ten cents a dozen. We had a gorgeous time this afternoon shopping in the French market along the wharves. It took the three of us to carry our purchases home—cabbage, potatoes, ground artichokes (did you ever taste them?), pounds of flour, and lard with which to make biscuits in the morning, and, most delectable of all—shrimps, which are fifteen cents a pound and huge and luscious. And the weather is perfect. We walked all afternoon exploring the docks dressed only in serge dresses, for no coats were necessary. The cold I had has disappeared entirely and I feel glorious.[7]

Mary Gordon soon found work selling women's apparel for fifteen dollars a week, plus commission.[8] Della, having been unable to find suitable employment, returned to New York within a few weeks of her arrival.[9]

Amidst the scramble for immediate employment, it is easy to imagine Day taking clippings of her previously published articles to various newspapers in New Orleans. She had done so earlier in her career, and landed a job on the Socialist *New York Call* in 1916.[10]

Day would soon encounter the "underworld denizens" of New Orleans—a phrase that she had derived from the literary works of Evangeline Booth and Thomas Burke. Many of these "denizens" were sadly addicted to vice—alcoholism, drugs, gambling, and sexual deviancy. New Orleans could be a tough city to live in, if one wanted to avoid succumbing to vice.

The goal of this work was twofold. On one hand, I wished to expand upon the context of Day's time in New Orleans. Although Day had mentioned New Orleans in her writings on several occasions, the events surrounding her three months in the Crescent City seemed like a mere footnote. I also briefly wished to show how dealing with the vice of the "underworld denizens" in New Orleans aided her, after her conversion to Catholicism in December of 1927.

The Thrills of 1924 contains seventy articles (twenty were signed by Day) from *The New Orleans Item*. *"All Around New Orleans"* contains an analysis of Day's unsigned articles, with

---

daughter's name was Rita Wilmuth. See "United States Census, 1920," database with images, *FamilySearch* (https://familysearch.org/ark:/61903/3:1:33S7-9R6P-F28?cc=1488411&wc=QZJP-1YZ%3A1036471301%2C1037714401%2C1037753001%2C1589332501 : 14 December 2015), Louisiana > Orleans > New Orleans Ward 5 > ED 76 > image 8 of 38; citing NARA microfilm publication T625 (Washington, D.C.: National Archives and Records Administration, n.d.).

[6] Day, "To Llewellyn Jones (December 4, 1923)," in *All the Way to Heaven*, 4.

[7] Day, "To Llewellyn Jones (Undated, 1923)," in *All the Way to Heaven*, 4-5.

[8] Ibid., 5.

[9] Day, "To Llewellyn Jones (January 2, 1924)," in *All the Way to Heaven*, 6.

[10] Dorothy Day, *The Eleventh Virgin* (1924; repr., Chicago, IL: The Cottager Press, 2011), 97.

ten separate indications that prove her authorship. *"Visiting Celebrities"* includes Day's articles relating to Italian tragedienne, Eleonora Duse, and interviews with the family of future Louisiana Governor Henry L. Fuqua. *Going Undercover in New Orleans* includes the fascinating, and oftentimes lurid, accounts of Day's exposé of vice found in three different dance halls. The section also includes an interview with heavyweight boxing champion, Jack Dempsey, and Day's coverage of his exhibition matches held in the Crescent City. Finally, *The Thrills of 1924* section contains Day's reporting upon the rampant rise of gambling undertaken by women.

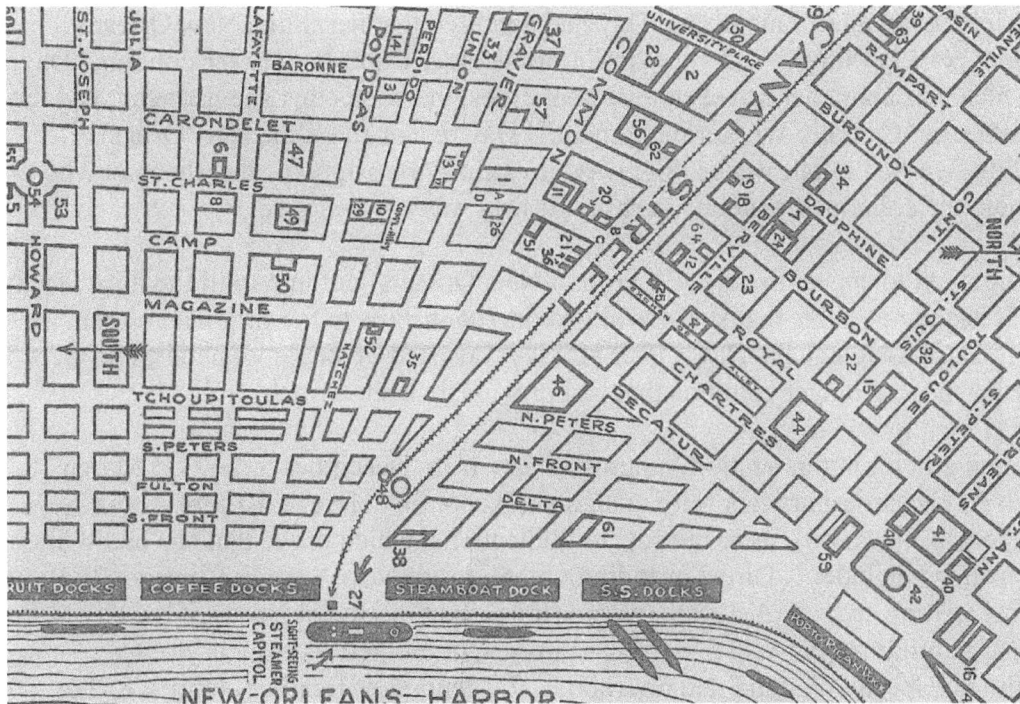

Figure 2-Map of New Orleans, from the *New Orleans Tourist Guide*, circa 1920s. Day and company lived on St. Peter Street, near the Spanish Cabildo and St. Louis Cathedral.

The Thrills of 1924: Dorothy Day Encounters the "Underworld Denizens" of New Orleans

"All Around New Orleans"

In early December of 1923, Dorothy Day had sought employment at the offices of *The New Orleans Item*. She was given work immediately, taking over a column that had been written by an unnamed man for the previous fifteen years.[11] The column, "All Around New Orleans," was published sporadically, several times a week, and consisted of observations of daily life in the Crescent City.

In a 1943 article for *Commonweal* magazine, Day had admitted that her initial New Orleans column was "about homely things," and very similar to her later *Catholic Worker* column, "Day After Day,"[12] which was about her travels to different cities, the books that she had read, and the struggles to maintain the Catholic Worker movement.[13] Day remained on the New Orleans column for roughly five-and-a-half weeks. She was temporarily reassigned when the man who had previously held the column, threatened to resign if Day was not removed.[14]

Day's articles continued to appear in the "All Around New Orleans" column until the third week of March 1924. It is quite possible that she was allowed to contribute to her original column while in-between major assignments. Day's later articles consisted of single vignettes, and were more than likely taken from longer columns that had previously been written.

There are forty-nine articles in this section, ranging in date from December 5, 1923 to March 18, 1924.[15] Although Day's earliest articles were unsigned (except for "Here and There About New Orleans," published on January 6), there are several indications, which prove that she had written them. These indications include: 1. Direct or indirect mentions of New York or Chicago, 2. A distinctly feminine writing style, 3. A degree of sarcasm against the social mores of the city, 4. The frequenting of familiar restaurants, 5. Familiar phrases, or themes, 6. Evidence of intermingling with diverse peoples and neighborhoods, 7. Mention of familiar authors, 8. The experiencing of new things, 9. A similar tone and writing style to later, signed New Orleans articles, and 10. Errata made by an author new to a particular city.

---

[11] Day had affirmed, "It was easy for me to find work in New Orleans," and one can imagine her immediately put into service. See Day, *The Long Loneliness*, 108. The man's name may have been Ashley Greene, as several articles in January 1924 were sub-titled, "WITH ASHLEY GREENE." See "All Around New Orleans," *The New Orleans Item*, January 16, 1924; "All Around New Orleans," *The New Orleans Item*, January 21, 1924.

[12] Strangely enough, *The New Orleans Item* also had a daily column entitled "Business Day by Day: In New Orleans As Seen by the Observer." Although this column was comprised of some observational anecdotes, it contained too much financial and statistical analysis to be considered as belonging to Day.

[13] Day, "About Mary," 62-63.

[14] Day, "To Llewellyn Jones (January 2, 1924)," in *All the Way to Heaven*, 6. Although Ellsberg dated Day's letter circa January 9, 1924, the actual date of composition was January 2, 1924. In the letter, Day had stated, "Tonight I try for this job, and if I don't get it at one place [dance hall] I will at one of the other two." Per Day's February 3, 1924 article, "Dance Hall Life of City is Revealed," her dance hall interview had occurred the evening after the New Year was celebrated.

[15] There was a definite break with the article of December 22, 1923 (not included in this volume), wherein the author had mentioned his wife on two separate occasions. It is possible that the original author of the column may have also served as Day's editor, and had filled in for her on this particular occasion. One indication that Day had an editor during this period concerned her usage of the word "cigaret," as opposed to the more conventional form, "cigarette." In the "All Around New Orleans" articles, the word "cigarette" appeared on fifteen occasions. However, over the span of Day's signed material, she used a form of the word on twenty-one occasions, nineteen as "cigaret," and two as "cigarette."

1. Direct or Indirect Mentions of New York or Chicago:

By the time that Day had settled in New Orleans at the end of 1923, she had traveled the country extensively, especially in terms of family relocations due to changes in her father's employment. The Day family had moved from Brooklyn, NY, to Berkeley, and then Oakland, CA. After the San Francisco earthquake of 1906, the family moved to Chicago, IL—living, on separate occasions, in both the north and south sides—and back to New York. As an adult, Day had traveled to Europe for nearly a year with her then-husband, Berkeley Tobey (circa 1920-1921); after the marriage had ended, Day resided in Chicago once again (circa 1921-1923).[16]

The articles contained numerous references to people and places, which could have only come from a "northerner." These included mentions of Northern emancipators ("Rights Respected," December 5), Broadway ("One-Armed Sentiment," December 6), and a sailor dressed "in clothes that would grace Fifth avenue" ("Neighborly," December 12). There was also a vignette about a visitor from Greenwich Village (who may have been Day herself), who felt robbed by the exorbitant prices charged at a tea room ("Villagitus," December 15), a response to the weather, called brisk, up north ("Cold Weather," December 17), and a mention of former New York Governor, William Sulzer ("Lafcadio Hearn," December 20).

Later articles included two references to Hobohemia ("Hobohemia," January 24; "Feelings Spared," January 30), which is a term used to describe the artistic or homeless people of a particular city. The vignette entitled "Exclusiveness Expensive" (March 5), included a reference to the Bowery.

2. Feminine Writing Style:

During the weeks that Day had contributed to the "All Around New Orleans" column, she had used a writing style that was distinctively feminine on several occasions. In other words, Day exhibited a verbiage that a male correspondent would not normally employ. In the anecdote entitled "What is the Moral?" (December 5), Day wrote about a "pretty little girl" who was feeding popcorn to the swans of City Park. In "The 'Mystery' Trunk" (December 12), Day described the contents of a case, which was left in an apartment (presumably her own) after the previous owner had died. She wrote that the old man's trunk contained "just baby clothes, locks of hair, letters, photographs, ribbons and a dozen and one of the little trinkets girls and boys carry in their purses and their pockets."

The vignette entitled "Femininity Survives" (December 14) is particularly interesting, not only for its feminine writing style, but also for its sarcasm. Here, Day mused:

> When "lady" ceases to mean anything except when allied with some descriptive adjective such as "cherub"—in other words when all women have thrown off the shackles of conventionality and taken their places in the business world with their sisters—already legion—what an awful world it will be.

---

[16] Day, *The Long Loneliness*, 18-20, 22, 94-95.

The Thrills of 1924: Dorothy Day Encounters the "Underworld Denizens" of New Orleans

The article on December 15 contained a vignette ("Tired") about a little girl, who stood in front of the Maison Blanche department store. She was enamored by a toy elephant, and refused the urgings of her mother to move along. Day had written that the defiant little girl claimed her legs were too tired. After her mother had offered to rub her legs, the girl refused, saying "'T'wouldn't do no dood. My legs is tired inside."

3. Sarcasm against Social Mores of the City:

Day had often employed sarcasm as a literary device. She did so, not to be malicious, but to shock her reading audience to a greater reality. On several occasions, Day had stated certain things about New Orleans that might seem offensive upon a cursory glance. As with other indications in this section, it is doubtful that a man who had been employed on a column for fifteen years would risk offending his reading audience.

In the vignette "'Ghost House'" (December 12), Day had described the decrepit conditions of the old United States mint building. She claimed that the desolate building was, "A lesson in waste; a damnably bad advertisement for government." In "Xmas" (December 19), Day described the competition of rival business owners, in the enticement of customers through Christmas decorations. After one owner had claimed that his display would make his rival's look sick, Day sarcastically stated, "That is the spirit of a lot of senseless giving." In "Ends at 'S'" (December 20), Day described the interaction between a librarian and a patron, in which the librarian admitted, with embarrassment, that certain volumes of a dictionary series were never purchased by the library. Day stated that New Orleans was, "not educated to the use of libraries and hasn't the facilities to be found in cities of the same size."

The untitled vignette of January 5 was also rife with sarcasm. The piece employed the contrast of a ragged former soldier, who stood in the cold outside of a restaurant, while the warm patrons inside stood in salute of the Star Spangled Banner. Day had exclaimed:

> Outside the poor, one-time soldier's head came erect with a proud snap, his shoulders straightened and the shuffling of his crippled foot stopped. For an instant, then, with the return of conscious thought, the head lowered, the shoulders sagged and the man limped dejectedly away from the lighted windows.

4. The Frequenting of Familiar Restaurants:

In one of her early articles ("One-Armed Sentiment," December 6), Day had stated that people from outside of New Orleans tended to visit restaurant chains that were familiar to them from their native cities ("…they yearn now and then for familiar surroundings"). She then mentioned Thompson's one-armed restaurant, which she would have frequented either in Chicago, or on Broadway in Manhattan. On December 13 ("Personality Has Value"), Day quoted a patron of Delmonico's on St. Charles Avenue, in New Orleans. Day would have also been familiar with the Delmonico's franchise in New York City, either on South William Street, or on Fifth Avenue and 44th Street. The article from January 1 ("A Visitor from Boston") also contained a mention of Childs' Restaurant, which Day would have frequented in Manhattan during her time as a reporter for the *New York Call* and *The Masses*.

5. Familiar Phrases or Themes:

Day had used similar phrases in several of the unsigned articles (e.g. "What is the moral," "oh, well," "passersby," "so-and-so," and "men of all…"). There were also recurring themes of romance (December 6, and 14), furniture stores (December 5, 14, 20, and January 2), observations from streetcars (December 5, 6, 12, and 24), and jewelry (December 6, 15, and 17).

The greatest indication that Day had written the forty-eight "All Around New Orleans" articles concerned two separate vignettes, which were published on December and March 18. The first piece (untitled, December 18) was eerily reminiscent to Day's "South Street," an article that had appeared in the November-December, 1917 issue of *The Masses*. In that earlier article, Day had stated:

> Then there is a tiny wave of laughter from one of the many ragged boys scurrying about the edges of things, as he succeeds in fishing out a bit of driftwood with a long stick. It's exciting,—fishing for driftwood. Little waves of imagination make the urchin's every sense more poignant. There's always the possibility of another fellow coming up behind him and pushing him into the thick water below. And there are wild chances of a bottle drifting in from the sea with a message in it from a shipwrecked crew or a submarine or something. And sunken treasure![17]

In *The New Orleans Item* article, Day described the pier off Elysian Fields Avenue: "Here, too, the kids can adventure, hunting around among the driftwood like beachcombers, for some sign of buried treasure, perhaps, or a bottle with a lost message in it." The common elements of children, driftwood, buried treasure, and a bottle with hidden messages are unmistakable.

In the second piece (untitled, March 18), Day wrote a vivid description of her landlady's African-American servant. She had remarked that:

> Early in the morning she is often seen coming from the river with a load of driftwood on her head, which she carefully hides in her room in order that her mistress may not get hold of it. Around her neck are a half-dozen necklaces made of safety pins, nails, bits of leather, rabbits' feet, teeth, wisps of hair and other strange twisted things. In her ears are twisted paper clips for earrings.

Day later used a similar description of the woman, identified as "Columbine," in an unpublished manuscript (circa 1940) held in the Dorothy Day-Catholic Worker archives at the Raynor Memorial Libraries of Marquette University (Dorothy Day, Dorothy Day Papers: Manuscripts, Ca. 1914-1977, Undated; Series D-3; Box 5, Folder 19).

6. Intermingling with Diverse Peoples and Neighborhoods:

Living in large cities, such as New York and Chicago, had allowed Day to experience peoples of diverse ethnic backgrounds. She had no difficulties in writing about people of color, and in New Orleans, she traveled through what would be considered African-American neighborhoods (e.g. South Rampart Street). Day's articles in *The New Orleans Item* contained several vignettes concerning African-Americans. Some of these articles had a social justice slant, which Day would become known for after her conversion to Catholicism.

---

[17] Dorothy Day, "South Street," *The Masses* 10 (November-December, 1917): 26.

In "Rights Respected" (December 5), Day sarcastically contrasted the empty seats on a trolley car, to the views society had of African-Americans in New Orleans. The message conveyed was that people of color were tolerated, as long as they remained invisible.

In "Diamond Teeth" (December 6), Day wrote of the former boxer, "Kid" Green, who had lost his teeth after a fight, and had them replaced with ones made of diamond-studded gold. The vignette also mentioned blues-jazz singer Ida Cox, whose songs Day had frequently mentioned in her early writings.

In "Diamonds and Old Shoes" (December 15), Day stated that people tended to borrow more money when the economy was good. She noted the irony found in the case of an African-American laborer, who was wearing old shoes, yet pawned a newer pair in order to purchase a keepsake. Day rightfully asked, once again, "What's the moral?"

7. Familiar Authors:

On several occasions, Day had mentioned authors and works that were familiar to her in her youth. In the December 12 article ("The 'Mystery' Trunk"), Day referenced characters from Robert Louis Stevenson's *Treasure Island* (i.e. Long John Silver and old Pew). On December 18 (untitled), she mentioned the prison escape found in Alexandre Dumas *pere's The Count of Monte Cristo*. Day had mentioned both of these authors in her semi-autobiographical novel, *The Eleventh Virgin*, which was completed shortly before her arrival in New Orleans.

In an untitled vignette from February 28, Day had compared an itinerant character in Lafayette Square to Sinbad the Sailor, whose tales were a late addition to *One Thousand and One Nights* (also known as *Arabian Nights*). Day had read this work when she was six-years-old.

In a most moving article regarding the potential suicide of a New Orleans artist (untitled, February 13), Day referenced Arthur Schopenhauer's essay, "On Suicide." Her description of the volume found in the man's apartment ("…little green leather book…"), identified it as the 1917 version of *Studies in Pessimism*, published by the same company (Boni and Liveright) that would issue Day's *The Eleventh Virgin* in the spring of 1924 (Albert and Charles Boni, who had bought Liveright's stake in the company). In Day's novel, she further mentioned reading Schopenhauer's essay, "On Women," which was also included in the 1917 work.

8. New Experiences:

In her article published on December 18 (untitled), Day mentioned visiting the French Market, and experiencing the "strange food for the first time." This mention is significant, because it is doubtful that a man, who had spent fifteen years working on a localized column, let alone his entire life, had never visited one of the biggest attractions that New Orleans had to offer.

9. Similar Tone and Writing Style to Signed Articles:

In addition to visiting familiar locations (i.e. The Roosevelt Hotel, City Park, the Maison Blanche building, the French Market, and the docks of the Mississippi River), Day had exhibited a similar writing style in both her signed and unsigned articles. Day had a habit during this period in her writing career, of beginning a paragraph with a two or three-word sentence, ending with an exclamation point. For example, in the "All Around New Orleans" articles, Day wrote, "Silent, Indeed!" ("Silent Partners," December 5), "'Hatchets!—Ha-a-a-tchets!'" (untitled, December 8), "'Crash!'" ("Names," December 15), "'A cigarette!'"; "'And a match!'"; "Adventures!" (untitled, December 18), and "Homesick!" (untitled, February 29). This pattern of writing was repeated in her signed articles: "And Dates!" (February 8), "The Thrills of 1924!" (February 24), and "But the musicians!" (February 26).[18]

There was also a marked similarity in the content of the "All Around New Orleans" article of December 14 (untitled), and "The Thrills of 1924" column of February 26. This included descriptions of soldiers and sailors from foreign ports (i.e. France, Italy, Spain, and Sweden), and the mention of romance. The "All Around New Orleans" article of January 2 ("Side Street Bargains") also contained a similar description of antique and furniture dealers: "Frenchmen, Germans, Italians, sometimes Americans."

The article of December 28 contained a short pantomime, or play ("The Prisoner of Sedan"), which was very similar in style to the beginning of the signed dance hall article of February 6 ("Danceland Girls Make Only 4 Cents…"). The resemblance of the two articles is even more remarkable when one considers that the signed piece was written on January 5, only a few days after the unsigned one had been published.

Day's first signed article was published on January 6. Consistent in content and style to her previous articles, the signed piece was even given a similar title, "Here and There About New Orleans."

Day's final major assignment for *The New Orleans Item*, "The Thrills of 1924," was written to expose the vast amount of gambling undertaken by the women of New Orleans, and its surrounding parishes. Curiously, the "Thrills" articles of February 26 – 27 were not about gambling, but were similar to her work on "All Around New Orleans." Each article had four or five vignettes of loosely related material. It is quite possible that Day had needed more time to research the gambling industry, and submitted unpublished articles that were originally intended for "All Around New Orleans."

Throughout her body of writings in New Orleans, Day had used several uncommon adverbs. For example, in the unsigned "All Around New Orleans" article of February 13, Day used the words

---

[18] Day had also done this earlier in her career. See Dorothy Day, "Girl Reporter, with Three Cents in Purse, Braves Night Court Lawyers," *New York Call*, November 11, 1916 ("Alas the 2 cents!"); Dorothy Day, "Nothing to Pawn But Her Body; Police Take That," *New York Call*, February 27, 1917 ("And the baby!"); Dorothy Day, "Mary, Mary, Quite Contrary," *The Masses* 9, no. 10 (August, 1917): 38 ("If she didn't—God help her!"). Day repeated this pattern of writing in her 1926 syndicated serial, "What Price Love." See Dorothy Day, "What Price Love," *Chicago Herald Examiner*, June 17, 1926 ("Heavens!"); Dorothy Day, "What Price Love," *Chicago Herald Examiner*, July 2, 1926 ("Silly!"); Dorothy Day, "What Price Love," *Chicago Herald Examiner*, July 17, 1926 ("Oh fudge!").

"brassily" and "lustily." Other uncommon adverbs included "cannily," "silkily," "sleepily," and "shabbily."

10. Errata Made by an Author New to a City:

Authors may sometimes make errors, in terms of names and addresses, when writing about a city that they have never before experienced. For example, in Day's first signed article on January 6, she mentioned a Rosa Pulissa who lived on Drive Street. This was more than likely Dryades Street, as there was no Drive Street in New Orleans.

There were also several examples of errata to be found in Day's "All Around New Orleans" articles. The article of December 24 ("The '400' in Shoedom") contained a vignette about rival shoe stores. Day had mentioned an S. J. Sepple, the manager of the South Rampart Street location of John C. Bright stores. The manager's name was actually Samuel J. Settles. Either Day had heard the wrong name, or her editor might not have been able to read her handwriting.

The article of December 31 ("From Newsboy Up and Back") contained a vignette in glowing praise of St. Bernard resident, Matt Reuter. The article lauded Reuter's many accomplishments, but failed to mention his 1920 arrest and imprisonment over a banking scheme known as "Monte." It is thought that Day had written the piece, unawares of Reuter's complete history. The man who had held the column for the previous fifteen years would have tempered the piece based upon previous knowledge of Reuter's legal issues—or perhaps not written it at all.

Day had used the word "sidewalk" on six different occasions. A reporter, who had lived in New Orleans for any length of time, would have known to use the more familiar term, "banquette." Day also misidentified the home of Jean and Pierre Lafitte as being in New Orleans ("Circumscribed," January 25; Evening Edition)—neither brother maintained a residence in the Crescent City, although they may have bartered slaves at a Bourbon Street blacksmith shop.

Why Day Was Possibly Removed:

One may wonder why the unnamed man, who had held the "All Around New Orleans" column for many years, threatened to resign from the newspaper unless Day was placed on a different assignment. Perhaps he was jealous of the number of articles that Day had published in *The New Orleans Item*, or he learned that she had written for Socialist newspapers and magazines, and did not agree with her politically. Secondary reasons may also be found in the list of indications proving that Day had written the articles, especially "Sarcasm Against the Social Mores of the City," and "Intermingling with Diverse Peoples and Neighborhoods."

As previously mentioned, the man may have been offended by Day's sarcasm. Perhaps he did not want to risk readership, or tarnishing the legacy he may have built during his decade-and-a-half on the column. Also, assuming the man was forty-years-old in 1924 (born, circa 1884), and had been a native of New Orleans, he may have had a father or grandfather who fought for the Confederacy during the Civil War. If that were the case, Day's willingness to mingle and write about diverse people of color may have caused the rift, and been a deciding factor in the man's demands to have Day removed from the column.

Silent Partners

The New Orleans Item
Wednesday; December 5, 1923 (P. 19)

All Around New Orleans

Unsigned

Silent Partners

Silent, indeed! Sometimes invisible, are the owners of some of the almost big stores of New Orleans. Shrewd business men, wedded to old methods, they have built up with the aid of their families the capital required to conduct big enterprises, and with the same shrewdness, have recognized that their methods are old fashioned, and unprofitable in this new industrial city. The owner of one big furniture house is never even seen there; he runs a little store, in the outskirts of the city, as he ran a similar store downtown fifty years ago. Nice looking young men, efficient salespeople, meet you, greet you, and sell you what they want you to buy; but the little old fellow who putters over dilapidated stock in the diminutive suburban shop comes in at the end of the week to count the cash and make-up the payrolls.

Rights Respected

Northern emancipators, who insist negroes are welcome in their restaurants, hotels and confectionery stores, then serve them quinine and charge them extortionate prices to prevent them coming again, may learn much in New Orleans.[19] The seats on the street cars are clearly marked, and the reservations for negroes are absolute. Even when the car is crowded, white people stand, while seats reserved for colored people are empty. Thus, there is consistency in the attitude which keeps members of the black race out of places where their presence is undesired.

---

[19] Quinine, although rarely fatal, was administered as a cure for yellow fever, or malaria. The insidious assumption here is that all people of color had yellow fever, and were liable to spread infectious disease. See "Things to Remember About Mosquitoes," *The Weekly Town Talk (Alexandria, LA)*, July 7, 1923.

In and Out

They tell this story around The Roosevelt.[20] Tuesday night, a prosperous appearing young man hired a large automobile and toured the boulevards and drives of New Orleans. He told the driver to return to The Roosevelt, and wait for him. The driver waited two hours. Finally, he went inside seeking information, and his money. "That fellow you drove is a little bit off," a friend told the driver. "Some of his friends took him out the other door about two hours ago."

What Is the Moral?[21]

Figure 3-View in City Park, New Orleans, LA, circa 1920s.

In City park a pretty little girl was feeding the black and white swans popcorn. Occasionally the greedy creatures clambered out of the water and frightened her so badly that she ran as fast as she could; and it was difficult to induce her to return. Swans are beautiful creatures, and no artist has ever been able to make a curve so graceful as their necks, in almost any position. Still, while they were squabbling over the little girl's popcorn, an awkward, dwarfish goose, with a short, thick neck swam up, pecked at two or three of them, and frightened them all away—but the little girl turned her back and ate the rest of her popcorn.

---

[20] The Roosevelt Hotel had been purchased from the owner of the Grunewald Hotel, and renamed in 1923. The Grunewald was established in 1893, at 123 Baronne Street.

[21] Day also asked the question, "What is the moral?" in a later article. See "Diamonds and Old Shoes," in "All Around New Orleans," *The New Orleans Item*, December 15, 1923.

The New Orleans Item
Thursday; December 6, 1923 (P. 26)

All Around New Orleans

Unsigned

Folks From Home

Everybody comes to New Orleans, or longs to come here. It is almost impossible to walk along a crowded street without observing a pair of united friends, one a resident, the other a visitor from the home town of both. "Just down to see the sights"—"On my honeymoon, old man,"—"Here a few days on business"—"I want to see the races"—"Say, where was that duel fought"[22]—"I'd like to meet some of these secret society fellows"[23]—"Let's go get some coffee"—wisps of conversation, clues to the universal attraction of the Metropolis of the South. New Orleans is the city of romance, the embodiment of sentiment. Not everybody comes to New Orleans; only those who love; those who are remembered. It is the mecca of those who yearn; the Venice of America.

---

[22] Many duels were fought near the "Dueling Oaks," located in City Park; only one oak tree remains there today. One of the more famous duels of New Orleans had occurred in January of 1804, when Robert Sterry shot Micajah Green Lewis to death. See *Historical Sketch Book and Guide to New Orleans and Environs* (New York, NY: Will H. Coleman, 1885), 181.

[23] New Orleans was rife with "secret societies" at the turn of the twentieth century. Many of them were harmless, and centered around control of Mardi Gras activities. These included such societies as Rex, Momus, Proteus, and Comus. The Order of the Mystic Shrine was another prevalent secret society, dedicated to the "respect for the Deity and love for humanity." This society established the Jerusalem Temple of New Orleans, where Italian tragedienne Eleonora Duse would later perform during her final tour in 1924. See "What Order of the Mystic Shrine is; Its History and What it Stands For," *The Times-Democrat (New Orleans, LA)*, April 10, 1910; "Silver Anniversary of Jerusalem Temple," *The Times-Democrat*, April 10, 1910; "South's Great City Fulfilling Its Destiny," *The Times-Democrat*, May 26, 1910; Dorothy Day, "Mme. Duse Here As Recluse; Even Sleuth Tactics Fail To Break Actress' Privacy," *The New Orleans Item*, January 14, 1924.

The Thrills of 1924: Dorothy Day Encounters the "Underworld Denizens" of New Orleans

Diamond Teeth

The "Rampart Street Blues"[24] floating from a Hawkins Music Shop[25] phonograph on the street of that name never sounds so in earnest, as when "Kid" Green, the pride of the colored fistiana, strolls past the door. Ida Cox, who sings the song, may have bells on her fingers and rings on her toes,[26] but she has nothing on the "Kid." He is noted as a tavern keeper, and, from his early years when he was a boxer, as a promoter and trainer of the world of pugilism.[27] He is known by his jeweled mouth. When his teeth were knocked out he secured new ones of gold, every one is 14-karat, guaranteed for twenty years, and in two front teeth are diamond studs. "Kid Green," by the way, is said to be almost as rich as he looks.

Seven Cents for Change

One of those merchandising experts who talks fluently about supply and demand ought to open a money-changing shop for the benefit of timid people. To thousands of every-day folks nothing is more embarrassing than to have to tender a ten or twenty-dollar bill in payment for a five to twenty-five-cent purchase. The clerks who are called upon to make change never feel so bad about it as many of those who ask it. On a Carondelet car the other day, a passenger tendered a five-dollar bill to the conductor, who glared at it and at the tenderer.

"I haven't change for that," he snapped. "Sit down and ride free. I ought to put you off."

"I am getting off at the next corner," the young man said, without the slightest confusion, "I didn't want a ride; I wanted change."

One-Armed Sentiment

One-armed restaurants, as they call those cafeterias where chairs are equipped with small table-arms, still are novelties in New Orleans, and it is noticeable that they draw their patronage largely from out-of-town people. Indeed, there, more than elsewhere in New Orleans, one rubs elbows with manners and characteristics of other cities of the United States. The reason is simple. Visitors have similar restaurants in their own cities; they yearn now and then for familiar surroundings. In Thompson's the other day, the consumer of a baked apple with cream payed his bill with a smile.[28]

---

[24] Day referred to the Lovie Austin song, "I've Got the Blues for Rampart Street," which was recorded by Ida Cox and Her Blues Serenaders, and released by Paramount Records (#12063) in November of 1923.

[25] The Music Shop was located at 600 South Rampart Street in New Orleans. See "'Carolina Mammy,'" *The Times-Picayune*, September 10, 1923.

[26] "Bells on her fingers…," is a reference to the 1784 English nursery rhyme "Ride a Cock Horse to Banbury Cross," the author of which is unknown.

[27] "Kid" Green operated a hotel for African-Americans at 538 South Rampart Street. See "Miscellaneous," *The Times-Picayune*, April 24, 1914. Green had also appeared in three boxing matches, with two losses and one disqualification. In January of 1917, he was involved in a street fight, wherein he was shot at twice, but otherwise unharmed. See "Orleans Man Jailed, Attempts Suicide," *The Town Talk (Alexandria, LA)*, January 4, 1917.

[28] Thompson's one-armed restaurant was located at 133 St. Charles Street, in New Orleans.

"Gosh, it was good," he said, "just like Broadway."

The Thrills of 1924: Dorothy Day Encounters the "Underworld Denizens" of New Orleans

The New Orleans Item
Saturday; December 8, 1923 (P. 9)

All Around New Orleans

Unsigned

Nine o'clock and a general alarm turned in at one of the Canal street fire boxes. Every fire engine in town, eight police trucks and thirteen taxicabs loaded with reporters hurrying to the locus. One of the clothing stores on a store-crowded block burning internally.[29]

Inside of five minutes after the first sirens interrupted professional entertainers everywhere, Canal street from sidewalk to sidewalk was spread over with zealous firebugs.[30] But no flames.

The crowding fire engines looked like a parade. From all sides poured firemen, hatted and gloved and spurred for the chase, their heavy slickers ballooning open as they ran, their boots swashing smartly with every step. Hundreds of them. It was better than a lodge meeting.

Five minutes more and the patent ladders were sprung open and fiercely attached to the building that had been decided upon. The front rank of firemen were already crowding the lower rungs, and the seconds were doing "down in front" hard at their heels.

---

[29] On the evening of Thursday, December 6, 1923, a fire caused heavy damage to the ironically named New York Waist Company. The business was located at 829 Canal Street, in New Orleans. See "Canal Street is Jammed during Fire in Studio," *The Times-Picayune*, December 7, 1923; "Stubborn Fire Does Big Loss in New Orleans," *The Shreveport Times*, December 8, 1923.

[30] Day used the word "sidewalk" on six different occasions. A true Orleanian would have used the more common term, "banquette." See "Invisible Clothes," in "All Around New Orleans," *The New Orleans Item*, January 3, 1924; "Warmth of Imagination," in "All Around New Orleans," *The New Orleans Item*, January 9, 1924; "The Lost Cake," in "All Around New Orleans," *The New Orleans Item*, January 31, 1924.

With what hurrah and circus the men scaled the walls! With what gusto they bawled to their maties below for hose and ladders and ropes and pulleys and pitch forks! But the crowd was dampened by the reticence of the fire. The great battle with smoke and flames was on, with the fire still quite incog[nito].

And then someone in the crowd discovered a wisp of smoke and a great cheer smote the night air, that these brave men had not left their beds in vain.

They themselves seemed to feel it, and the shouting and the ladder raising and the wall scaling and the rope shinnying doubled in fervor. One splendid man of action appeared as by magic on the very crest of the façade, where he stood, bravely outlined, like an arm-swinging weather-vane.

"They say they's a heap of magnesia stored on one of them floors," confided one of the spectators to the rest. "It'll sure be a heap a trouble if the fire gets to that!" The crowd vibrated to the thought, and many a silent prayer of encouragement to the weakly flames rose into the night air.

More stir on the ground, and the largest truck, the flower of the department, hurried importantly forward. Its huge round canvas case bore the words "Life Net." Again the crowd thrilled to the image of beautiful femininity in distress. They pictured the headless models that are wont to wear the endangered garments casting themselves in a frantic jostling procession from the upper windows into the ready net.[31]

"Let's stand back a little," suggested the gentle policeman from the Dumaine street beat. More firemen, more devices rushed up the ladder.

"Oh, Charley! Git me a small hook!" bawled the star on the crest, and all the way down the ladder could be heard the forceful echo—"Small hook!"

"Let's have another small line here," cried another figure, that appeared for a moment—and got stuck—in one of the small third-story windows.

"Hatchets!—Ha-a-a-tchets!" implored another, while the querelous voice from the top rank continued to cry for Charley's attendance with a small hook.

By this time two or three chemical lines were going beyond control, several larger water hose were out and at work, and in lieu of the conventional flames, the crowd was contenting itself with pictures of "what it must be going to look like inside tomorrow!" Crisp strokes of hatchets and sounds of Charley's friend visiously wielding the small hook sounded above the shouted pass words and the business of the meeting. But it was plain that the flames had been cowed and that the fire had nothing more to offer.

---

[31] The image of mannequins jumping to the street to avoid the fire makes more sense when one considers that the fire began in a clothing store (New York Waist Company).

The brothers were beginning to pile out of the windows and descend whence they had risen. The crowd sneered and straggled. They had come to see a finished performance, with all the incendiary properties, and all they had witnessed was a spirited dress rehearsal. They couldn't know that Fate had set the hour of the real production for three-thirty that same night, when a $500,000 building was to burn to the ground.[32]

---

[32] On December 7, 1923, a fire did extensive damage to the Newman building, which was located on Dryades and Gravier Streets. See "Newman Building is Burned; Loss Estimate is Placed at $500,000," *The Monroe News-Star (Monroe, LA)*, December 7, 1923.

The New Orleans Item
Wednesday; December 12, 1923 (P. 10)

All Around New Orleans

Unsigned

Neighborly

City folks become accustomed to strangers—they see so many of them, and often are not on speaking terms even with their neighbors. There are certain places, and occasions, though, when a sort of kinship protrudes itself into gatherings, makes them friends for a moment then disappears. A pleasant surprise awaits those who have never ridden on the City park trolley car. While it is waiting for patrons, or the whim of the operators, at the Canal street terminus, the conductor and motorman sprawl over the seats, and greet each new arrival with a warmth that has nothing to do with seven cents. A war veteran, his fearful experiences recalled by "Powder River,"[33] speaks entertainingly with the motorman who served in a home camp—a sailor in clothes that would grace Fifth avenue, tells how he got them by the customs collector—a little colored girl is informed regarding the destination of a big hat box in her hands—a traveling man adds a few remarks about commercial improvements in New Orleans—a newsboy hops on the car, grabs an iron bar from behind the door, gets out, pushes over the switch and takes his place on the platform. The motorman stretches himself leisurely, and starts the car. The conductor goes down the aisle and formally collects fares. The passengers settle themselves in their seats and turn their faces toward the windows. Bells ring, steel grates on steel, faces become stolid. The moment of leisure is past; acquaintanceships are abruptly broken. Strangers sit side by side.

---

[33] The "Powder River Expedition" occurred during the summer and fall of 1865. The U.S. Army, led by Brigadier General Patrick E. Connor, left Fort Laramie in Wyoming in August in order to drive the Arapaho, Cheyenne, and Sioux out of the Montana Territory. By the end of the expedition, an estimated 400-500 Native Americans were killed, as opposed to twenty-four U.S. Army casualties. See "Successful Indian Expedition," *The Daily Clarion (Meridian, MS)*, October 19, 1865.

The Thrills of 1924: Dorothy Day Encounters the "Underworld Denizens" of New Orleans

The "Mystery" Trunk

In an uptown rooming house, lived for a few months an old man. Friends of his better years sent him there. The owner of the house took a great interest in him and did what she could to make his last few weeks of life pleasant. Then he died. His children whom he had written, and wired, frantically, pleadingly, beseechingly to come to him in his infirmity, never came. They let him die among strangers. Then, afterward, someone's curiosity let him to examine a canvas bound, sole leather, trunk in the old man's room. It was sturdy and had seen long service. Everything about it suggested mystery—piracy, secret papers, buried treasure. Long John Silver and old Pew lurking near the house—only that was needed to complete the picture.[34] Inside the trunk, however, was little that was valuable—just baby clothes, locks of hair, letters, photographs, ribbons and a dozen and one of the little trinkets girls and boys carry in their purses and their pockets. These were the treasures of an old man who died among strangers.

"Ghost House"

The old United States mint building on Esplanade[35] to most people is not overly attractive for residential purposes but it meets the description of a "Quartier" inhabitant who was seeking rooms in the vicinity recently.[36] She said she wanted to live in a house with a ghost in it.[37] Those who yearn, not infrequently devise peculiar extravagances. Still, the old mint building has a certain fascination, which it is difficult to disregard. The walls are blackened and crumbling; dark windows stare out upon the observer, as though to engulf him. There are no trees around it; and without shade, even the grass is dead. It is a picture of desolation; a lesson in waste; a damnably bad advertisement for government.

---

[34] Long John Silver and old Pew are characters from Robert Louis Stevenson's *Treasure Island*. In her youth, Day had often read the works of Stevenson, listing him as one of her favorite authors. See Day, *The Eleventh Virgin*, 59; Day, *From Union Square to Rome*, 29; Day, *The Long Loneliness*, 25.

[35] The old U.S. Mint building was located at 400 Esplanade Avenue, in New Orleans.

[36] Seemingly, a "Quartier" inhabitant is a person who lives in the French Quarter of New Orleans.

[37] While there may have been haunted houses in the vicinity of Esplanade Avenue in 1923, the U.S. Mint building itself is rumored to be frequented by the ghosts of William B. Mumford, and his mother. During the Civil War, Mumford was hung outside of the U.S. Mint by Union forces, for disrespecting the American flag. See Thomas O. Moore, "Address to the People of Louisiana," *The Daily Picayune*, July 1, 1862; "Old U.S. Mint-New Orleans, LA (from Fort to Fed)," http://hauntednation.blogspot.com/2016/09/old-us-mint-new-orleans-la-from-fort-to.html (accessed January 2, 2018).

The New Orleans Item
Thursday; December 13, 1923 (P. 18)

All Around New Orleans

Unsigned

The Cheaper the "Sweller"

Fashion's step-sister Fad is a democrat, heart and soul; a republican sole and head, for she is awed and subdued [n]either by wealth nor poverty. Billy Sehrt, whose specialty is sweet cakes and candies, says he does not cater much to children because their likes and dislikes change so rapidly; and the novelty of today, tomorrow is spurned; but adults are just as bad.[38] Milady has become accustomed to beaded handbags, with the richness of King Tut's tomb—now she swings on her arm a revamped worn-out automobile inner-tube.[39] Yvonne, who cashiers in [a] Rampart street store, has made several of them for her friends for $1.50 each. Anyone with a piece of rubber, a pair of shears and a weird imagination can duplicate the best to be found—and the cheaper, apparently, the "sweller."

Personality Has Value

Elsie now serves the two front tables in a Royal street restaurant, instead of the girl who a few weeks ago began appearing with flowers in her corsage. Rose is married now. Elsie wears flowers too:

---

[38] William Sehrt and Son, "Makers of 'Sehrt-ainly' Good Cakes," were located at 924-926 North Claiborne Avenue, in New Orleans. See "New Easter Candies," *The Times-Picayune*, March 31, 1923.

[39] The tomb of King Tutankhamun was discovered by Howard Carter in November of 1922. See "Gem-Studded Throne Found," *The Ogden Standard-Examiner (Ogden, UT)*, November 30, 1922. Day had used the name "Mary Milady," in her semi-autobiographical novel, as a pseudonym for the Day family's domestic helper, Mary Manley. See Day, *The Eleventh Virgin*, 3, 18.

"A waiter gave them to me. I stop every night at Delmonico's on St. Charles for supper, and he brings them to me with my check—every night he brings flowers—I have been going there five years now—maybe—[40]

"I used to be at a restaurant on Canal street, and only tonight the manager said I must have brought all my customers here with me—and I did; that is why I get more money than the other girls here—oh, the flowers? Maybe—he gives them to me every night."

"Tiger" D'hote

In a tavern on Bienville, Francois waits—for that is his occupation. Tourists and patrons of the Vieux Carre who go there, at first stare at him curiously.[41] His face is familiar—they have seen him somewhere—still they may be mistaken. One woman did remember him. "You used to be at the La Louisiane," she said, "I remember seeing you there fifteen years ago."[42]

"Yes, madam," Francois returned, "I was there thirty-forty years—we were there, you and I— now we are here. Is it not so?"

Francois is his name; but ask his compatriots. "Him. He iss Clemenceau." That is the secret of his personality. He is a dead ringer for the "Tiger of France."[43]

Delicatessen

Lonesome people—the world is full of people yearning for a home they don't know how to make. Sunday morning you find them chasing to the corner for the ingredients of a luncheon which they can prepare in their rooms. In a St. Charles delicatessen, there is human interest in every purchase.

"Give me some tea—the smallest package you have—gosh, I only want to make three cups, that much will last forever. O, well, it is cheap—give me a small quantity of sugar, a box of Graham crackers—how much are oranges?[44] That's not a bad breakfast is it? Tea, crackers and fruit—my sister is visiting me—she has her breakfast sent to her room at home—she will be surprised when she awakens—gosh, I will never use all that sugar."

---

[40] Delmonico's was located at 1300 St. Charles Avenue.

[41] "Vieux Carré" is a French term, which roughly translates into "old square." The term is also used to describe the French Quarter of New Orleans.

[42] The La Louisiane was a hotel-restaurant located at 725 Iberville Street. For the history of the business, see Lyle Saxon, "The Story of La Louisiane," La Louisiane pamphlet, circa 1930s, http://old-new-orleans.com/NO_LaLouisiane.html (accessed December 27, 2017).

[43] Georges Clemenceau, the combative "Tiger of France," was the former French Prime Minister who presided over the Paris Peace Conference at the end of World War One. See "Warns of German Militarists," *The Town Talk (Alexandria, LA)*, November 22, 1922.

[44] The cost of sweet Florida oranges in nearby Shreveport, LA was twenty-one cents per dozen, or less than two cents per orange. See "The Big Chain Stores," *The Shreveport Times*, December 15, 1923. Day had mentioned, in a letter to Llewellyn Jones, that oranges cost ten cents per dozen in New Orleans. See Day, "To Llewellyn Jones (undated, 1923)," in *All the Way to Heaven*, 5.

A little meat for the dog, a sandwich, a quarter of a pound of liverwurst; ten cents worth of olives—"Which are the best to serve with oysters?" "My husband always wakes up hungry." "Next week, mister, the wedding bells ring; then no more delicatessen for little Mary." There is a story in every purchase.

The New Orleans Item
Friday; December 14, 1923 (P. 25)

All Around New Orleans

Unsigned

It is a commonplace to Orleanians, but none the less interesting to people who have spent most of their lives inland, that all the world meets on the water front of New Orleans.

Briton and Japanese, French, Spaniard, Swede and Portuguese, Jamaica negro, rich American, you will see them all in a twenty-minute walk through the great sheds that help to make New Orleans the proud port.

Romance? There is so much of it, one is bewildered.

Consider, if you will, where these ships of a dozen different countries, with sailors of a dozen more aboard each ship, and sweethearts in heaven only knows how many countries—consider then the kaleidoscope of pictures of different corners of the world these ships and men call up.

To them the outposts of the south are commonplace; they've been in places that are mere names to most of us; Singapore, India, Cape Horn, the River Platte, Siberia, the ports of the Red Sea.

They have rubbed elbows and bought drinks with yellow men and white and brown in the Orient, the Mediterranean, The Gold Coast of Africa. They know so many good stories that you do not know where to begin and consequently, in many instances, do not begin at all.

You find these men, when they are off duty, in various places, from the dim groggeries along the water front to the equally dim little missions that seem to appeal almost timidly to sailor folk to enter.

Their officers you find in more cosmopolitan corners and cafes of the town; hail fellow well met, well able to take care of themselves in a fight or a frolic and normally ready for either.

Is it any wonder that many a youngster from the interior beats his way to New Orleans to ship out, most anywhere where he can find a berth. All the world lies before him, and youth would not be youth if it did not yield sometimes to the call of somewhere else.

Femininity Survives

When "lady" ceases to mean anything except when allied with some descriptive adjective such as "cherub"—in other words when all women have thrown off the shackles of conventionality and taken their places in the business world with their sisters—already legion—what an awful world it will be. Doughty bachelors in the Young Men's Gymnastic club and those other haunts of romance-rebels, shrug their heads over their coffee cups, and sigh, "What an awful world it will be."[45] The riddle perplexes them. That is one reason why Mrs. Weil is interesting. She is part owner, and manager of a bustling furniture store, which is holding its own, and more in the business life of the city. Still, with all the cares of an executive, she appears at the office each day, modestly but tastefully dressed, in clothes Baronne street's exclusive shops would be delighted to display in their windows. She makes them herself.

---

[45] The Young Men's Gymnastic Club was located at 224 North Rampart Street, in New Orleans.

The New Orleans Item
Saturday; December 15, 1923 (P. 9)

All Around New Orleans

Unsigned

Villagitus

In New Orleans, every one can find his level—his own people. That is one of the advantages of a large city and the reason why economists and social workers stay awake at night studying how to lead immigrants inland. That is another problem. This one concerns the visitor from Greenwich Village. She pattered down Royal street, as though guided by a silver thread to a haven of familiarity, and poked her way into a little tea room, decorated with grotesque sketches, and with a color scheme of chlorine-gas-green.[46] Inside were a number of women seated at garishly painted tables, eating little portions of nothingness. One smoked a cigarette which she held in a long green glass tip; several others took their nicotine straight. The visitor ordered luncheon, ate it in silence, then called for cigarettes, smoked a while and finally asked for her bill. When she had pursed the 25 cents left of her two dollar bills, she sauntered out: "It is just like home," she observed. "Extremely artificial and indecently expensive."

Diamonds and Old Shoes

People borrow when times are good; not when they—that is, times—are bad. When people have money or the hope of getting it, they will pledge their dearest possessions in the belief that they can get them back again. When out of work and broke, they hold on to those treasures, like life

---

[46] The Sazerac Tea Room was located at 116 Royal Street, in New Orleans. A period newspaper advertised a Merchants Lunch for fifty cents and a Plate Lunch for thirty-five cents ("Special Attention to Ladies"). See "Sazerac," *The Times-Picayune*, December 17, 1923.

itself—rather to die than lose them. That is one idea. Loan offices are full of them. On South Rampart just off Canal are a dozen such shops, and the first one in particular seems ablaze with the diamonds displayed in the windows.[47] People are buying diamonds now; but the little, dark booth in the rear of the store, labeled "Loan Dept." is the major part of the business. A colored laborer in worn out shoes, comes in, takes two dollars on a pair of brand new shoes and spends it all for a keepsake. What's the moral?

Tired

Maison Blanche's big toy elephant is worth a paragraph by itself; but this is about a little girl, who stood in the crowd before the window gazing with fascination at the stacks of playthings.[48] Mother had her arms full of bundles; and was impatient to be off, but the baby resisted all efforts to pull her away, and in answer to pleadings said: "Mummy, I tant walk any more—I'se tired— my legs is tired."

"Well, come, let me rub them," the mother conceded, but the little girl in a tone of pathos entreated:

"'T'wouldn't do no dood. My legs is tired inside."

Names

"Crash!"

Traffic comes to a standstill, pedestrians stop as if by electricity, and a policeman blows his whistle. At St. Charles and Canal streets a big limousine and a flivver are telescoped together. The colored driver of the big car and the flivverer both hop out with pencil and paper, berate each other and question onlookers. Who saw the wreck? Those who did disappear quickly; they haven't time, they say, to go to court. Others are loquacious but they are no good for witnesses. Two or three names are obtained; then the flivverer steps on the gas, slides off the mud guard of the big car and glides away. It is merely a ten-minute incident; the big one or the little one is at fault; but there is no arrest. It is up to the insurance company. Men and women stroll on their way with that rather satisfying thought. Their children may be playing on the streets; and they may pay accident premiums every month; but "it is up to the insurance company."

---

[47] One such shop was located at 442 South Rampart Street, in New Orleans. The owner, a jeweler named Richard Schromestein, was subpoenaed by a federal grand jury for "using the mails to defraud." Schromestein failed to attend the hearing, because he claimed he was too busy. See "Business Good, Can't Testify, Pays $25 Fine," *The Shreveport Times*, June 13, 1924.

[48] The Maison Blanche building was located at 901 Canal Street. See "The Department Store Museum: Maison Blanche," www.thedepartmentstoremuseum.org/2010/05/maison-blanche-new-orleans-louisiana.html (accessed December 15, 2017).

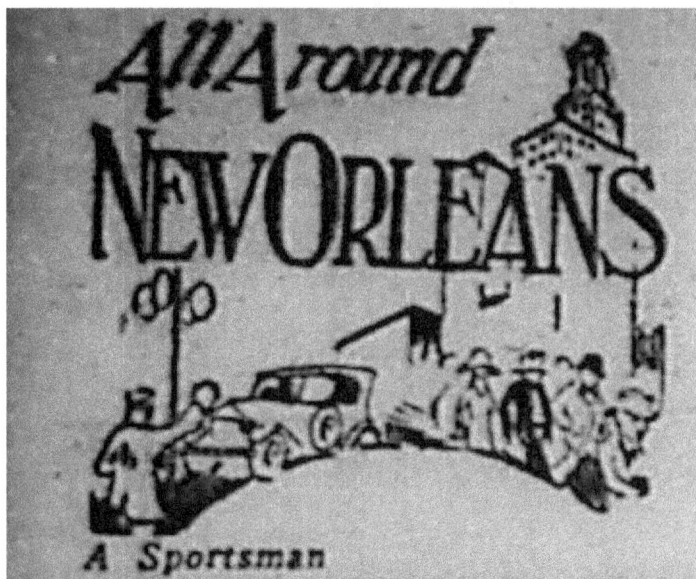

The New Orleans Item
Monday; December 17, 1923 (P. 13)

All Around New Orleans

Unsigned

A Sportsman

In the Arts and Crafts club, a set of impressive etchings, attracted the attention of visitors.[49] One woman glanced at them and said she knew the artist—Anne Goldthwaite.[50] Nearby stood the owner of a stable of race horses, fastidiously dressed, open in his admiration of the etchings, one of which pictured a cock-fight.[51]

"Would you mind telling me her address?" he ventured.

"Yes," the woman said, and gave it to him, and added, "I suppose the cock-fight appeals to your sporting instinct?"

"Oh, no," he said. "I do not like fighting—strife—bloodshed. I am a sportsman. I want her to make an etching of one of my horses."

---

[49] The Arts and Crafts Club of New Orleans was then located at 520 Royal Street.

[50] Anne Goldthwaite was an artist and, for many years, an art instructor for the Art Students' League of New York. She died in 1944. See "Anne Goldthwaite, Artist, Dies," *St. Louis Post-Dispatch (St. Louis, MO)*, January 31, 1944.

[51] Anne Goldthwaite's etching, "The Cock-Fight," was published in International Studio, circa 1914. See Anne Goldthwaite, "The Cock-Fight," *The International Studio: An Illustrated Magazine of Fine and Applied Art; Volume 52, March, April, May and June, 1914* (New York, NY: John Lane Company, 1914), LXXIX.

The Customer Sometimes Wrong

In a Baronne street jewelry shop presides a most interesting individual, for his business methods are his own.[52] He relies on low prices for patronage—salesmanship jumped out the window when he came in. The other day he was making some effort to sell a diamond and the prospect balked on the price—then said he did not want it anyway. The dealer walked to the end of the counter, took out a twenty-dollar bill, and held it around the corner of the case:

"Here, take it," he whispered hoarsely, "and give me a dollar."

"What is the matter with you?" demanded the patron.

"Don't talk so loud—take it," the dealer insisted. "Give me a dollar and take it."

"I don't want it," the patron said, "what in the world is the matter with you?"

The dealer shrugged his shoulders and gave the bill to a clerk. She took it out and brought back change.

"There you are," the dealer said, closing the argument. "I can't even sell you a twenty-dollar bill for a dollar. How can I sell you merchandise."

Cold Weather

They call it "brisk weather," up north—just a crisp, invigorating chill, that makes people step lively and puts a smile on even hardened faces. It means a lot to New Orleans. It opens the buying season, and brings a paradox. Customers pass by open doors, but as soon as they are closed, business picks up. That means good fortune for everybody—except—

Samuel Williston Calhoun McCarthy, knight of the road. He stood on the pavement on Canal street, his ragged coat collar turned up, his hands in his pockets, his feet clad in broken shoes, topped with burlap, stamping restlessly—veritably, too cold to move. There is no story in it except that he looked sort of odd, standing there, while three feet away, in the store, a dapper, well fed, and gloriously happy little merchant smiled genially as he counted his receipts for the day.

Buy Now

Turkeys at 28 cents a pound are a novelty—and the dealers who have gone down to that figure are selling all they can get.[53] That is why a Dryades street dealer, with a 33 cents sign in front of his store, smiles confidently.

---

[52] Antin and Richard, Jewelers and Gift Counselors, were located at 11 Baronne Street, in New Orleans. See "Old Jewelry House Moves to Baronne," *The Times-Picayune*, October 6, 1923.

[53] On December 17, 1923, turkey was selling for twenty-three cents per pound, as reported in Chicago, IL. On the same day, an ad in an Alexandria, LA newspaper sought to charge thirty-five cents per pound. See "Butter,

"Sure I can't meet that price," he conceded, "and I am not selling many—but just wait. Next week these fellows blow up—then I come in. They can't get many more. Thirty-three cents now—but just wait. I get fifty cents before Christmas. Forty-five years I have done it, right here. Fifty cents a pound."

Eggs, Poultry," *The Monroe News-Star (Monroe, LA)*, December 17, 1923; "For Sale—Turkeys," *The Town Talk (Alexandria, LA)*, December 17, 1923.

The New Orleans Item
Tuesday; December 18, 1923 (P. 19)

All Around New Orleans

Unsigned

At the western end of Esplanade avenue, there is a fine place to dawdle and taste the beauty of these December days with only the gulls and perhaps some small boys to keep you company. You cross Elysian Fields avenue, across the railroad tracks where there is always an engine and cars being shunted to the ferry and away from it; and then if you brave the mud and climb a red earthy hill, you'll find the place. The small boys like it because there [is] a long inclined slope down which they can coast on their bicycles. The pier juts out into the river and there is always the delightful danger of being taken possession of by some perverse instinct to pay no attention to the brakes and go whirling off the pier into the river. This pier is curved like a protecting arm around a little bit of river and beach, and all through the sunny afternoon the gentle waves murmur among the piles of driftwood and shingle. Here, too, the kids can adventure, hunting around among the driftwood like beachcombers, for some sign of buried treasure, perhaps, or a bottle with a lost message in it. You can sit on the pier, with your back against a post and your legs dangling over the water and watch the gulls that are so thick around some of the steamers that they look like whirling snowflakes in the distance. There is smoke streaming from every smoke-stack, derricks are at work, loading and unloading, but the steamers are so far down the river, that you can't hear the noise of the machinery or of the men. There is only the cries of the gulls, the shouts of the small boys, and an occasional shrill whistle of a tug.

———————

Speaking of small boys, there is a grocery store on a corner not far from the house, and this morning when we were buying coffee, one small swaggerer walked in with a penny clutched in his murky hand.

31

"A cigarette!" he cried boldly, and slapped his penny on the counter.

While the Italian storekeeper reached for our coffee with one hand, he tossed a single cigarette from a pile of loose ones in the show case, with the other.

"And a match!" He got it. Brazenly, with the gestures of an adult, the child lit the cigarette, and with his hands in his pockets, and school books clutched firmly against his side, he puffed out of the store.

——————

Adventures! The old French market is a place for them. Aside from the place itself, encountering strange food for the first time, brings with it a sense of adventure. At one of the most exciting meals we ever ate, the main dish was whelk. Cooked and garnished, the Italians call it Conchiglie. Fresh from the market, whelk come in their shells—large shells, big enough to hold to your ear to hear the sea in them. If you lift up the paper which covers them to look at them, they will rear at you, poking out of their shells like snails, with horns on their heads and strange, blind faces. They say that if you put them in the bath tub, they will come out of their homes and swim around. You will not linger over their antics in the bath tub, without giving up the idea of conchiglie and taking up that of starting an aquarium. If you wish to eat, you will not look at them at all, but leave their preparation to a ruthless cook.

There aren't any whelk over at the French market, but there are other strange fish. The most adventurous time to shop is at dusk when there are only a few spluttering lamps here and there, and brawny men with grotesque shadows on their faces, leaning against wet marble or wooden tables, gossiping in foreign tongues. There are piles of palest green shrimps, curly, beautifully formed little things; scallops, which we have never seen in their shells and we don't know where they got their name; large, handsome pink fish, stubby looking fish, fish with brutal heads—you could almost write a free verse poem about them. The smell of this end of the French market is so frankly fishy that you don't mind it at all, but wander down the dark corridors between the huge tables, peering into barrels and baskets on the way.

——————

Along one of these dark alleyways in the market we had a strange encounter yesterday afternoon. A dark patch squirming along in front of us was found on closer scrutiny to be a huge crab, making his slow and painful way towards the vegetable stalls, perhaps attracted there by the light and color. Oh, to know the adventures of this harsh, horny creature—that we might write the story of his escape which was doubtless as thrilling and interesting to him as the escapes of the Count of Monte Cristo or Casanova were to those heroes of history![54] Was he dropped by the careless hand of some marketman, or did he overcome, by Herculean effort, the lethargy induced by the ice packed all around him, and crawl precariously down the side of the barrel to the

——————

[54] Alexandre Dumas *(père)* wrote *The Count of Monte Cristo* in 1844. Day had read works by Dumas, *père* and Dumas, *fils*, circa 1918-1919. See Day, *The Eleventh Virgin*, 283. Giacomo Casanova's prison escape was detailed in his 1787 work, *Story of My Flight*.

freedom of the pavement? And what will be his end? Will he gain temporary peace and security in the shade of some Christmas tree in the market, or will he fulfill the destiny which man has imposed on him and which he has tried to avoid, and be eaten?

The New Orleans Item
Wednesday; December 19, 1923 (P. 10)

All Around New Orleans

Unsigned

Few of us get the whole story of many things we see and hear, but sometimes one gets enough of it, to see the comedy and the tragedy involved in fun-making.

Three young men and a man a little less than middle-aged are the characters in scene one. The youngest of the young finds a quantity of tobacco store coupons, theatre checks and two restaurant receipts in his overcoat pocket. He puts them in the left-hand overcoat pocket of the married and middle-aged man. As the orchestra plays loudly, he tells another of his prank and all dispose of their pocket garbage into the overcoat pockets of the unsuspecting friend.

The next day a wife calls on a friend.

"My dear, I wish some advice," she says. "I picked up my husband's overcoat last night and a lot of theatre checks and receipted restaurant bills fell out of it. He told me before I went away to see mother that we could not have a new car this year because he was short of money. What should I do about it?"

"Well, don't do anything," the woman friend advised. "He's a good man at heart and maybe he was lonely while you were gone.

"Besides, you will not get the truth from him. He will tell you some of his friends put those things in his pockets as a joke."

The wife decided to take her friend's advice. She agreed that for many years her husband had been devoted to her and that since he had not been out alone in the evening after her return, there was certainly very little seriously wrong. But women sometimes change their minds.

"My dear," she said to her friend a week later, "I intended to do as you said but I simply could not.

"I asked him how those things came to be in his pockets and he said just what you said he would say.

"'That's just what Agnes said you'd say,' I told him. And now he is furious with you and does not seem to be displeased at all with me. And somehow or other, I don't care. He still refuses to buy a new car, but he has not been out without me since I got back."

Xmas

It is in the air; and in the faces of people. Christmas is coming soon. Tony, the bootblack, is infected and his competitors are catching it. One of them stood on a stepladder in his shop the other night stringing red and green streamers, when Tony chanced to pass and look in: "Oh, ho, ho," he said, "Guess I gave you a new idea, huh?"

"All-a right," said his competitor, "just wait till I get through and my place will make yours look sick!"

That is the spirit of a lot of senseless giving.

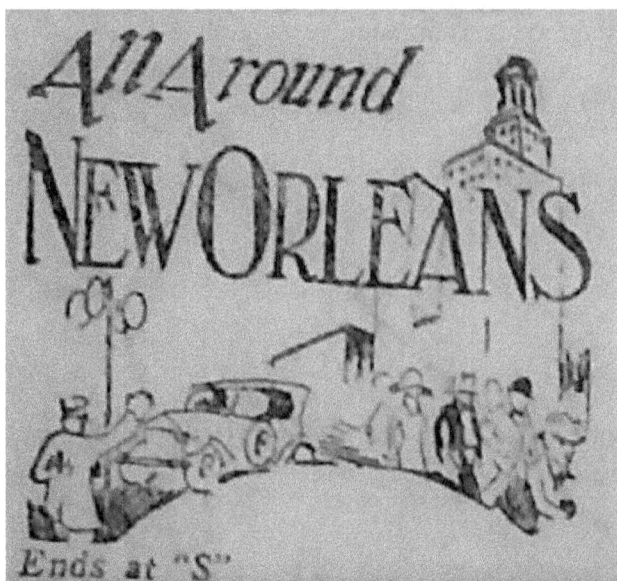

The New Orleans Item
Thursday; December 20, 1923 (P. 24)

All Around New Orleans

Unsigned

Ends at "S"

Truly New Orleans is a city of homes, and in its confines are some very fine libraries, most of them privately owned, and certainly few cities boast of a finer receptacle than this—still, New Orleans is not educated to the use of libraries and hasn't the facilities to be found in other cities of the same size. This is not a plea for funds to procure standard fiction for the starving masses—it is simply an introduction to a rather humiliating discovery. A visitor at the public library asked for Volume "W" of the Dictionary of National Biography, a set which is considered by many experts to be as essential to a library as cheese to a cheese sandwich.[55] The librarian turned toward the shelves, then came back with this startling explanation: "Oh, I forgot," she said, "we purchased our set at an auction sale and the volumes run only through 'S.' I am sorry we have not what you wish. Much education begins with "H" and ends with "T".

Youth Stumped

Youthful marriages are all wrong anyway—Avana says so, and she speaks from experience. She was married ten years. Then her husband ran away with someone else, and Avana got her old job back at the five and ten. "Of course," she says, "it sounds pretty—growing up together and that sort of stuff, but it ain't on the level. It is in the movies, that's all. In life saps and saplings planted side by side get further apart as they grow up, and each tries to push the other over."

---

[55] *The Dictionary of National Biography: Founded in 1882 by George Smith*, ed. Sir Leslie Stephen and Sir Sidney Lee, vols. I-XXI, vol. XXII Supplementary (London, England: Oxford University Press, 1921-1922).

Still, many people do believe in early marriages—here is one that even old man Economic Pressure can't prevent. They were standing in front of a furniture store window in which was displayed a set for "Three Rooms for $119."

"Louis, love," she whispered, "if we are married by a priest without a wedding and a lot of fuss, we can buy that—then we won't have to live with mamma."

Lafcadio Hearn

Darkness settling over the city, a haze of fog and in the light of the big sign over The Item doorway, a stranger.[56] A slender figure, austere he seemed, distinguished by a big black felt hat drawn over his eyes, and a peculiar wistfulness of manner as he peered through the glass doors.

"I was recalling my memories of The Item in the old days—when my friend Lafcadio Hearn was here.[57] My association with that brilliant mind is one of the sweetest memories of my life."

The voice, soft and pleasing, was that of William Sulzer, former governor of the state of New York.[58] He stopped here for a few days after a tour of Texas and Mexico, on his way home for Christmas.

A Prayer Answered

The speaker is Francois:

"No, sir—you will not find St. Roch's chapel open so late—but it will be open tomorrow—next Sunday also. There you will find most interesting—crutches strewn about, wonderful gifts from those whom St. Roch has favored.[59] You, too, may leave a lighted candle—and your prayer will be answered. Only yesterday a lady and gentleman with a little girl came in and sat there. 'Do you remember, Francois,' she said 'seven years ago we were here and we told you we had come to make a prayer to St. Roch and to leave a candle.' Oh, yes, yes, I remembered and she pointed to the little girl and said, 'Our prayer was answered, Francois.'"

---

[56] *The New Orleans Item* offices were located at 336 Camp Street, in New Orleans.

[57] Lafcadio Hearn, who once maintained a home in New Orleans at South Villere and Gasquet Streets, worked for *The New Orleans Daily Item* from 1878 to 1881. Hearn also wrote several books regarding Creole culture. He died in Japan, in September of 1904. See "Lafcadio Hearn Dies in His Japanese Home," *The Times-Democrat (New Orleans, LA)*, September 29, 1904; Lafcadio Hearn, *Creole Sketches* (Boston, MA: Houghton Mifflin Company, 1924).

[58] William Sulzer was the thirty-ninth Governor of the State of New York. He was impeached in 1913, ten months after his inauguration, charged with falsifying documents relating to campaign contributions and committing perjury. See "Sulzer Ousted; Glynn Seated; Vote for Removal is 43 to 12," *The Sun (New York, NY)*, October 18, 1913.

[59] A site of many miraculous healings, the chapel is located within the confines of St. Roch's Campo Santo, at 1725 St. Roch Avenue in New Orleans. See "Society Notes," *The Times-Democrat (New Orleans, LA)*, February 5, 1899.

Figure 4-Saint Roch Chapel Altar, 1920. Photograph courtesy of John Tibule Mendes.

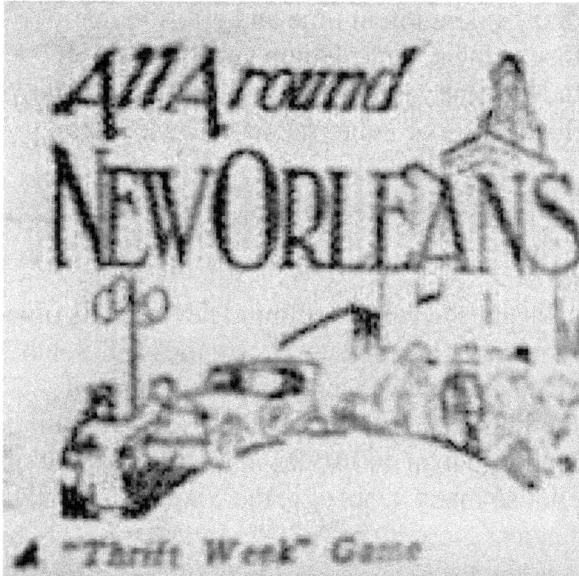

The New Orleans Item
Monday; December 24, 1923 (P. 11)

All Around New Orleans

Unsigned

A "Thrift Week" Game

Spending wisely is profitable; here is a way to spend nothing at all in a most amusing manner. Two little girls invented it. They said they stopped in their Christmas shopping, to decide just how much they needed to spend and how much they had. Their assets consisted of eighty-seven cents. Their Christmas lists totaled $5.90. So, they decided, since the spirit of the gift is the thing that counts that they would give only the spirit, and blow the eighty-seven cents for candy and ice cream. Down Canal street they went, "window shopping"—"there is a lovely ring for Mary Jane," one said, making a note on a pad, "and that rug is wonderful for mother—look, Anna, there is no price on that smoking set—I'll just put down five dollars for daddy—oh me, oh my, I have spent $530 already—goodie, goodie, look, an automobile—five hundred and fifty-three—I am going to give myself that doll—isn't she adorable?—goodness, Anna, how much have you spent?"

No Stop

In Union there is strength, children are taught in school, but on Union street there is only indignation. Every morning every day some passenger whose business leads him to that thoroughfare arises at Poydras or Gravier street, and goes to the platform only to see the car rumble on by the place he wishes to alight; every evening every day someone waits patiently for a car at Union street, only to have it sail by him, with frantic arm waving on the part of the motorman as his only consolation and explanation that the cars do not stop at that particular corner. Of course the no-stop schedules were prepared after careful deliberation; and for the good of the service in general, but an extra block is a consideration in time and effort to many workers, and there is no explanation that is satisfactory to them, since Union street is the only one in the business district where cars do not stop. Indeed, one irate patron voiced the opinion that the cause was the belief that only Yankees and Federation of Labor men are employed on Union street.

The "400" in Shoedom[60]

Mr. Warner's five-foot shelf of styles,[61] on which is displayed each week brand new models of men's hats now has a rival in the windows of the John C. Bright stores on St. Charles and South Rampart.[62] This rival in a shoemaker's bench on which are displayed a half a dozen shoes of different appearance. S. J. Sepple, manager of the South Rampart place, says shoes shown will be changed at intervals and that in the course of a year more than 400 styles in men's footware will be exhibited.[63] A chiropodist friend recalls that not so many years ago, there were, generally speaking, only two kinds of shoes—brogans, and Sunday.

Letters

Even those who have reason to conceal their addresses look for them anxiously—a letter is a direct contact with a memory world. In the post office an interesting half hour is always available to those who read faces—stand near the general delivery window. A negro approaches respectfully: "Boss, will you come tell dis man who ah is—he says I got to be identified before I can cash dis here blue ticket Melissa sent." A woman in heavy mourning, touches her handkerchief to her eyes as she turns away—there is no letter for her. A girl with a tired face, painted cheeks and expensive clothes, quickly conceals a white envelope in her dress and hurries out. A broken old man, leaning heavily on a cane, hobbles to the window, hope, too frightened to express itself, on his face. The clerk shakes his head, and as the disappointed figure goes out: "Poor devil, every day he comes for a letter—it never comes—his name is Johnson—there are many Johnsons."

---

[60] The "400" was meant to denote the elite members of a particular community. In December of 1916, Day wrote a scathing article for the *New York Call* wherein she chastised the elitists of Manhattan for their excesses concerning food. Amidst rampant food shortages in Manhattan during World War One, Day had asked, "But why not spite the '400' and build up their [the poor] strength and courage that is latent in them on the money that they have, so that they may fight for a top place and be fit to hold a top place when they get it?" See Dorothy Day, "Call's Diet Squad is Accused of Gluttony by Experts," *New York Call,* December 15, 1916.

[61] A tongue-in-cheek reference to Dr. Eliot's Five Foot Shelf of classic literature, which consisted of fifty-one volumes, published by the P. F. Collier and Son Corporation in 1909.

[62] The John Bright Shoe Stores Company had three locations in New Orleans, 414 St. Charles Street, 140 South Rampart Street, and 1410 Dryades Street. See "Announcing Spring Styles," *The Times-Picayune*, March 23, 1923.

[63] The South Rampart Street location of John Bright Shoes was robbed on the day this article was published. Samuel J. Settles was mentioned as the manager of the store. See "Thieves Active Over Week-end," *The Times-Picayune*, December 25, 1923.

The New Orleans Item
Thursday; December 27, 1923 (P. 17)

All Around New Orleans

Unsigned

Pride

A real boy, sturdy, self-reliant and alert, distinguished most by ears pink with cleanliness, in the uniform of a Boy Scout, was helping out at the distribution of toys. He and his chum were not invited to participate in the work; they just thought there might be something they could do to help out. There was. This one was helping other kids bundle their toys, keeping his eyes peeled for "repeaters," and otherwise making himself useful to those in charge of the distribution. Then into the picture came another real boy, slender, his narrow, white face peering curiously from a mass of rags, one eye wide the other half closed, an inherited or acquired deformity which added to the grotesqueness of his appearance. The two youngsters surveyed each other appraisingly, then their eyes met.

"These toys are for my kid brother," said the ragged youngster, half in defiance half in apology. Then he went on his way.

Still Walking

They called him "Daddy," and if he ever had a name he is probably glad it is forgotten. Just an old soak he was halting in gait, shabby in appearance and sort of feared most of the time of being kicked out of the way, but Ed took care of him; made him master of ceremonies at his backwash saloon; then gave him the additional title of "carrier of keys" with instructions to lock up everything in a hurry at the approach of trouble. When trouble came in the persons of prohibition officers "Daddy" walked briskly out of the cafe and continued down the street. At last reports he was still walking. Ed had been good to him; he is good to many others in the same way; one boy he is putting through school, but when the old man deserted him in his need, Ed laughed. He is not critical of ingratitude. Helping others is a pleasure; the profit it returns is velvet.

Resourcefulness

Getting a story about Christmas printed after Christmas is as about as difficult as borrowing money on New Year's eve; but this one will be just as good then. It is a scrap of conversation picked up on Union street.

"Charley, doggone it, old man, I am up against it bad. Little Mary Anna has got her heart set on a great big doll for a present and I am telling you straight. Charlie, I haven't got a nickel. The wife and I decided we could get along without eating all right—but Charley, you know how to fix things—what am I going to do about that great big doll for Mary Anna?"

"Tell you what you do, Jim," Charlie said after a moment of reflection, "go home and tell little Mary Anna you just got a wire from Santa Claus and he said he had a blowout and can't get to her house until New Year's. That will give you time to grab off a job and get the money. Don't mention it old man. See you again some time."

A Person of Consequence

He stood at the corner of Lafayette and signalled a Carondelet car to stop. Immaculately dressed, with the personality of a man of years he seemed, and, indeed, so marked was his distinction, that people looked twice at him, and wondered. A passenger on the inner platform of the car put the imagery into words. "Who is it?" he asked the motorman, "Statesman or business man."

"Him?" returned the motorman contemptuously, "He's a four-flusher and one of the biggest mobsters in town. He ought to have been in jail ten years ago."

The New Orleans Item
Friday; December 28, 1923 (P. 11)

All Around New Orleans

Unsigned

***THE PRISONER OF SEDAN*[64]**
(A Pantomime)

Characters: Italian gentleman who could have shaved with the creases of his trousers; Italian gentleman's son, two years old; friends, garage men, innocent bystanders and others.

Place: Inside, but mostly outside of the big sedan parked at Union and Carondelet streets.

Time: Half-past eight to nine-fifteen last night.

Enter I. G. and son by driving up in a big sedan trimmed with spot lights, side lights, headlights, tail lights, extra windshields and three extra tires.

I. G. gets out of sedan, waves to son inside, slams door and enters saloon at left.

Five minutes pass during which son blows horn of sedan loudly.

Enter I. G.

---

[64] The title of this article was a play on Anthony Hope's classic work of fiction, *The Prisoner of Zenda* (Bristol, England: J. W. Arrowsmith, 1894).

He tries to open door of sedan. It will not open. It is locked. As I. G. goes through pockets for keys he sees them on dashboard. He wig-wags for son to open door. Son wig-wags back gleefully and backs away from door. I. G. tries the windows and windshields of sedan. They will not budge. More wig-waggins.

Enter friends, innocent bystanders and others.

I. G. slips as he tugs on windshields and falls to wet street.

All laugh except I. G.

Innocent bystanders help I. G. up and give him advice.

I. G. tries to crease trousers with hands. No luck.

Exit I. G.

Enter I. G. with garage men.

I. G. makes final attempt to get son interested in opening sedan door from within. Son wig-wags as before. Exhibits no interest in door.

Exeunt I. G. clinging to running board of sedan in tow of garage men's car. He is wig-wagging to keep son from crying at being taken away from innocent bystanders and others.

Friend Alex:

"There's just us in the house," says Owen.

Alex looks up and blinks an eye in confirmation. He likes to have Owen rub his back with his shoe.

"You know how you get to feel," goes on Owen.

"I caught him 32 years ago and he's been about the house every day since. He goes everywhere and sleeps under my bed at night. Comes when I call him; won't let anyone in. You bet he'd give a burglar a dirty crack with that tail of his."

Alex has a big tail. It is seven feet long. Alex's head is three feet long. Alex, so Owen says, is the biggest captive alligator in New Orleans.

During the day Alex clatters about Owen's courtyard far down on Royal street.[65] He paddles in the pool and dozes in the sun. Now and then, when he is sure he is dry, he makes a tour of the

---

[65] In April of 1904, *The Times-Picayune* reported on Herman Levi, an antique dealer who had a shop on Royal Street. Levi, who actually lived on Basin Street, had been housing alligators in his home since 1894. He claimed to have an alligator that was 250-years-old and, based upon his growth formula, would have measured

house and when Owen comes home in the evening, Alex eats a pound or two of raw meat. Then he goes to sleep under Owen's bed.

"He's just like a dog to me, I guess," says Owen, stroking his beard and tickling Alex's ribs with his shoe.

---

twenty-five feet in length. Perhaps Day had changed the name of the antique vendor to limit curiosity-seekers. See "Alligators a Passion with One Orleanian," *The Times-Picayune*, April 3, 1904.

The New Orleans Item
Monday; December 31, 1923 (P. 6)

All Around New Orleans

Unsigned

Casey Jones, Florist[66]

Steady eyes, nerves of steel and the endurance of a giant bring the limited snorting into the station; the thrill of the small boy on his first journey is only a spark of that experienced by the locomotive engineer a dozen times a day. Who answers the call of the steam whistle is doomed to spend his life in its service. The fascination of the calling makes all others seem commonplace. That is why it seemed odd to see Martin Gunthier in a dainty little florist's shop on Esplanade selling a bouquet to a debutante. He has driven more than one engine from its maiden trip over its course to the junkpile and has fifteen years or more seniority to his credit. The shop adjoins his modest but comfortable home, and is owned by his wife but Martin does most of the work connected with it.

"But driving a locomotive breeds an incurable desire to keep doing it," he says. "I shoveled coal that would make a pile higher than the Delgado school and carried my locomotive through storm and fire on time day after day, year after year, for what I have, but still about once a month, I get homesick and I have just got to get back into my cab, if it is only to ring the bell."[67]

---

[66] In late April of 1900, Illinois Central Engineer Casey Jones died in a rear-end collision due to a misinterpretation of train signals. His heroism, in saving his passengers, was later eulogized in song. See "Railroad News from All Around," *The Times-Picayune*, May 1, 1900.
[67] The Delgado School, now Delgado Community College, was located at 615 City Park Avenue, in New Orleans.

From Newsboy Up and Back

Years ago there was a husky young hustler who carried papers downtown; and in the whole city there was hardly to be found the like of him. Later he went into business for himself and prospered. St. Bernard parish liked him so well they made him president of the school board, and he also was elected bank director, then he retired, content with the share of worldly goods he had accumulated. Years of training in the school of experience, however, and its demands upon vitality and nervous energy, made him restless and he yearned to step to harness again. That is why he returned to his first occupation and took charge of newspaper distribution in his section of the parish. Day and night, summer and winter, sunshine and rain he is on the job directing the efforts of a crowd of newsboys; helping them to earn a livelihood and pocket money; giving them good advice and compelling them to follow it. He has two grown sons whose success is adequate testimony of his ability to guide boys right. A block from his corner is his pretty home, surrounded by flowers and fruit trees and a great big yard. Inside is some of the richest, finest and most nourishing milk procurable; well worth a pilgrimage to St. Bernard.

Mr. Reuter, banker and newsboy, keeps five cows to supply milk for his family.[68]

Tantalia

Even punishments survive. Today, not grapes suspended just beyond the reach of the condemned, not cool fresh water so close to his lips that he could feel but not taste it; indeed, the victim is not one who has offended the gods or otherwise transgressed. She is just a little girl, whose greatest wish was a bicycle. She has it, so her happiness should be complete, but it is kept up in the playroom where is hardly enough room to turn it around, and she is not permitted to remove it. It is so dangerous for children to be on the streets and far more hazardous for them to ride bicycles, mother says, and she trembles when she thinks of what might happen to the little girl who means so much to her. So, in the playroom, it remains. The little girl has jacked up the rear wheel. She gets on it, closes her eyes, and turning the raised wheel at lightning speed, just imagines she is going down Canal street, and at every hundredth revolution sings a cheery

---

[68] Mathias J. "Matt" Reuter was at one time the President of the St. Bernard Parish School Board. He was also elected a Director of the Bank of St. Bernard. In January of 1920, Reuter was indicted by the Grand Jury of the 29th Judicial District on charges of aiding and abetting in an illegal banking scheme ("Monte"). Reuter claimed his innocence, and appealed his case to the Supreme Court. When his appeal was denied, Reuter faced either a $2,500 fine, or six months in the Parish prison. Reuter resigned his position at the School Board in January of 1921, choosing to serve the prison sentence in lieu of paying the fine. In March of 1921, a petition was circulated on Reuter's behalf to the State Board of Pardons in order to grant him an early release. Reuter was pardoned in April of 1921. See "School Board to Meet on Saturday, July 5; President Reuter Looking Into Finances," *The St. Bernard Voice (Arabi, LA)*, June 28, 1919; "Bank of St. Bernard Holds Annual Election; Simon Leopold Member of Directorate," *The St. Bernard Voice*, January 17, 1920; "Grand Jury Work," *The St. Bernard Voice*, May 1, 1920; "Fined $100, 30 Days in Local Jail," *The St. Bernard Voice*, May 15, 1920; "District Court," *The St. Bernard Voice*, May 29, 1920; "New Trial Denied," *The St. Bernard Voice*, June 12, 1920; Supreme Court of Louisiana-State V. Reuter (No. 24173), November 29, 1920, rehearing denied January 4,1921; "Local Happenings," *The St. Bernard Voice*, January 22, 1921; "School Board Meets in Quarterly Session on Saturday and Organization is Effected," *The St. Bernard Voice*, January 29, 1921; "Friends Seek Pardon in Matt Reuter Case," *The Times-Picayune*, March 3, 1921; "Friends Greet Matt Reuter on Return from Prison," *The Times-Picayune*, April 25, 1921.

greeting to a startled traffic officer. Had Tantalus been a little girl, tantalize would have meant something besides temptation.[69]

---

[69] Tantalus was a figure of Greek mythology, who had been eternally damned to Tartarus.

"Go-Get-'em" Kelly

The New Orleans Item
Tuesday; January 1, 1924 (P. 22)

All Around New Orleans

Unsigned

"Go-Get-'em" Kelly

It is a hard beat, and one who covers it deserves a swell funeral, nevertheless. Traffic Policeman Kelly maintains his good humor. His post is Carondelet and Howard. When he crosses the center park to stop traffic a dozen violations crop up on the other side. Often he is compelled to personally escort children, elderly people, limousines and trolley cars past the intersection as a measure of precaution. The other morning, a car driven by a woman cut around the park in defiance of signals; and Kelly started after her, while bystanders shouted "Go Get 'Em Kelly— Take her number and let the judge apologize." A pedestrian, amused, said Kelly once stopped a car in which was a prominent politician and as he upbraided the driver he was informed he was treading on uncertain ground: "I don't care whose car it is," he exclaimed, "another violation and I'll lock all of you up. My self-respect is worth more to me than my job."

Property Rich

Some day someone will write an epic on the hardships of being wed to a real estate operator. Meanwhile, a mere notice will suffice. In a large office on Carondelet two women met. "I am mad—downright mad," one exclaimed, "here I have just completed furnishing my home and I come down to the office to learn that my devoted husband has sold us out—sold the roof from over our heads, bag and baggage—and this is the third time this has happened in six months."

The Thrills of 1924: Dorothy Day Encounters the "Underworld Denizens" of New Orleans

"My husband did exactly the same thing," the other woman said, "and I told him I didn't want anything for Christmas except trunks—my heavens, if I have to move every three weeks on two days' notice. I might as well be prepared."

"Well, I won't live in a trunk," her friend continued, "I am going right out this afternoon and rent a house from my husband's rival—and by George, I will sign a lease on it for five years. Come on, Helen."

And Helen went.

Yellow Mud

Someone said the mayor's edict on better streets should be punctuated with handsful of mud—but this is not political—it is a condition.[70] A ride on the Clio trolley line is as pleasant as a pink tea in the Okeefenochee swamp—but Frank Costley's newly painted fence is worth the trip to see. It is yellow—bright, gloriously, incandescently yellow, and in contrast to the coal piles behind it strikes the eyes so forcefully that for half an hour after looking at it everything around the rider is mud, suddenly turned yellow. If Mr. Costley's neighbors were as industrious, there wouldn't be any mud there, one car passenger said, but if they were, everybody would order their coal, building materials and similar products of the neighborhood by phone.[71]

A Visitor from Boston

He was eating beans in Childs' and stopped to inquire if a sightseeing trip was worthwhile for a visitor with only a limited time to see the city.[72]

"Great town," he said, "no I am not here on business; was working down in Texas and had just a few days for Christmas, not enough time to go home, so I decided to come here—I'd heard so much about New Orleans, and, believe me, it was all true. The first night I went to the Orpheum and I saw the Palace also.[73] Yes, I have been up Royal street, stopping there at the Monteleone—is there anything worth seeing further up than that?[74] Last night I fell in with a bunch of coo-coo New Yorkers, who had seen everything and done everything, so I took them over to the hotel and

---

[70] The Mayor of New Orleans during this period was Andrew J. McShane. On December 19, 1923, McShane advocated for a city commission dedicated to the supervision of street maintenance and construction, citing that improved transportation related to increased real estate values. See "Advocates Commission for Street Supervision," *The Shreveport Times*, December 20, 1923.

[71] This passage makes more sense when one considers that the Costley family operated the Gulf Coal and Coke Company, Frank D. Costley, President-Treasurer, Frank G. Costley, Vice-President. The Costley's business was located at Clio and Willow Streets, in New Orleans. See "You Can't Be Chilly and Cheerful," *The Times-Picayune*, December 16, 1923.

[72] Childs' Restaurant was located at 620 Canal Street, in New Orleans. See "Hold-Up Epidemic in New Orleans," *The Clarksdale Press Register (Clarksdale, MS)*, October 7, 1929. As a young reporter for the *New York Call* and *The Masses*, Day had spent much time in Childs' Restaurant on 21-27 Park Row in Manhattan. See Day, *The Long Loneliness*, 53.

[73] The Orpheum Theatre is located at 125-129 University Place, in New Orleans. The Palace Theatre was located at 201 Dauphine Street, in New Orleans.

[74] The Monteleone Hotel is located at 214 Royal Street, in New Orleans.

50

we played cards. Now here I am shaved and shined, tickled to death with what I have seen of the Crescent City, and anxious to see the rest of it. Guess I will have to leave tonight."

Oh, well if importations satisfy, why worry?[75]

---

[75] The first of three usages of the phrase "oh, well." See "A Chicken Sermon," in "All Around New Orleans," *The New Orleans Item*, January 14, 1924; "Truant," in "All Around New Orleans," *The New Orleans Item*, January 28, 1924.

The New Orleans Item
Wednesday; January 2, 1924 (P. 8)

All Around New Orleans

Unsigned

It's open season in New Orleans for tourists, as you can see any day by a trip down Royal street where the wily antique dealers and purveyors of old and curious furniture, pewter, China, Arab swords and Chinese Lord-knows-whats are arrayed with a view to attracting the customer—particularly, of course, the customer from the North.

The season for profit is short, like that of the trappers who go after fur-bearing animals—and some of these Northern beauties might be mistaken for that, in their heavy coats.

But sometimes the pickings are rich.

Again, there are dull days when one doesn't take in rent.

But as one devout old dealer whose store has dust enough to furnish all the atmosphere the ardent seeker of the picturesque could demand, says: "Often the Lord delivers them into our hands.[76] And they can pay without feeling it—so why not?"

Why not indeed?

There isn't any reason.

The ramifications of the antique business are odd.

---

[76] A reference to Joshua 10:8 [KJV].

Dealers From New York

Dealers come to New Orleans from far-away New York to pick up furniture at what they still consider very reasonable prices, though the average Orleanian who knows his town knows that the crafty New York buyer pays just three times what anybody who knew the game here in New Orleans would.

For instance, a reporter who has furnished his home since coming to New Orleans with second-hand furniture went out one day recently to gather accurate data on price variations here.

It goes without saying that the highest prices are to be paid on upper Royal street, where the blithe tourists flock and shed their gold and greenbacks for something "so picturesque, my dear—such a characteristic little bit of old New Orleans—and really, you must go there to appreciate it."

Usually the "something" is genuine enough. But the funny thing is that the tourist pays anywhere from two to three times what he needs to.

Side Street Bargains

Were he patient enough to poke about side streets and into stores that do not pretend to be antique emporiums, but just second-hand furniture stores, he could save some money. That's where the antique dealers go when they get an order for something not in stock.

The chair that fetches $15 on upper Royal street goes for $2.50 or $3 on lower Royal, down toward Esplanade, or on any of the innumerable side streets, or on Magazine street this side of Jackson avenue. Of course, it isn't refinished when you buy it at these cheap places. It isn't even repaired. You take it "as is," and depend on your own ingenuity and diligence to make it look like a chair that costs $35 in New York.

"I buy cheap and sell cheap and in a hurry," said one side street dealer. "In the long run, I find I make more money that way. I haven't enough capital to afford to have any of it idle. I'm not an antique dealer, mind you, though I know antiques when I see them, and sometimes buy them. My father, now, he's an antique dealer, a real artist. He won't handle anything else. There's nothing in his store that isn't beautiful. But lots of it waits a long time before it's sold. It's all right. He's made his money and can afford to run an antique shop, and make money only when heaven sends him tourists who have the rare combination of taste and treasury notes. He likes to do it."

They are of all nationalities, these dealers in antiques and old furniture—Frenchmen, Germans, Italians, sometimes Americans.

One old German told a delightful story on himself, serenely unconscious, apparently, how good it was.

He was showing an inlaid mahogany desk of his own building—this man was by way of being a cabinet maker, the sort who takes odds and ends of old furniture and creates something wholly new and pleasing from them.

"I made a desk something like that once," he said reflectively. "It took me six months, working off and on. It was a beautiful thing. Then I sold it to a lady for $75. Next week a friend of hers came to me. She wanted to know how much I would charge her to make a desk exactly like Mrs. B's. I told her $400. 'But that's ridiculous,' she said, 'I know Mrs. B. paid only $75.'

"'Quite true,' said I, 'but I enjoyed making the first desk and it would be just drudgery to make a copy.' She couldn't see it, and she didn't buy."

Which goes to show that the artistic temperament asserts itself sometimes even among such practical folk as a good many of the antique dealers are.

The New Orleans Item
Thursday; January 3, 1924 (P. 22)

All Around New Orleans

Unsigned

Hogly Woglying[77]

Everybody is doing it—trying to save enough on necessities to pay the wages of the cook, the upkeep of the car, to support this or that charity or because they are infected with the thrift malady. Even Mrs. St. Charles has joined the ranks of the initiated. She was discovered in a self-service grocery at Jackson and St. Charles, doing her own shopping, while a limousine, with engine running, awaited her at the door, a liveried chauffeur at the wheel. A liveried footman preceded her through the turnstile and around the labyrinth where shelves of eatables are arranged; he carried a basket in which to put purchases. Mrs. St. Charles, with great deliberateness, inspected the offerings through a lorgnette: "Two of those, William," she said pointing the lorgnette at cans of peas, "One of this; two of those; sardines, my goodness, how bizarre!"

A river front worker, also shopping, watched her for a while, then grinned: "She's hogly woglying," he said.

---

[77] "Hogly Woglying" was a playful derivative of "Piggly Wigglying." The Piggly Wiggly Delicatessen was located on the corner of St. Charles and Jackson Avenue. See "Dividends Paid Promptly," *The Times-Picayune*, March 21, 1925.

The Thrills of 1924: Dorothy Day Encounters the "Underworld Denizens" of New Orleans

Worthy of Citizenship

The gods help those who help themselves—so long as people have the capacity to get "up in arms" and stay up until they get what they want, there is hope for the democracy.[78] New Orleans is cursed with acres of mud which serve for streets. Most people say "politics" is responsible; some hint at graft; a few are well informed enough to know that the growth of the city, even were waste eliminated, has outstripped its resources for public improvements. Wise men wag their heads; fools rave and the mud remains. There is, however, a way out. On Coliseum street above Second will be found a short stretch of well kept highway. Abutting property owners, tenants and their employes, chauffeurs, butlers and cooks procured materials and fixed the street themselves.

Climate Cured

She owns a beauty parlor and recently opened a branch in an exclusive neighborhood. "I came here 13 years ago," she said, "because I had tuberculosis and had to have a change of climate. Then I went back to Chicago, stayed two weeks and returned. The doctors said I had not long to live. I thought I would make the most of my time. I had six dollars then. Gradually I accumulated funds and finally went into business for myself and have prospered. I have my own house uptown, my own car, and something to leave my children. The other day I decided to take out an insurance policy and I went down for an examination. The doctors said I was sound as a dollar. The disease had eaten into my lungs before its ravages were stopped, and there is a cavity in one of them big enough to hold a hen egg but the injury has healed and my health is perfect. Do I like New Orleans?"

She smiled. If that smile could be caught and broadcasted, the population of the city would be a million before 1925.[79]

Invisible Clothes

A little boy in a theatre, when a rather gawky looking girl was on the stage, nudged his companion and whispered: "She can't sing and she can't dance; I bet she comes out in tights." The professional performer has been criticized severely for her tendency to discard wearing apparel but according to Bill, the truckman, she has had to do it to meet competition. Here is a bit of sidewalk gossip.

"I went to New York to represent my company—they are wearing tailor-mades there—they look smart, maybe, but awfully stiff—guess what, I bought some of these new nude stockings—honey they look like you haven't any on—they are a dream."

---

[78] The phrase, "God helps those who help themselves," was attributed to English political theorist Algernon Sidney, and later popularized in Benjamin Franklin's *Poor Richard's Almanack* (1736).

[79] As of the 1920 census, New Orleans ranked number seventeen in terms of the largest 100 urban places in the United States. The population of the city was 387,219. See "Population of the 100 Largest Urban Places: 1920," U.S. Bureau of the Census, https://www.census.gov/population/www/documentation/twps0027/tab15.txt (accessed February 23, 2018).

Fashion, which for several years has pursued fairly consistently a policy, the aim of which is to make clothing invisible, apparently is soon to arrive.

The New Orleans Item
Saturday; January 5, 1924 (P. 9)

All Around New Orleans

Unsigned

Outside the wind was bitter cold.

Shuffling before the brilliantly lighted windows of a restaurant in Chartres street was a man, poorly dressed in rough trousers and an old army blouse on the arm of which showed dirty red, his discharge chevron.

Inside was warmth, light and well-dressed men—sons of illustrious forefathers who fought in the War of the Revolution.[80]

Suddenly from the orchestra came the strains of the Star Spangled Banner.[81]

Inside well-dressed men were standing at attention. Some of them raised hands to their heads [making] the salute. Others hastily choked down last bites of food and stood rigid. Waiters paused with their trays of smoking food.

Outside the poor, one-time soldier's head came erect with a proud snap, his shoulders straightened and the shuffling of his crippled foot stopped. For an instant, then, with the return of conscious thought, the head lowered, the shoulders sagged and the man limped dejectedly away from the lighted windows.

---

[80] The American Revolutionary War was fought from 1775 to 1783.

[81] Francis Scott Key wrote the lyrics to the "Star Spangled Banner" in 1814, toward the end of the War of 1812 (1812-1815). Key's lyrics were adapted to John Stafford Smith's 1773 song, "To Anacreon in Heaven."

Here and There About New Orleans
By DOROTHY DAY

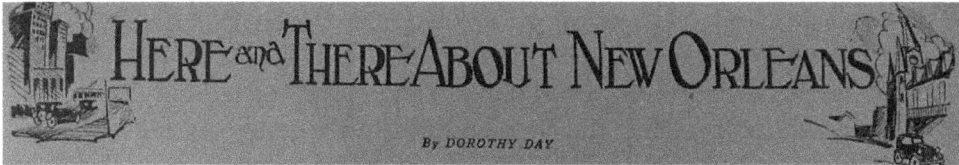

The New Orleans Item
Sunday; January 6, 1924 (P. 11; Special Section)

Here and There About New Orleans

By DOROTHY DAY

IN ALL cities may be found music in the sounds of the streets, but New Orleans has a rich and consistent melody of its own which other cities in the United States have not. Often it reminds you of old Paris, where the hucksters do not cry their wares, but sing and chant them. In Paris there is the song of the strawberry vendor, the chant of the flower sellers, and wailing tune of the cream cheese women. They used to sell cream cheese in Old New Orleans, too, in little heart-shaped pats, with a dash of cream poured over it from a claret bottle. But those days have passed. Other songs remain, however. Every day, throughout the French quarter, you know the scissors grinder man is trundling his old wheel down the street by the little tune which he plays on a flute, and which you can hear a block away. It is a simple little tune, and by its repetition insinuates itself in your mind, so that it becomes a motif, in the song of the streets, like that simple and endless motif, which sings its way, over and over again, through one of the arias of Manon Lescaut which, once heard, you can never forget.[82]

Yesterday we heard a huckster, singing a song of his cabbages and potatoes, a simple homely song, all the way down the street, and two little children, sitting on the curbstone, imitated the tune, till it was cast back and forth, between the huckster and the children, like a chant.

Occasionally comes a long, deep note from one of the steamboats on the river, that is like the throbbing note of an organ. In the night, the thrilling, long drawn-out emphasis of a certain kind of automobile horn comes like the opening of a symphony, and you listen expectantly for more, but the sound is stilled in the blackness of the night, and merged with the infinitesimal tunings of hundreds of other city instruments.

City music is like a modern symphony, soul wracking and restless, leaving you always listening, waiting for some simple tune that you can catch and hold to. And you find the simple tune in the city, where you don't in symphonies by modern composers. You will find it in the flute of the scissors grinder, and you will find it in the less subtle and rollicking tintinnabulations of the street organs.

*   *   *

---

[82] Day referred to Giacomo Puccini's 1893 operatic adaptation of Antoine François Prévost d'Exiles' (a.k.a. Abbé Prévost) 1731 novel, *Manon Lescaut.*

The Thrills of 1924: Dorothy Day Encounters the "Underworld Denizens" of New Orleans

The street organs deserve a paragraph by themselves. In New Orleans, they have a full and happy jazziness, with none of the undercurrent melancholy which you hear in other cities. We have listened to hurdy-gurdies in New York, San Francisco, London and Paris, and the only ones which have the fullness of tone which you get in the New Orleans hurdy gurdy, are those of London.[83] Every other night or so, an old negro and a little boy trundle a street organ to the front of our house, and play their entire repertoire, and we were so intrigued at finding London hurdy gurdies in New Orleans, that the other night we were forced to run down three flights of stairs, to find out about it.

But this was not a lone instrument, as we had thought it, brought by some Cockney from across the sea. "No, ma'am, this heah ain't mine. This heah piana belong to Mis' Rosa Pulissa down on Drive street. Yes'm, she has twelve o' them, and they comes from New Yawk."

But why aren't they played in New York instead of the plaintive, tin-panny instruments you hear there?

At the foot of St. Ann street, there was a huge steamer, trussed up to the dock, being stuffed and loaded like some huge fowl. You could hear the rolling thunder of an organ in the loading of the boat, and above the bass notes the shrill soprano of a derrick cried out. Settling ourselves comfortably on a bulkhead, we watched and listened while the rhythmical work went on. At fore and aft, barrels were rolled up gang planks and lowered into the bowels of the boat. And at two other gang planks, resinous logs were lifted and swung gracefully into the ship, giving forth an odor sweeter than incense. Far below the level of the dock, two sailors sat on a precarious plank and painted the rusty sides of the boat, gracefully and leisurely, while the gulls swung like separate notes of music around them.

We were not without company that afternoon. Other loungers sat along the dock and after a time a pleasant old man with a basket and baiting his two lines with tiny shrimp, lowered them between the planks of the pier close to the shore and sat beside them waiting. "It's no use sitting at the edge of the pier in winter time," he answered our query. "You either catch 'em out in the middle of the stream, or as close to the shore, under the pier, as you can get. Sure, I catch enough for supper and tomorrow morning's breakfast." And he lit his pipe and settled his back against a bulkhead, and the calm expression of the fisherman settled on his face.

All of those who sit by the water have this still look of peace on their faces. They are not waiting for anything, not even for the fish to bite. They are as still as though in prayer, and without watching the mother-of-pearl clouds on the horizon across the river color their thoughts, the silent motion of the driftwood enters their souls. Perhaps they, too, without listening for it, hear the dimmed music of the city by the river.

---

[83] In addition to living in New York and the San Francisco area (Berkeley and Oakland), Day spent nearly a year abroad during her honeymoon with Berkeley Tobey (circa 1920-1921) visiting England, France, and Italy. As the article implied, she had experienced hurdy-gurdies there. See Day, *From Union Square to Rome*, 102.

The New Orleans Item
Wednesday; January 9, 1924 (P. 6)

All Around New Orleans

Unsigned

Warmth of Imagination

A cold snap is the touch of nature that brings out the soul of New Orleans. Neighbors who have been strangers for years, suddenly begin speaking to one another. Chance acquaintances exchange stories of frozen pipes and chilled rooms. Newsboys, usually alert and on the job, withdraw from the street corners seeking protection from the cold in stores and doorways. Drivers desert their vehicles and scurry for cover. Soft drink dealers and coffee purveyors do a rushing business.

On Poland street a dozen workmen cease digging, shoveling, mixing and laying to gather around a fire on the edge of the sidewalk, extending their big hands into the warming rays. The fire consists of three small pieces of wood and two or three pieces of wrapping paper. The heat generated is insufficient to warm a spoonful of porridge; still, flames suggest warmth; imagination does the rest.

"Goat Giver"

The "goat-getter" has become more or less familiar—here is a woman who specializes in "goat giving." She is manager of a candy store on Carondelet.[84] A stately figure she is, with gray hair

---

[84] In July of 1922, the Fuerst and Kraemer Company opened a confectionary and lunchroom at 316 Carondelet Street, in New Orleans. The manager was a Mrs. Antoinette Darms. See "New Tea Room Opens," *The Times-Picayune*, July 5, 1922.

and a most charming manner. She has a grown son. Perhaps that is why most of her customers are boys. She exchanges pleasantries with them; meets them on their own 'ground. "Say," one of these patrons said after a wordy engagement with the hostess, "I come in here four or five times a day for coffee, just to get her goat.[85] Watch me, I'll have her raving before I go away." The manager smiled indulgently. She has found "goat getters" come back to harass their victims. She sees to it that "her goat is gotten" as frequently as desired.

Roller Skaters

On the campus of Tulane university is a sign prohibiting roller skating on the sidewalks and roadways—perhaps it is intended as a warning to freshmen.[86] At any rate, roller skaters are becoming numerous throughout the city, and children are not the only adepts. Two girls of debutante age boarded a St. Charles street car. They wore sweaters, knickers and sports hosiery, like those seen at St. Moritz or on the snow clad hillsides of Maine. On their arms were roller skates. "Oh, it is lots of fun," said one of them, "you shut your eyes and it's just like being on the ice."

Drawn Blinds

Like a deserted city, it seems, at times as you pass through residential districts. Doors are closed, blinds are drawn, and all is still and lifeless. Automobiles speed by, but flowers bloom, green trees droop, and shadows fall on silent homes barren of movement. A vigil of hours is sometimes rewarded. A fleeting glimpse of the figure of a maid or chauffeur in the rear garden is reassuring. A limousine draws up at the curb; the door opens; people come out, enter the car, and in a twinkling are gone. In winter, mild though it is, New Orleans lives indoors. Sometimes it seems that beautiful exteriors, for which the city is famous, are wasted. Too often, however, that is all that the uninvited visitor sees. The blinds are drawn tight.

An Understudy

Downtown a little girl was amusing herself by making faces at a dog, while her mother chatted with a friend. The youngster screwed up her eyebrows, shivered and shook, heaved and hissed. Mother smiled approvingly. "You know," she told her friend. "Everybody tells me Yvonne is just like Mae Murray.[87] She too may have her name in electric lights."

---

[85] The expression, "get one's goat," was attributed to a convict residing at Sing Sing; the expression means "Anger; to exasperate." See Number 1500, *Life in Sing Sing* (Indianapolis, IN: The Bobbs-Merrill Company, 1904), 248.

[86] Tulane University is located at 6823 St. Charles Avenue, in New Orleans.

[87] Mae Murray was an actress and dancer during the silent era of films.

The New Orleans Item
Thursday; January 10, 1924 (P. 19)

All Around New Orleans

Unsigned

The Star Boarder

His presence in the house would hardly be noticed, were it not for the marked deference shown him by the owner of the house; and her anxiety to please him. He arrives home when others are leaving for their places of employment, and is going out when they return. During the day his sleep must not be disturbed; the landlady sees to that. In conversations with other roomers, she never fails to speak of him and to mention incidentally the rather high rent he pays for his comfortable room in very modest surroundings. He, however, is a person of means and consequence and might be expected to live in a marble palace furnished with gold trimmed mahogany and ivory. He is said to be the manager of one of the most prosperous gambling establishments in New Orleans.

The Lure of Lucre[88]

Not everyone in New Orleans is a gambler; it just seems so to the visitor. The races have hundreds of followers who never saw a thoroughbred. Money and white slips change hands on every street corner; the wise salesman soon learns that the most appreciated courtesy is a good tip on the contests. The widow of an army officer bets two dollars a day. She lays her wager on the jockey rather than the horse he rides. A stenographer shares her meager salary with her "best friend" who pools it with his own earnings and places the total with bookmakers. If they ever

---

[88] "The Lure of Lucre" vignette was more than likely the impetus for Day's later article series, "The Thrills of 1924," which exposed the large number of women connected to the gambling industry in the New Orleans area.

make a "killing," she says they will be married and go on a honeymoon. A waitress puts in all her gratuities conservatively, and realizes a small profit. She is looking forward to an old age of idleness. Some shops depend for the bulk of their trade upon racing people. Easy come, easy go. A poor woman spent a thousand dollars she had won in a Baronne street shop for ornamentation. In almost every establishment will be found someone anxiously reading newspaper predictions and results. For every sportsman there are ten gamblers paying a heavy price for chances to get rich quick. It is a characteristic. Whether it is good or evil depends on the point of view.

Tailor By Proxy

It was a big clothing store, whose reputation is not questioned. A patron selected a suit and the tailor was called to insure a perfect fit. It was during the rush season, and the workrooms were packed with clothes ordered altered, and tailors had all they could do to keep pace with salesmen. The individual who responded to the call carried three tape measures on his shoulders and danced around the customer, measuring every breadth and width visible, but his procedure was more of a burlesque than a finished job. The patron viewed him with suspicion.

"Are you a good tailor?" he demanded.

"Oh, no," said the poseur with frankness, "I am not a tailor at all. I am the substitute. I am a measurer. I can measure ribbon, cloth, horses, coal—anything that is measurable, and I can lick any tailor who does not follow my directions explicitly. If you have any doubt about it; pay for your suit after you receive it. You will be satisfied."

The clerk confirmed the confession and promise, and the patron was mollified. To his great surprise the suit was delivered at the time promised and fitted perfectly.

On New Year's eve the measurer went out on Canal street selling horns and ticklers. On another occasion he was seen taking up tickets at a bazaar. Apparently he is a man of parts.

Cleanliness Underfoot

In the sections where colored people make their homes, and the district is most difficult to define, houses are sometimes dilapidated, badly in need of paint and surrounded by weeds, but an almost general characteristic is the cleanliness of floors and steps. Every day, it seems, this part of the house is scrubbed and in many places the wood has been worn down to half its thickness by the relentless scrubbing brush. It is a practice to sit on the steps during the day; perhaps there is a saving in clothes. Ants and roaches, however, are a more relentless incentive. Cleanliness is their most formidable foe.

The New Orleans Item
Monday; January 14, 1924 (P. 2; Evening Edition)

All Around New Orleans

Unsigned

A Chicken Sermon

Preachers sometimes complain that those who need sermons most never come to hear them. Chickens in the window of Bruce's poultry and seed store on Poydras street cannot make that complaint.[89] In the window a head of lettuce is suspended on a string, as high as the chickens can jump. All day long they busy themselves pecking at the lettuce, and, as a result of the exercise, are sinewy, strong and contented. At all hours idlers watch them. Some of them smile sympathetically, others with blank faces peering from ragged clothes, stare blankly as though entranced, possibly amazed at fancied complexities, or fascinated by movement in the window. Past them hurry throngs of preoccupied individuals in a maddening pursuit of lettuce leaves, but for them—oh, well, something may turn up tomorrow.

Welcome Winter

Water, water everywhere and not a drop to drink;[90] only Gunga Din water in which to wash dishes;[91] undoubtedly water pipes were frozen. Colds, ugly tempers and pneumonia are other by-

---

[89] The Bruce Seed and Poultry Company, Incorporated, was then located at 727 Poydras Street, in New Orleans. See "Advertisements," *The Times-Picayune*, March 23, 1924.

[90] "Water, water…" is a line from Samuel Taylor Coleridge's poem, "The Rime of the Ancient Mariner," published in 1798. Day had used this same quote earlier in her career as a journalist for the *New York Call*. See Dorothy Day, "Reporter Looks into Fads, Facts and Fancies, and Things at Rand School," *New York Call,* November 12, 1916.

[91] "Gunga Din" was a poem written by Rudyard Kipling, circa 1890.

products of the brief taste of water just passed, but it is an ill winter that brings no one happiness. In the midst of confusion and complaint, Charley's little girl danced with glee.

"No water," she exclaimed, "I am so glad I could bust. Don't have to wash my face. I don't have to wash my face."

Hobohemia

They had the grandest apartment. He said so, she confirmed his statement. It was downtown, right in the center of the artistic colony, and had a real, honest-to-goodness patio where parties innumerable could be held. They have had the whole place "done over" and have spent three weeks and more than a thousand dollars furnishing it, but though the end is not yet, they still cherish their dream of comfort. Indeed, annoyances seem to add to the joy of living.

"We never had so many callers before," she exclaimed rapturously, "you see, our bell is right on the street. School boys ring it in the morning, at noon and in the afternoon. Today three house-to-house canvassers called, and a party of tourists rang, begging permission to see our 'garden.' I showed them the brick pile in the patio and our brand new hot water heater. Just before you came a drunken man rang the bell and beat on the door, but I would not let him in. I used to get lonesome uptown."

Hard Luck

On North Claiborne avenue seated leaning against a tree near a trolley stop was a little colored boy. In his left hand was a woman's card case, open and empty. Between the fingers of his right hand he held a small white card. He studied it patiently, spelling out the words printed on it, one by one. Apparently he had just found the case and had sat down to ascertain its value. A frown gathered on his face as he read, and finally he threw down the card with disgust, shoved the leather case into his pocket and shuffled away. On it was printed: "Mrs. B. Hall, beauty specialist."

Trolley Aristocracy

Habitual "rush hour" trolley patrons occasionally oversleep or for some other reason are thrown with late comers. The difference between the two groups of workers is not clearly defined, but is marked to a degree. The nine o'clock riders are leisurely in their manner and more considerate of their fellow riders. Seldom does a woman stand. Faces are bright and interesting. Conversation is a little more than chattering. These are not job holders or clock slaves. Some perhaps are shoppers, some are in business for themselves, still, others by adroitness, kinship or long service go to work when they please. You will find them in every office. They are the aristocracy of trolley patrons.

Municipal Magnificence

Just beyond the viaduct over the Industrial canal to the left is a quaint little building. Set back from the road, it is surrounded by evergreen trees and sheltered with vines, seemingly, in its colorful picturesqueness, the work of an artist blind to a limited background. Frequently visitors stop there, thinking it is a church, a school or a library. It is really a municipal sewage pumping station distinguished, the watchman will tell you, by the fact that "the pipes are twenty-five feet underground, and the engines were overhauled a few weeks ago for the first time since the station was opened."[92]

---

[92] Municipal Pumping Station Number Five is located on Florida Avenue. See "Detailed Map of City's Drainage System," *The Times-Picayune*, May 9, 1926.

The Thrills of 1924: Dorothy Day Encounters the "Underworld Denizens" of New Orleans

The New Orleans Item
Friday; January 25, 1924 (P. 2; Evening Edition)

All Around New Orleans

Unsigned

Circumscribed

Some people live in a world apart from their environment. One of them is a girl who came here a year ago from the North. She lives with her aunt on lower St. Charles and is employed in a restaurant on Royal street. Every day she goes from one place to the other and back, occasionally going two or three blocks across town to shop or to moving picture shows. That is her world, and even in its narrow borders, she is a stranger. The house where she lives is old, shutters are loose but there is a shadowy grandeur remaining and quaint whisperings under the eaves—she does not hear them. Where she spends her day was formerly a bar-room. There gentlemen clicked their glasses, dealt cards, planned fortunes, toasted success, confessed ruin, quarreled and renewed friendships while rapier wounds were still fresh—they still seem to stroll between the tables, booted and spurred, and longing—but she does not see them. A few minutes walk would bring her to the Cabildo, historic treasure house, the great river, the home of Lafitte,[93] the United Fruit company's palatial home,[94] the public library, or Dryades street's bargain counters[95]—but she

---

[93] Day mentioned what was believed by many to be the Lafitte brother's "blacksmith shop," located at 941 Bourbon Street. Although Jean and Pierre Lafitte may have bartered slaves at that location, there is no evidence that the property ever belonged to the infamous duo. In fact, there has been no evidence that either Lafitte brother ever resided in the Crescent City. A reporter, native to New Orleans, would not have made this error. See Stanley Clisby Arthur, *Old New Orleans* (1936; repr., New Orleans, LA: Harmanson, 1955), 136-137.

[94] The offices of the United Fruit Company were located at 321 St. Charles Street, in New Orleans. Sam Zemurray, the founder of the company, held a palatial estate at 2 Audubon Place, in New Orleans. The property is now part of Tulane University. See "Many Big Features on Club's Program," *The Times-Picayune*, March 4, 1923; "For $250," *The Times-Picayune*, April 23, 1923.

never deviates from her beaten path. It is not her fault, altogether. She has little time and when she does have a moment she wants happiness quick and at a low expenditure of effort. At the movies she finds enjoyment in another life that is perfect and ready made. She does not know the richness of the world around her.

Appreciation

An etching shown at the Arts and Crafts club of dancers at Montmartre, wonderfully graceful figures, almost dancing out of their frame, so lifelike they seem, has attracted considerable attention.[96] One who looked at it was a woman. Then she took her husband there to see it, and both of them went back several times. True appreciation of the beautiful is more rare than might be supposed. Others became interested in the couple. Finally, they made themselves known. He is secretary of an ice company. He said they wanted that picture but they really could not afford to buy it. He wanted to know if the club would not hold it for him if he would make a deposit. Can you picture the home in which the etching will be placed?

Milk Elevator

The driver of a milk wagon hasn't time to climb stairs, and he is so early on his rounds, in many places he would wake everybody up if he tried it. Still, people who live on the second floor must have milk and it is a whole lot of bother walking downstairs for it every morning.[97] In Carrollton the problem has been solved in this fashion: A basket with a string is lowered from the window to the ground. The milk bottle is put into it and when the originator arises, he hauls his milk up to his apartment.

Samaritan[98]

"Will someone help me."

A tall, slender, rather handsome young man tapped the pavement on Canal street with his cane and waited. Dozens of people passed him, wondering. They did not observe that he was blind. A school girl, with an art portfolio, dressed in gray with soft cloth hat to match, pretty, young and

---

[95] Dryades Street bargain counters included the Famous Electric Co., Inc. (fans and lamps), at 1423 Dryades Street; Grand Leader (dresses, hats, and shoes), at 1626-1628 Dryades Street; Handelman's (general goods), at 1824-1832 Dryades Street; Harris Ice Cream Company, at 1300 Dryades Street; and, Chas. A. Kaufman Co., Ltd. (women's wear, shoes), at 1700 Dryades Street. See "Shop on Dryades Street," *The Times-Picayune*, June 11, 1924.

[96] Day had written about the Arts and Crafts Club in a previous article. See "A Sportsman," in "All Around New Orleans," *The New Orleans Item*, December 17, 1923.

[97] The St. Peter Street apartment that Day and Gordon had lived in was located on the second floor. Strangely, Day had claimed, in a previously signed article, that she had had to run down three flights of stairs to hear the hurdy-gurdy players. See Dorothy Day, "Here and There About New Orleans," *The New Orleans Item*, January 6, 1924.

[98] A reference to "The Parable of the Good Samaritan," Lk 10:25-37 [NRSV]. Day had written about the Good Samaritan in her final article for the *New York Call*. In describing the people who refused to help a poverty-stricken old man, Day stated, sarcastically, that "The story of the Good Samaritan was enacted yesterday morning, not on the road from Jerusalem to Jericho, but on 19th street between Second and Third avenues." See Dorothy Day, "Europe's Moloch Claim's Old Man's Son; He Comes to America and Starves," *New York Call*, April 19, 1917.

vivacious, hesitated and looked at him, then offered him her arm. "I am going across," she said, cheerfully, "come along." She chatted gaily as they walked, and the blind man smiled. Perhaps he was conscious that the attention of passersby was directed not at him but his companion.[99]

---

[99] The first of six references to "passerby" or "passersby." See "All Around New Orleans," *The New Orleans Item*, February 27, 1924 (Evening Edition, twice); "All Around New Orleans," *The New Orleans Item*, March 5, 1924; "All Around New Orleans," *The New Orleans Item*, March 15, 1924; "All Around New Orleans," *The New Orleans Item*, March 17, 1924.

The New Orleans Item
Saturday; January 26, 1924 (P. 4)

All Around New Orleans

Unsigned

Late for Church

A chill wind whipped through the tree tops, and around the church tower silhouetted against a silvery sky. Automobiles with lights darkened flanked the curbing, black shadows in the glaring light of a street lamp. From the church came voices singing, but the doors were closed as though to reprove late comers. An elderly man, hurrying, suddenly paused, looked at his watch, glanced at the church doors, then more slowly walked on by, apparently disappointed but glad tardiness furnished an excuse for absence. A young man overtook him and walked beside him.

"I often go to church outdoors," the elderly man said, "and I don't know that it is not the best place for prayer. No cathedral is so great as God's magnificent heaven, dotted with myriad candles; indeed, sometimes symbols seem to obscure a broad and understanding view of the Throne."

Some twenty blocks the walk led past beautiful homes, where lights glowed invitingly, by little houses built like steamboats, darkened and cold, under palms and oaks, and beside wonderful gardens, over brick, stone slabs and concrete walks. The Churchman was silent after a time, looking at the moon and the stars, and speaking softly to himself; then he began to hum a hymn, and soon started singing the words. Spiritually he was uplifted, physically he seemed to gather strength and an added height as he walked. At any rate, it was with a clear conscience that he finally turned toward home, for then he talked of the governorship, of himself and his work, of the street car system and many other matters of interest. The hymn was the recessional.

The Thrills of 1924: Dorothy Day Encounters the "Underworld Denizens" of New Orleans

Anishia

If a colored girl with that name applies for a job, pull her in the house and lock the doors. She is cheerful, industrious and resourceful, a household wonderworker. However, she is now employed. This is about her name.

"Don't know what it means—guess it don't mean nothing but me," she said. "My mother was working in a place before I was born for a lady that always used big words and she just liked Anishia better than any other she heard."

A Reminder

A crowded car. One seat in front of the car was left vacant. A young man asked a woman who was standing with her back turned to it if she did not wish to sit down.

"No," she said shortly, and continued talking to a friend.

An older man asked another woman if she would have it, and she, too, preferred to stand. The older man looked at the younger man and waited.

"You sit down," the younger man said.

"No, you take it," he returned.

"You're older than I am."

The older man regarded him from head to foot, as though debating the question.

"I guess you are right," he admitted, and sat down, seeming a little regretful the precedence was his.

The New Orleans Item
Monday; January 28, 1924 (P. 14)

All Around New Orleans

Unsigned

Truant[100]

A faint light drifted through the windows, falling full on the raised bench of the judge, and beyond to the heavy seats reserved for spectators. A stenographer was within the railing. In the aisle were three parents with children, who had been commanded to appear there for an interview respecting the right of their children to remain away from school. They were poor mothers. The children were wage earners. The dreadfully worded summons had brought them to the appointed place through a downpour of rain. An attendant said the judge would not be there; that the summons had been issued by an employe of the board of education. Telephone calls brought the information that the employe was sick and would not be there either. Oh, well! When everyone who is not graduated is incarcerated, perhaps officialdom will be more considerate of its victims.

Homesick

Sunday afternoon Orthodox Creoles sleep, and callers are not always welcome; so when Fred, who is a Philadelphian, first called on Mrs. Rosa, he thought her rather cool and inhospitable. Now he makes his calls Saturday afternoons. Homesick, even with the thousand delicacies from the kitchens of New Orleans, he longs of just a reminder of the food he was raised upon, so when

---

[100] Day had trawled the Jefferson Market night court, in Greenwich Village, for her first assignment for the *New York Call* (1916). She would later work for the City News Bureau in Chicago (circa 1921-1922), covering the events of the children's court, the court of domestic relations, and the morals court. See Day, "Girl Reporter, with Three Cents in Purse, Braves Night Court Lawyers," November 11, 1916; Day, *From Union Square to Rome*, 101; Day, *The Long Loneliness*, 95.

he calls he brings a steak, vegetables, a salad—enough eatables for a full course dinner. For the evening he becomes housekeeper, cook and servitor, and when he is through, washes and replaces every utensil and dish that has been used. Mrs. Rosa is mighty fond of good food. She hates housework. Fred never has to ring the doorbell but once.

The New Orleans Item
Wednesday; January 30, 1924 (P. 22; Evening Edition)

All Around New Orleans

Unsigned

Reproved

At the corner of Jackson and St. Charles in the hours when the streets are congested are two policemen both on the "uptown side." One is at the intersection, the other is a little further down. His job is to "hurry 'em on." Mrs. Prytania, driving her own sedan, was "hurried on" right up to the white line, then the whistle blew, and she slammed on the brakes.[101] The policeman glared at her and shouted something she did not hear. When the signal changed, she had difficulty starting then swerved till she almost struck the policeman, and came to a standstill, apparently intending to tell him what she thought of him. The policeman looked at her sympathetically.

"Please hurry along, sister," he said.

Mrs. Prytania stiffened haughtily, stepped on the gas and was gone.

Feelings Spared

It is a peculiarity of many of the old Creole families that they do not like to hurt people's feelings. Indeed, "white lies" are quite common. One woman, a native, had a room uptown. During the cold spell, she could not get hot water, then the cold water was shut off for a week.

---

[101] This is the second occasion that Day had substituted the name of a nearby street in place of the person's name, which would have been unknown to her—the other being "Mrs. St. Charles." See "Hogly Woglying," in "All Around New Orleans," *The New Orleans Item*, January 3, 1924.

Service was bad all around, so finally she decided to move. She did not say she was dissatisfied with her rooms; she said she was going downtown to live with a relative, which she did not. In another instance, two Hobohemian girls from the North succeeded in getting rooms with an old and very respectable French family.[102] After two weeks they were asked to move to make room for a "sister of their hostess."

"Oh, my sister?" the hostess said to someone else who went to look at her rooms, "that was just a story. They were nice girls, but they had visitors in their rooms instead of the parlor, which was all right—but, well, I did not think it was quite proper."[103]

---

[102] This represented the second mention of the term "Hobohemia." See "Hobohemia," in "All Around New Orleans," *The New Orleans Item*, January 14, 1924.

[103] Although Day and Gordon may have been asked to vacate their apartment, there is no evidence that they were actually evicted. Perhaps after a stern warning, Day and Gordon began adhering to their landlady's rules. Day later admitted to having several gentlemen callers, "…one a wounded cameraman from Hollywood who had gone through the war and come back with many scars and minus a leg, and another silent, mysterious young man on his way to South America who had told me he carried a revolver in a holster under his arm and slept with it under his pillow." See Day, *The Long Loneliness*, 108-109.

The New Orleans Item
Thursday; January 31, 1924 (P. 21)

All Around New Orleans

Unsigned

The Lost Cake

In the home of a prominent insurance man in Audobon street, a cake was baked—a big cake, with delicious white icing, enough to tempt even a boy prodigy nursed on truth serum. The cake was left on the rear balcony to cool. A few minutes later it had disappeared. Mother with the girls got out the car and cruised around the neighborhood looking for the cake or the culprits. Neither could be found. No one had seen it walking away. Apparently, as a police reporter might say, it was shrouded in mystery. Meanwhile, however, another member of the family had organized herself into a posse and joined the pursuit. In the neighborhood is only one street that is impassable for automobiles, and down that way she directed her steps. To her amazement, she found the cake sitting unceremoniously in the middle of the sidewalk, a little lump of sweet whiteness with a background of mud. "Maybe the angels just swooped down and toted it" there. At any rate, there were no fingerprints to identify the culprits. Tomorrow the police reporter is scheduled to write: "The police are still seeking" and so forth. The cake is being held as evidence.[104]

Memories

A few brief moments with one who remembers makes New Orleans even more interesting. Between Bienville and Canal street, there was little time, but as Mrs. Ruby picked her way

---

[104] See Footnote no. 100.

cautiously, in deference to her lameness, along Royal street, she graciously made the most of fleeting minutes.

"When I was a little girl," she said, "there were beautiful residences here. We girls used to come by, and one would say: 'Oh, come let's stop and see Mrs. So-and-so,' and we would troupe in to be greeted warmly in French.[105]

"Mr. Monteleone owned a shoe store on the corner there, and he used to rent a few rooms on the second floor. That was the beginning of the hotel.

"Do you know, the change in the city is almost startling. Then the Esplanade car line circled the city. The homes of the elite were for the most part on Esplanade. Poor people saw them, admired them, and envied the owners, and perhaps became ambitious to be like them. Most of those homes are owned now by the people who were poor when I was a girl.

"There is something that will interest you—those urns in the doorway of Sern's auction rooms.[106] When I was young, urns like that were kept on the lawns on Esplanade. We used to stop on our way to and from school to drink rain water from them. Maybe it wasn't healthful but it tasted better than that which comes from a spigot. Still, doctors have learned much since then; I have, too."

Fit Punishment

He was a good boy and a devoted son, but a little careless in his habits and not easily disciplined. He knew not fear and was mildly tolerant of favor. There seemed to be no way to reach him by pleading, threats or persuasion. So, he often stayed out late at night, forgetful of his mother's anxiety. One night, however, he came home to find the house full of excitement. There were calls for the doctor and restoratives were hurriedly fetched and applied. Mother had become hysterical, she was having a fit—and all because he stayed out late at night. The boy was properly frightened. He hurried for the doctor himself, and stayed right at the bedside until the danger had passed and vowed then and there never again to cause such commotion. The mother is wise. As the days passed and the vow was kept religiously, an inward satisfaction provoked a smile, with just the suggestion of shame for her deceit, but only over a coffee cup with an old friend did she admit the fit was a hoax.

---

[105] The first of two references to "Mrs. So-and-so," the other occurring in March of 1924. See "All Around New Orleans," *The New Orleans Item*, March 18, 1924.

[106] Stern's Art and Auction Rooms (Jac. H. Stern, Auctioneer) were located at 235 Royal Street, in New Orleans. See "Auction Sales," *The Times-Picayune*, April 20, 1924.

The New Orleans Item
Monday; February 4, 1924 (P. 11)

All Around New Orleans

Unsigned

Tonsillitis

It was a hopeless case. In Shreveport he was a bright boy and always led his class. He was ambitious and industrious and a great help to his mother. Then she brought him to New Orleans. Soon he lost interest. He did not want to go to school any more. He was brought up for truancy. He preferred to work or do nothing at all. He really wished they would send him to one of those homes for delinquent boys. He thought he would find there a life of ease. He was invited to go to one of the homes and see how the boys live, but he declined.

That would require mental and physical effort. He was not impressed with a recital of the discipline and hardships to which such boys are subjected. Fatherly advice from his elders was received with indifference. He felt that he was alone against all the world, battling for his right to be indolent. He breathed heavily, and now and then gasped as though inhalation of air was difficult. A physician was asked to examine him.

"It is an ordinary case of swollen tonsils," the doctor said, "that is all that is the matter with him. I will treat them, but a simple operation would afford permanent relief."

It is really an ordinary case. One door leads to the physician's office, the other to the house of detention.

The New Orleans Item
Wednesday; February 6, 1924 (P. 8)

All Around New Orleans

Unsigned

The lady with the sedan bearing the Alabama license drove straight between the long lines of traffic at St. Charles and Howard avenues. The autos skidded on the wet streets and honked danger signals.

The lady took out a cigarette, and a match. She lit the cigarette.

And, so doing, she took both hands off the wheel.

The autos kept on honking. Drivers of other autos looked wild-eyed at the lady, and kept their hands on the emergency brake.

But the lady was oblivious of all noise, all danger. She puffed at her cigarette, and sighed in content. Then she put her hands back on the wheel.

A Wise Boy

A certain rich man was so impressed with the courtesy of an Item newsboy that he stopped one day to talk to him.

"Young man," he said, "I have been buying a paper from you every day for some time, and I notice that no matter how busy you are, you always say 'thank you.' I'd like to know why you do it."

"Oh, it don't cost nothing and don't take no time," the boy returned, evasively.

"But why do you do it?"

The boy regarded the patron with more attention.

"Tell me," he said, "why do you buy a paper from me every day?"

"Well, I don't know," the patron said, "unless it is because you say 'thank you.'"

"That's why I say it," the boy returned.

Somebody's Mother

Captain Eugene Casey, of the police department, was in the midst of an enthusiastic explanation of a new traffic plan at St. Charles and Louisiana avenues with a committee of inspection when he suddenly stopped short.[107]

"Great Scott," he exclaimed, starting off at a run. "They will never let her across."

A woman with a baby carriage had stopped at the curb and waited patiently for an opportunity to cross. Automobiles raced up the street, a moving mass of danger. Captain Casey rushed into an opening and extended both arms to the sky, as though he would push the stream of traffic back down the avenue. He stood in that position while the woman leisurely lowered the carriage over the curb and walked to the other [side]. She was somebody's mother.

---

[107] Captain Eugene Casey was the first chief of the traffic division for the city of New Orleans. A member of the police force since June of 1907, Casey was considered a national traffic expert. He retired in November of 1929. See Edgar Boutwell, "Amateur Describes Life of Traffic Cop," *The Times-Picayune*, January 20, 1924; "Captain Casey's Funeral Service to be Held Today," *The Times-Picayune*, May 5, 1942.

The New Orleans Item
Wednesday; February 13, 1924 (P. 8)

All Around New Orleans

Unsigned

He had a rendezvous with death, and in his well-bred way was willing to take any sympathetic soul into his confidence about it. I met him in the middle of lower Royal street, at 1 o'clock in the morning.

He came and urged me to beat on the door of a writing person's house until in desperation the writing person came down and let us in. My new found friend sat down recklessly and by a miracle managed to hit the chair. Not that it would have bothered him much if he hadn't. He was beyond bothering about these mundane trifles.

For, announced the young man, this was to be his last night on the earth. Before another sun came up he intended to be sleeping forever in the Mississippi river—launched on the Great Adventure—anyhow, dead.

His fellow roomer and I remonstrated with him in a mild way over his decision. It was too hot to protest very hard. Why hurry this death thing, said we. The river was always there. It never freezes over.

Our levity offended him a little, but he was still polite. He told us with unsteady gravity that he must be getting along with his arrangement for the river. They were delightfully simple. He had some whisky and was out of money.[108]

He would sit and drink the whisky and play Chopin's funeral march on his phonograph, and when the whisky was gone and he had achieved the proper frame of mind, then for the rendezvous.[109]

"Won't you join me?" he urged pleasantly.

"Why not?" said I. After all, there was a chance he really meant it. One couldn't just sit back and let him make his "gesture."

How true to type runs Youth, how artlessly conventional in its defiance of convention, how touching its confidence that it is different. The boy was reading Schopenhauer, of course.

The little green leather book lay open at the chapter on suicide.[110]

It was the central object on a flimsy table littered with burnt matches, squeezed out lemon halves, books, dirty collars and cloudy glasses, holding the dregs of drinks.

He told me something of himself. He was 20 and an artist. There was a girl, of course. One gathered, without his saying so, that she was the reason for the rendezvous with death. Wouldn't marry him. He was tired of living.[111]

She must have been a nice girl, judging from the letter he showed me. It was a fine, brave, tender, kindly letter. Somehow, it seemed as out of place, that letter, in that littered room, as apple blossoms in a charnel house.

Heavens, what frightful stuff they sell as whisky down on lower Royal street!

---

[108] Over the course of her *New Orleans Item* articles, Day had used the word "whisky" (nine times) and "whiskey" (five times) interchangeably. Either usage was acceptable, but it must be wondered whether the discrepancy in usage was due to an editor, or lack thereof.

[109] Composed by Frederic Chopin in 1839, the "funeral march" is more properly known as Piano Sonata No. 2 in B Minor, Op. 35. This represented the first of two of Day's articles mentioning Chopin's funeral march. See "The Thrills of 1924," *The New Orleans Item*, February 27, 1924.

[110] Day's description of Schopenhauer's book identified it as the 1917 edition of *Studies in Pessimism*, published by Boni and Liveright. Albert and Charles Boni, who later bought Liveright's stake in the company, published Day's *The Eleventh Virgin*, shortly after she left New Orleans. See Arthur Schopenhauer, "On Suicide," in *Studies in Pessimism* (New York, NY: Boni and Liveright, Inc., 1917). In *The Eleventh Virgin*, Day also mentioned reading Schopenhauer's essay, "On Women," from the same volume. See Day, *The Eleventh Virgin*, 265.

[111] Day had experienced a similar situation, in Greenwich Village in January of 1918, with the suicide of Louis W. Holladay. She had been present when Holladay, a good friend of Eugene O'Neill, ingested a vial of heroin after being jilted by a lover. Holladay's death was ruled a heart attack by officials, because Day had withheld the empty vial from the police. See "Died," *The New York Sun*, January 24, 1918; Agnes Boulton, *Part of a Long Story: Eugene O'Neill as a Young Man in Love* (Garden City, NY: Double and Company, Inc., 1958), 39-40; Day, "To Donald Powell (April 9, 1959)," in *All the Way to Heaven*, 325-327; Louis Sheaffer, *O'Neill: Son and Playwright* (Boston, MA: Little, Brown And Company, 1968), 410-411.

He pulled out a half pint flask, and gravely poured me a drink—on top of some of the dregs. It reeked to heaven, reeked of everything bad and new and poisonous and rotten. I told him I wanted to look at the stars from his balcony, and gently poured the drink into Royal street.

He drank his, though. In the next room three girls and a young man were talking, listlessly. It was breathless and hot in Frenchtown, and the tin-pan piano of a cabaret jangled brassily.[112]

He showed me the things he had drawn, and told me about critics who had said they were "nice things." He was tall, pale and slim; well-mannered, Irish.

A Bible with his name lettered in gilt lay among the cigarette butts. It had been a present for two years' unbroken attendance at Sunday school, said an inscription on the fly-leaf, written by the Sunday school teacher.

He played Chopin's funeral march, and one by Beethoven, and assured me only Germans could understand them, and one of the faults he had to find with life was that he was Irish.[113] He bumped into an easel, and an oil study in still life fell to the littered floor and nobody bothered about picking it up.

The phonograph played some more dirges, and the boy drank some more Royal street whisky, and the perspiration ran down his white face and behind his ears.

Wicked stuff, that Royal street whisky. Calculated to make one forget everything—even a rendezvous with death, and how theatrical is one's "last night on earth."

He reached for something on the mantel piece, knocked down an empty flask, fell over it, got up, very wearily, and said it didn't matter.

The young man came in from the next room, and the boy told him about the things he wanted him to have, after he'd kept his rendezvous with death. The young man thanked him gravely, and went out.

And then the reader of Schopenhauer and drawer of pictures leaned over and collapsed in a limp heap on the floor.

There was only one bed in the room and I thought I had earned it. I straightened him out and tossed the flask of overnight whisky out the window and went to sleep.

---

[112] "Brassily" and "lustily" were the first of several uncommon adverbs used by Day in her New Orleans articles. Other uncommon adverbs included "cannily," "silkily," "sleepily," and "shabbily." See "All Around New Orleans," *The New Orleans Item*, February 14, 1924 (Evening Edition), "cannily"; Dorothy Day, "Boxers Seem Fine Fellows by Comparison After Sleek Sheiks Mincing at Cabarets," *The New Orleans Item*, February 12, 1924, "silkily"; Dorothy Day, "The Thrills of 1924," *The New Orleans Item*, February 25, 1924, "sleepily," and "shabbily."

[113] Beethoven's funeral marches included the second movement of Symphony No. 3 (*Eroica*), and the third movement of Piano Sonata No. 12.

The rendezvous with death was off.

The letter from the nice girl lay on the table, under the cloudy glass and next [to] the Bible, and the phonograph had stopped and the lights were out. A policeman, coat tightly buttoned, strolled leisurely on his rounds, and a rooster at [the] French market lustily proclaimed the coming dawn.

The New Orleans Item
Thursday; February 14, 1924 (P. 20; Evening Edition)

All Around New Orleans

Unsigned

The street fakir was selling two-bit fountain pens, "unbreakable, guaranteed not to leak and to last a life time." His "spiel" was cannily humorous, revealing a deep knowledge of the vagaries of human nature. While delivering his monologue the young man would demonstrate the writing qualities of the pen by inscribing elaborate designs upon paper. To illustrate the unbreakable qualities of the pen he would place one upon a board, pause a moment to impress the crowd, then hit the pen with a brick.

It was an impressive demonstration. He sold many pens. But to give his "spiel" he had first to attract a crowd. Upon his table in the gutter were two upright pieces of wood. Between these were two cylinders, placed close together, like the cylinders of a printing press. The fakir would impressively demand silence, place a strip of blank paper between the rolls, turn the crank and the paper would emerge as a crisp new one dollar bill.

The crowd thickened. Again the peddler demonstrated the art of making good money out of blank paper. He elaborated upon how easy it was to do it. Negroes and boys gazed in pop-eyed wonder as the crisp bills came out. Only one, a snub-nosed newsboy, was cynical.

"Say, boss," he called, "if it's as easy as that to make them, let's see you tear a few of them up."

That broke up the demonstration.

————————

This is the only social club of its kind in the city. The members meet each day at noon on the corner of St. Charles and Poydras streets. All are deaf mutes working in the neighborhood. Every day during lunch hour they congregate at that corner. About 15 of them meet regularly. They stand on the corner and converse in signs for half an hour.

Pedestrians pause to stare at them. All human beings are curious. Sometimes the hearing people form a ring about the mutes, a ring of "rubbernecks." The mutes are too accustomed to it to be bothered much. When a too curious person stares too long, one of the mutes will point to his neck and make the motion of stretching an elastic band. The gesture is so vivid, so contemptuous, that even the too curious hearing person understands. He blushes and passes on, followed by the grins of the mutes and others.

The policeman on the corner apparently knows them all. He never makes them move on. Perhaps he knows that they have no other place in which to meet, and that this noon hour meeting is their only chance for conversation. Most of them work among hearing people and this noon hour social is the bright spot of the day for them. Even the clerk in the cigar store, whose doors they sometimes block, offers no objection. In fact, he encourages them.

"They're an attraction," he told one who inquired. "I like them, they give me their trade and some of those who pause to watch them also are reminded of smokes that they need."

That's a new form of advertising.

The New Orleans Item
Friday; February 15, 1924 (P. 20; Evening Edition)

All Around New Orleans

Unsigned

He was evidently celebrating something. His face was expansive with good humor. He was clad in holiday attire. A flower bloomed in his buttonhole. He hung from a strap in a crowded Carondelet car downward bound. His smiles were for all in sight.

Two friends occupied the long end seat before which he stood. They were joshing him about his festive appearance and humor.

"Why the great joy?" queried one.

"I'm celebrating an anniversary."

"Wedding?"

"No."

"Birthday?"

"No."

"What sort of an anniversary are you celebrating?"

"Listen. I've been riding this line for years. You know how it is, you've been riding with me. Well, one year ago today, I caught the regular 7:30 car to work. The car was not delayed. I had the correct change ready. The conductor didn't slam the door on my heels and, listen, man! I had a seat all the way to town. Can you believe it? Well, that's the anniversary that I'm celebrating. I don't expect it to happen again in my life time."

His seated friend was equal to the occasion.

"Congratulations, old man. You're right. And to aid in perpetuating a tradition, the observance of a historical occasion, here, take my seat."

———————

New Orleans harbors an embryo financial magnate, a young man destined to control the pressing and cleaning business. He has a small pressing shop on Magazine street.[114] Monday night he called at the home of one of his regular customers to get a suit.

"Boss," he said, "I'm going to move my shop this week, but I want to keep your trade. I can send for your suits regularly."

"Where are you going to move to, Sam?"

"Over on Freret street."

"Why the change? Don't you like your present location?"

"Yassuh. I likes it all right but I think that I can do more business over on Freret. You see, boss, this street has been torn up for over two years. Every time it rains, everybody gets muddy and that's good for my business. But this part of the street is finished now, and I'm losing trade.

"Yestiddy I went over to Freret. They been working on it for about a year but it's still tore up. Boss, that street's worse than Magazine was. There's lots of mud to boost business. So I'm gwine to move over and boss, if they's as slow about fixing Freret as they was in fixing Magazine, I'm gonna get rich."

———————

The advance carnival guests are here—some in rags, some in tags and some in velvet gowns. The professional carnival men, the troopers, the pitchmen and the gypsies have come to plan their participation in Mardi Gras. Licenses to beg, to play hurdy gurdies, to sell street corner novelties and to erect amusement stands have been requested. Beggars explore the city for profitable looking corners. And pitchmen in cheap unfurnished rooms manufacture tin whistles and feather ticklers to vend. They expect in a few days to make enough money to indulge themselves in extended rests of unaccustomed luxury and drink.

---

[114] In late December of 1923, a curious advertisement appeared in the pages of *The Times-Picayune*, which read: "Colored man with $300 to buy half interest in cleaning & pressing establishment and laundry. Good opportunity for right party. Call at once. 4105 Magazine St." See "Business Chances," *The Times-Picayune*, December 27, 1923.

The Thrills of 1924: Dorothy Day Encounters the "Underworld Denizens" of New Orleans

Behind curtains of bright rugs and colored shawls gypsies have established themselves in empty store buildings. What part they play during Mardi Gras can only be imagined, but in their eastern costumes they are a fitting and picturesque addition to any carnival crowd.

That shoppers are temperamental weather vanes is the opinion of the oldest stall owner at the French market. "In the summer people buy more fruit for the making of cool drinks I can understand that and why women are attracted to bright colored fruits and vegetables on gray stormy days. But why fish is in demand on windy days and nuts in hot murky weather—well, it's beyond me."

The New Orleans Item
Saturday; February 16, 1924 (P. 9; Evening Edition)

All Around New Orleans

Unsigned

She lives in the Home for Incurables, on Henry Clay avenue.[115] She weighs 200 pounds. Her mind is that of a child. In her heart is music. For hours at a time, every day, she sings, sings queer little songs, not always sensible, but in them all is a weird music.

Two others share her room. They are mute, unable to utter a sound. Each day they come to hear her sing. Their eyes gleam with enjoyment. Their faces twist with their efforts to speak. One rocks steadily in rhythm with the music.

She sings. And they, who are dumb, listen.

The day of the pretty girl has passed. They stand on an equal footing with the men, in the crowded street cars. New Orleans, for better or worse, has adopted the habits of the northern cities. The great majority of the men retain their seats while women stand. On a car yesterday, a man seated conversed pleasantly with a standing woman friend. He did not offer her his seat.

Chivalry, however, is not dead. Men of New Orleans still retain some of the instincts and courtesies of their fathers. The pretty girl may stand, but the aged or the mother with a baby ever receives the cheerful offer of a seat.

----

[115] The New Orleans Home for the Incurables was located at 612 Henry Clay Avenue.

The Thrills of 1924: Dorothy Day Encounters the "Underworld Denizens" of New Orleans

Many women of the city have adopted the cigarette. The sight of one smoking in a public restaurant no longer attracts much attention. They appear to be at ease and unconcerned. They have developed a grace of movement and use the cigarette as an artifice to display their hands. Two things most of them have not learned. They are embarrassed as to where to strike a match and what to do with the burned fragment afterwards. They cannot adopt the old-fashioned masculine method. Men seldom use their method any more either. It is too hard upon the trousers.

————————

It is said that 50,000 Orleanians came originally from Mississippi. Mississippians are fond of fresh pork sausage, particularly those from the hill sections. That may explain the popularity and rushing business of a Carondelet street lunch stand. This stand makes a specialty of fresh country pork sausage sandwiches. They sell for a dime. The place during the noon hour is crowded beyond capacity.

A newspaper man once asked Fred, the manager if he advertised his specialty. He laughed and said it was not necessary.

"Most of my patrons once lived in the country. When the sausage[s] are frying, I just open the doors wide. The odor goes all over the street. That's all the advertising I need. Folks smell, their memories are aroused, their boyhood appetites return, and they come in and order sausage."

————————

Speaking of lunches, for the first time since the advent of prohibition and the passing of the free lunch, the regular 15-cent hot "merchants' lunch" has appeared again in the city. An ex-saloon features it and the patrons are mostly longshoremen and shipping clerks.[116]

————————

There are men who are too proud to beg or steal even when they are half starved. Such a man walked the streets for days hunting for work. He found none. He applied to no charity organization. His money was gone. He had missed four meals. Walking the docks in search of work, he reached the fruit wharf. They were unloading bananas. Half-ripe fruit sometimes drops from the conveyors. The man in question retrieved half a dozen such bananas. No one objected. He ate them all, on a stomach half famished.

Two hours later they carried him to the hospital.

---

[116] This would be the Sazerac (116 Royal Street), which Day had written about in December of 1923. The Sazerac was the saloon where the Sazerac cocktail was invented. See "Villagitus," in "All Around New Orleans," *New Orleans Item*, December 15, 1923; Arthur, *Old New Orleans*, 25.

The New Orleans Item
Tuesday; February 26, 1924 (P. 2; Evening Edition)

All Around New Orleans

Unsigned

Known By Their Coughs

This paragraph is written with no intention of duplicating the success of "Ten Nights in a Bar-room," or "Uncle Tom's Cabin," it is merely to note a peculiarity.[117] Into a Carondelet cigar store rushed a rather nervous looking business man, eager to make his purchase and be gone.[118] As he entered, he coughed. The clerk without a word selected a package of cigarettes for him, and returned him his change with thanks.

"Sure, I knew what he wanted," the clerk said, "though I never saw him before. You see that particular brand of cigarettes induces a sort of siren cough, that is distinguishable. This brand here gives a hoarse, whispering cough; this one, a deep bass. I heard a cough that fooled me the other day. It was crossed with a sneeze. I found out that the customer changes off every day or so on Turkish and American brands."

---

[117] "Ten Nights in a Bar-Room, and What I Saw There," was a novel written by Timothy Arthur Shay, in 1854. "Uncle Tom's Cabin or, Life Among the Lowly," was a novel written by Harriet Beecher Stowe, in 1852, although serialized in an 1851 abolitionist newspaper. Both novels have underlying themes of temperance.

[118] Possibly U. Koen's Cigar Store, which was located on the corner of Canal and Carondelet Streets. See "Tonight—Boxing—Tonight," *The Times-Picayune*, November 16, 1923.

The Thrills of 1924: Dorothy Day Encounters the "Underworld Denizens" of New Orleans

Jelly Bean

One of Messrs. Fuerst & Kraemer's happiness girls is responsible for this bit of more or less confidential material:[119]

"He ain't anything but a little old Jelly Bean! Do you know what he did last night? He swiped my vanity! I don't care. He can have it. Maybe he will give the powder, the paint and the rouge to some other girl, but I don't care. He can keep the case. If he gives that away I'll cut off his toes. Say, I swiped his handkerchief! It is a great big one, embroidered. Every night I wring it out just like it was his neck. I sure do love that Jelly Bean."

Matched

After the ball was over Mary took off her cork leg, but John Debelo,[120] proprietor of the bakery shop at 2401 Palmyra, puts his on when he starts for a dance.[121] John served eight years in the navy and got out with only a broken nose, received in a boxing match, to show for his work.[122] Then he slipped when he was attempting to board a train, fell underneath it, and lost his good tight leg.[123] Cork replaced it. He still likes a good time, and his handicap often serves as a source of amusement at dances and in athletic encounters. One evening he was dancing at the Alberta Pleasure club with a girl he liked very much. They kept dancing as one after another of the other couples dropped out. Finally John realized that they had the floor almost to themselves.

---

[119] Fuerst and Kraemer was located at 828 Canal Street, in New Orleans. See "Miscellaneous," *The Times-Picayune*, March 7, 1924. Fuerst and Kraemer's candies were billed as having "Happiness in every box," hence the reference to "happiness girls." See "Fuerst & Kraemer Candies," *The Times-Picayune*, December 20, 1924. Day had indirectly mentioned the Fuerst and Kraemer Company in a previous article. See "'Goat Giver,'" in "All Around New Orleans," *The New Orleans Item*, January 9, 1924.

[120] This article is more than likely about John Debelo, Jr., as John Debelo, Sr. was married to Marietta Mascari. It is doubtful that she was the same "Mary" in this vignette.

[121] The Debelo Bakery Company and residence were located at 2401 Palmyra Street in New Orleans. A bankruptcy notice, from May of 1923, listed the entire contents of the bakery for sale, with Nicholas H. Debelo named as the owner. John Debelo (not specified as to Jr. or Sr.) had assumed control of the assets, and the bakery remained in the family. Nicholas Debelo later regained control of the bakery, per a newspaper article concerning vandalism of the property, in May of 1938. See "Bankruptcy Sale," *The Times-Picayune*, May 13, 1923; "Sanitary Inspections," *The Times-Picayune*, April 25, 1925; "Christmas Greetings," *The Times-Picayune*, December 25, 1929; "Creosote Spray Smears Freshly Painted Bakery," *The Times-Picayune*, May 29, 1938.

[122] Per John Debelo Sr.'s 1928 obituary, he had "shipped before the mast" for eighteen years. See "Father Dies Trying to Save Two Sons in Squall on Lake," *The Times-Picayune*, August 27, 1928. John Debelo, Jr. had also enlisted in the United States Navy, in July of 1912. See "Thirteen Recruits," *The Times-Picayune*, July 9, 1912.

[123] The journey of the Debelo family was one of epic tragedy. In October of 1923, John Sr.'s son, Francis Debelo, died. Four months later, another son, Joseph V. Debelo, was killed by a policeman (Lemmie L. Fortenberry) during a botched robbery attempt. The twenty-one year old Debelo had been an auxiliary patrolman, but he had been suspended for drunkenness. Fortenberry would also die as a result of being shot by Debelo. In March of 1927, sons Nicholas and Thomas Debelo were slightly injured when their truck was struck by a Southern railroad switch engine. In February of 1928, twenty-nine-year-old Thomas Debelo was accidentally shot to death by a family friend. In August of 1928, John Debelo, Sr. drowned in Lake Pontchartrain while trying to save two of his sons. The family boat had capsized when a sudden squall hit the lake. One of the sons, twenty-four-year-old Vincent Debelo, died; the other son, thirteen-year-old Emil Debelo, survived. See "Died," *The Times-Picayune*, October 4, 1923; "Policeman, Former Patrolman Killed in Burglar Battle," *The Times-Picayune*, February 18, 1924; "Two Brothers Hurt in Crossing Smash," *The Times-Picayune*, March 11, 1927; "Housewife Faces Charge of Killing Family Friend," *The Times-Picayune*, February 19, 1928; "Father Dies Trying to Save Two Sons in Squall on Lake," August 27, 1928.

"What do you think of that?" he demanded, "everybody is quitting just as I am getting started—and me with a cork leg."

His entrancing young partner gazed sweetly into his eyes, and naively: "I have one, too," she said.

The New Orleans Item
Wednesday; February 27, 1924 (P. 22)

All Around New Orleans

Unsigned

In a dusty old shop on lower Royal street lives a German cabinet maker.[124] His is not at all a fashionable shop; it is cluttered with broken furniture, as his life is cluttered with broken hopes. He tells a curious and vivid story, which he believes implicitly.

"Some fifteen years ago," says the cabinet maker, "I was desperately ill with pneumonia. All my life I had been fond of good living and gayety; I took my liquor when occasion offered, and spent money on good times with friends. All that didn't improve my chances any when I got pneumonia. I got worse and worse. The doctors thought I was unconscious, and one day I heard them telling the nurse—I was in a hospital—that I would be dead within 24 hours.

"Then they sent for the priest, and he gave me the last sacraments. I remember how he looked, in his black robes, and his voice sounded as though it came from a long way off. And though it was broad daylight, with the sun streaming into the room, I saw the black shadows drawing closer, closer to my bed, and I knew they were the shadows of death. The priest went out.

"Then I prayed to God to spare me a few more years, because my family has need for me. Never had I prayed like that before; it was like talking to some one in the room with me. As I finished my plea, there was a light among the dark shadows, and I saw a woman standing before me. Her

---

[124] Day had presumably interviewed this same German cabinetmaker in an earlier column. See "Side Street Bargains," in "All Around New Orleans," *The New Orleans Item*, January 2, 1924.

face was the face of Margaret Haughery,[125] whose statue stands in Margaret Place, the woman who did so much good to the poor.[126]

"In her hand she held a book, and I knew it was the book of my life. The book was open, and she turned it toward me, and held it out, and on the left I could see scrawled pages, the years that I had lived, and on the right new, clean pages, with no writing, and then I knew that God had granted my prayer, and that the book of my life was not finished. There were still pages, on which I could write good or evil.

"The figure of the woman disappeared, and the black shadows drew back; I could see trees in purple silhouette against the sunset, and a great sense of peace descended on me, and I fell asleep.

"Next morning, when I awoke, I heard the doctor tell the nurse that I would live. I made up my mind since God had granted my prayer, I would show my appreciation by giving up the gay, useless life that I had lived. I gave up drinking altogether, and tried to write in the remaining pages of my life book those things that would be pleasing to my Master.

"Only God knows whether I have succeeded in that, but in 15 years I have not ceased to try."

In a jeweler's window on Canal street is a diamond ring containing a steel blue diamond weighing 10.19 karats. It is said to be priced at $65,000, but few have the nerve to go in and ask.

"Gee, ain't it a knockout?" said a little shopgirl, gazing reverently at the solitaire. "Kid, you have to wear smoke glasses to look at it."

---

[125] This article incorrectly listed the woman's name as Margaret Houghty. Margaret Haughery (1813-1882) was known in New Orleans as the "mother of the orphans." A member of the Roman Catholic Church, Haughery devoted her life to charity concerning orphans, and the poor. An orphan herself, Haughery was instrumental in the development and funding of the Poydras Female Orphan Asylum, the New Orleans Female Orphan Asylum (at the junction of Camp and Prytania Streets), the St. Vincent Infant Asylum (on Magazine Street), and the St. Elizabeth Asylum (on Louisiana Avenue). Haughery funded these institutions with profits from her dairy (on Seventh Street), and, later, Margaret's Steam and Mechanical Bakery (on New Levee Street, now South Peters Street). See "Margaret's Steam and Mechanical Bakery," *Daily Picayune*, September 26, 1879; "Margaret," *The Times-Picayune*, February 10, 1882.

[126] Margaret Haughery's statue, dedicated two years after her death, is located on Margaret Place, near the intersection of Camp and Prytania Streets. See "Presiding Over a Wreath Dedication," *The Times-Picayune*, February 7, 1965.

The New Orleans Item
Wednesday; February 27, 1924 (P. 8; Evening Edition)

All Around New Orleans

Unsigned

It was young Arthur O'Keefe, son of the Tenth ward leader, speaking. A typical American of the new generation college bred, a lawyer, and a man one would expect to find as far as possible from the ways of the old days.[127] But, listen:

"My father went to every wake in the Tenth ward for nearly 20 years.[128] Now that I am grown-up, he only has to go to the big ones. They are perfectly satisfied if an O'Keefe is there—father or son."

And he left me to go to one; to meet his fiancée there as was done in the days gone by.

A Smell Costs Nothing

Incense shops—there is one on University Place—where the concentrated odors of the finest flowers, in vari-colored cubes, are offered for sale. Sandalwood, orange blossoms, cherry blossoms—perfumes that bewilder and entrance. Burned sweet herbs sometimes save the trouble

---

[127] Arthur J. O'Keefe, Jr., a former state senator, and First City Court judge, was a leader of the Old Regular Democratic Organization in the Tenth Ward, located in the Irish Channel section of New Orleans. He had received his law degree from Loyola University. See "Arthur J. O'Keefe Jr. Dies; Former State Senator, Judge," *The Times-Picayune*, April 6, 1988.

[128] In addition to serving as a state senator, Arthur J. O'Keefe, Sr. held a number of positions in New Orleans, including alderman in the city council, city treasurer, and finance commissioner. O'Keefe later served as the thirty-seventh Mayor of New Orleans, from 1926 to 1929. See "Arthur O'Keefe, Ex-Mayor, Dies," *The Times-Picayune*, November 14, 1943.

of cleaning rooms, or camouflage the evil of closed windows and odoriferous kitchens. Still, the stores where they can be purchased are inviting and the acme of cleanliness. One luxury-hungry youth stops there every day, just for a smell.

_____

There is a man in this city who grades the parties he gives according to the predilections of his guests. The other day, he was telling a lady about one he had just given.

"And you didn't invite me!" she pouted.

"Oh, no. That was one of my D-parties."

"D-party?"

"Yes, you see it's like this: The A-party is literal and musical and all that. The B-party is a little livelier. At C, we begin to get a little pep. And D—well, you know!"

"At any rate, I'm glad," she answered, "that you didn't try to D-grade me."

_____

Yes, spring is on its way, but surely the six young men stationed on the avenue at each corner between Walnut and State street on this drizzly Sunday morning were rushing the season a bit. Dressed in white flannels barely covering the knee (possibly the effect of the damp weather on flannel) with straw hats and red neck ties, these young men grinned sheepishly at the startled passersby. Aside from clutching suspicious looking suitcases they appeared otherwise normal.

Passersby were at loss as to whether they were escaped maniacs from the nearby asylum or merely hicks arriving at the big city. Both surmises were wrong, however, for they were only the six new pledges of a Tulane fraternity undergoing the miseries of initiation.

_____

While waiting to telephone in a department store, the following conversation was heard within the booth:

"Yeah, kid, ain't it a shame he ditched her flat—Ain't men awful tho?—Yes, can't be too careful tho—."

"And so you know she's going to raffle off her trousseau tomorrow? The lingerie at 10 cents a chance and, kid, I mean to tell yer she has 'em all colors. And the towels and tablecloths at $1. Gee, she oughta clear a hundred easy."

"But ain't he a brute to break her heart that way?"

The New Orleans Item
Thursday; February 28, 1924 (P. 22)

All Around New Orleans

Unsigned

The nerve of some people!

A likeable but impecunious young man was trying to persuade a storekeeper to cash a personal check after banking hours. The proprietor was rather doubtful. He hesitated. The young man persisted, earnestly argued and produced a letter from his bank to clinch his argument.

"See here," he told the other. "Here's proof that I have an account in the bank and can be trusted."

The storekeeper read the letter, looked puzzled and an angry expression crept across his face. Then he laughed.

"You win," he chuckled, "I'll take a chance and cash that check on your nerve."

The letter that the young man had produced as evidence that he could be trusted was a notice from his bank that he was $4.95 overdrawn.

A modern Ananias,[129] Sinbad the Sailor[130] and Diogenes,[131] all in one person, sat on a bench in Lafayette square. He was a friendly chap, gregarious and given to talk. He introduced himself

---

[129] Ananias and his wife, Sapphira, were Disciples of Christ who were killed for lying to the Holy Spirit. "Ananias and Sapphira," Acts 5:1-11 [NRSV]. Day would later reference Ananias in *What Price Love*, to

with a request for a cigarette. In return he gave his name, which was Reynolds, and he said that he hailed from "little old New York." After that came tales, boasts and display of trophies.

"I've been traveling around for 20 years and I've never scabbed yet.

"I'm 40 years old and I've never taken a drink."

These were his proudest, oft-repeated boasts. The first was made after he told why he was hard up. He was a machinist and strikes had put him out of a job. The only work that he had been offered in New Orleans was as a "scab." In telling it he made his boast and followed it up with a dissertation on the evils of bootleg booze. That man had a poor opinion of New Orleans.

The sun was warm in the square. Under the mellow influence of the cigarette the genial Reynolds expanded, and so did his stories.

"See this stick pin? That stone is the pupil of a tiger's eye. I shot him in South America.[132] And say, listen, do you know anything about pearls?"

Fishing into his inside pocket he produced a dirty handkerchief. Unwinding it he took out a handful of shiny shell-pebbles.

"These are real pearls. I got them out of the head of a fish that I caught in Florida last month. Sure, they're genuine, rough but can be polished. I'm saving them to fall back on if I get real hard up.

"I thought yesterday that I would need them. Had been working for two days on the new Western Union building.[133] Slipped from a third floor beam and fell. That's why I'm limping, but it didn't hurt me much."

The pupil of a tiger's eye as a stone for a pin; pearls from the head of a fish, a fall of three floors without injury and 20 years of traveling without a drink! That was an entertaining guy. But the queer part was that in all the talk he didn't try to sell the pin, the pearls or ask for a loan on the strength of his injury.

Lafayette square has heard weirder stories.[134]

---

demonstrate the guilt that the main character (Tamar) experienced at deceiving her sister (Ruth). See Dorothy Day, "What Price Love," *Chicago Herald Examiner*, June 19, 1926.

[130] The fabulous tales of Sinbad the Sailor were a relatively late edition to *One Thousand and One Nights* (also known as *Arabian Nights*). Day had admitted to reading *Arabian Nights* when she was six-years-old. See Day, *From Union Square to Rome*, 21.

[131] Diogenes (circa 412-404 BC – 323 BC) was a Greek philosopher, and a founder of Cynic philosophy.

[132] Reynolds' statement is quite ironic, given that tigers are not indigenous to South America. Perhaps he had shot one that was escaping a zoo or circus.

[133] The Western Union Telegraph building was located at 334 Carondelet Street, in New Orleans. See "Chain Store Firm Leases Valuable Business Place," *The Times-Picayune*, May 24, 1923.

[134] Lafayette Square is located at St. Charles Avenue and Camp Street, in New Orleans.

The Thrills of 1924: Dorothy Day Encounters the "Underworld Denizens" of New Orleans

The New Orleans Item
Friday; February 29, 1924 (P. 28)

All Around New Orleans

Unsigned

To "mooch" means to beg change from passing pedestrians. A "moocher" differs from the street beggar in that he has no regular station and does not beg openly. The police do not molest the street beggar, those who have no obvious handicap or infirmity. They are vigilant for the "moocher" who is an able-bodied man out of a job or too lazy to work. He mooches with one eye on the lookout for a cop. Usually he selects a busy street, walks slowly with the crowd, and whispers his appeal to some person with an "easy" look. They are expert physiognomics, these moochers. Seldom do they ask for more than a dime.

One night recently, five moochers were at work on St. Charles street between Canal and Poydras. They reaped a harvest from the theatre crowds.

———————

New Orleans has a reputation among the hobo fraternity of being an "easy town." Many winter here regularly without working. With the approach of the carnival season they arrive in flocks. In addition to the hoboes, who become moochers, crippled professional beggars come in. One of the signs of approaching Mardi Gras is the increased number of beggars and the swarms of street peddlers with their trinkets, gay balloons and miniature toys.

———————

With spring fever comes homesickness.

In a yard on Lowerline a grove of plum trees are in full bloom. The scent of the cloudlike blossoms wafts for a block in either direction. Just before twilight a little Newcomb freshman leans against the fence, her eyes upon the trees, drinking in the scent of the blossoms.[135] A look of unutterable misery, of loneliness, wrought upon her face. It may have been shadows, it may have been tears that dimmed her eyes. A letter peeping from the pocket of her sweater bore the postmark of a little Mississippi town.

Homesick!

[135] Day had previously mentioned the H. Sophie Newcomb College in relation to her Jack Dempsey interview. See Dorothy Day, "Dempsey Scores Another Knockout When He Calls Dorothy Day 'Little Girl,'" *The New Orleans Item*, February 11, 1924.

The New Orleans Item
Tuesday; March 4, 1924 (P. 12)

All Around New Orleans

Unsigned

Shoes and Sheep Skin

In a small Dryades street store wanders Mr. Johnson, veteran traveling salesman to receive a hearty welcome from Mr. Weil, a former customer.[136] "Nothing to sell you this time, Mr. Weil," he exclaims, "as I get old people are getting educated. Do you remember when I sold you good, substantial shoes for all the family at $1.50 and less? No more of that. Flapper shoes; that's my line now.[137] A piece of baby sheep skin, tacked to a cardboard with a ribbon on it and a trade mark—that's the stuff that keeps 'em coming, even at $10 to $18 a throw.[138] The girls must have a pair for each dress; the style changes before they wear a pair out; and back they come for more. The shoe business ain't what it used to be, Mr. Weil—I am like old business methods—rheumatism and indigestion."

---

[136] Day had mentioned a Mrs. Weil, manager of a furniture store, in an earlier article. Perhaps Mr. Weil was her spouse. See "Femininity Survives," in "All Around New Orleans," *The New Orleans Item*, December 14, 1923.

[137] As a taxi-dancer, Day may have encountered Mr. Johnson while purchasing "Flapper shoes." Johnson possibly worked for the Chas. A. Kaufman, Co., located at 1700 Dryades Street in New Orleans.

[138] A period advertisement for "Flapper shoes" sought to charge anywhere from $8.50 to $12.00 per pair. See "Holmes Store News," *The Times-Picayune*, April 3, 1924.

The New Orleans Item
Wednesday; March 5, 1924 (P. 12)

All Around New Orleans

Unsigned

The other day a young man deliberately walked underneath a ladder placed in front of the Boston club, where they were whitewashing the temporary gallery constructed for the carnival season.[139]

"Oh, seven years bad luck," warned a feminine passerby.

The smiling young man then fearlessly determined to pass underneath the ladder placed at the other end and as he turned to see the effect of his bravery he knocked over a whitewash bucket and got completely spattered with its contents.

Flirting Doomed[140]

God bless them just the same—but it is becoming increasingly more hazardous to tell them so. A stony stare which succeeded the fawn-like look of fright as women became economically independent, was bad enough—then there has always been the danger that she will call a cop and commit the courageous gallant to the rock pile. Now she carries a cane. Gold, silver and ivory handled, too short to facilitate walking or to investigate strange objects seen along the street; just the size to whack someone over the head. Style is a facetious dictator. She puts a club into woman's hand a couple of thousand years or so after it was broken over her head.

[139] The Boston Club is a well-known gentleman's organization, located at 824 Canal Street in New Orleans. See "Dry Agents Raid, Make No Arrests in Boston Club," *The Times-Picayune*, May 17, 1924.
[140] This vignette was similar in tone to "Femininity Survives," of the December 14 article. See "Femininity Survives," in "All Around New Orleans," *The New Orleans Item*, December 14, 1923.

Exclusiveness Expensive

Below Canal street, on St. Charles and in other parts of the city are smug little shops known only to patrons. No signs outside indicate the nature of the business. Often the door is locked, and sometimes customers are required to ring three times or twice as a signal. The operators, however, are not bootleggers. They are dressmakers. Hour after hour limousines stop in front of such places and well dressed women enter the buildings to have their gowns fitted, or to purchase odd little knick-knacks imported from France, the Bowery and Royal street. Such places usually do little advertising, yet they succeed. Customers pay for the advertising they don't do.

Misfortune An Asset

Near a Roman Catholic church downtown, almost every day will be found a miserable looking beggar woman with an aged and calloused hand extended for alms. New Orleans has many beggars, but this one has a peculiar affliction that is appealing. Her ankle is swollen until it appears to be that of an elephant. Try to get her to tell what is the matter, and she will talk of other misfortunes. The ankle attracts attention for it is a freak, and the reason is her secret. She puts her worst foot forward; but many supposedly successful business men could learn a lot from beggars.

The New Orleans Item
Thursday; March 6, 1924 (P. 2)

All Around New Orleans

Unsigned

More That Is Feminine

If you have an idle hour some time, drop into a restaurant in automobile row and see another side of the picture.[141] There you will find waitresses; where a week or so ago men were the servitors. Mr. Reinhardt, the manager, says: "Among my customers are many girls, who can't afford to pay big tips, but they are attracted here by the inexpensive luncheons, and are good customers because they come back later. There are not so many lunch rooms open to them as to men. My waiters treated them rather contemptuously; and served them only when there was no one else from whom a big tip might be received; threw food down in front of them and let it go at that. My waitresses instinctively like to please whether they are paid for it or not. They are more careful and considerate of patrons; and not less important is the fact that they give to my place an air of respectability and decency which it would not have otherwise." Bless them again.

---

[141] The heart of automobile row was located at St. Charles and St. Joseph Streets, in New Orleans. See "Announcing the Opening of Our New Home for Nash Cars," *The Times-Picayune*, December 16, 1923.

The New Orleans Item
Tuesday; March 11, 1924 (P. 20)

All Around New Orleans

Unsigned

For twenty-two years three cats lived in the Cafe des Quatre Saissons on Chartres street, near the Cathedral.[142] This winter they died; Brother first, Socks next, Dick last.

Dick left a legacy.

One day he rose from the sun-patch in the courtyard where he was dozing with the younger cat, who had been washing his face for a month and sleeping alongside of him to keep the cold away. He took the youngster with him and went to the door connecting the courtyard with the cafe.

Only Dick had ever learned to open the door. The other cats tried it every day, but they always failed to push the latch over as well as down.

At the door, Aunt Rose, who presides over the cafe, came upon the aged cripple and the youngster.[143] Dick was working the latch.

---

[142] No record of a Cafe des Quatre Saissons, or Four Seasons, could be found on Chartres Street. Perhaps what Day actually meant by this reference was that the cats lived, and were cared for, all year round.

[143] "Aunt Rose" was Rose Lee Arnold, who owned a cigar store and a sailor's rooming house at 625 Chartres Street, in New Orleans. Arnold died on November 25, 1929; her estate was valued at over $73,000. See "Aunt Rose's Wildcat Disappears! French Quarter Trees Searched," *The Times-Picayune*, April 12, 1929; "Court Petitioned for Property Sales," *The Times-Picayune*, November 27, 1929; "'Aunt Rose' Leaves $73,136 of Property," *The Times-Picayune*, December 18, 1929; "Arnold Estate Decision Given," *The Times-Picayune*, December 19, 1929; "Contempt Charge in Arnold Estate Continued," *The Times-Picayune*, December 24, 1929; "State Falls Heir to Woman's Effects," *The Times-Picayune*, January 3, 1930; "Contents of Famous Old Vieux Carre Residence," *The Times-Picayune*, January 12, 1930.

Both ran away to their sun-patch when she disturbed them. And the next day Dick died.[144]

Now the youngster can work the latch.

---

[144] A few months before Aunt Rose's death in November of 1929, a strange article appeared in *The Times-Picayune* wherein she had claimed that someone had stolen her eight-week-old wildcat, "Hoover." Hoover had come from Mexico, and he had attacked several of her stray cats. Although residents of the French Quarter searched their trees and courtyards, there was no record of Rose's wildcat being found before her passing. See "Aunt Rose's Wildcat Disappears! French Quarter Trees Searched," April 12, 1929.

The New Orleans Item
Thursday; March 13, 1924 (P. 24)

All Around New Orleans

Unsigned

There is an opening in the green dock shed at St. Peter street which frames the gray sweep of the river, the yellow and black funnels of a ship and the circling gulls.

On afternoons when the sun brightens the hulls of the ships across the river a Spanish girl and her husband come and stand at the head of St. Peter street and look out through the shed's great doors.

They have been seen there every day for two years.

————————

Near the junction of the Industrial Canal and Bayou Bienvenu there is a camp such as might be found in any tropical jungle. The swamp comes down close behind it. The dead bayou crawls in front of it. The houses are built of old poles and tin roofing and are thatched. The families get their sustenance from the swamp and the men are nearly always caked with the swamp-mud. The children play in the stagnant puddles clad in the remnants of a suggestion of clothes.

The New Orleans Item
Thursday; March 13, 1924 (P. 2; Evening Edition)

All Around New Orleans

Unsigned

The Stone Age persists in Jackson Square. A fierce warfare is carried on there incessantly. There are no rules.

Yesterday a tourist stopped to have his shoes shined. Two negro boys with a bootblack's box undertook the task. Before they had gotten the first shoe polished three Italian boys came, kicked the negroes, took the box and continued shining the shoes.

They had the polish on the first shoe when two larger boys came, hit the Italians, claimed the box and continued the shining of the shoes.

They had come to the final flip of the polishing rag when the two negro boys came back with a policeman.

The large Italians saw the battalion and fled.

The negro boys finished shining the shoes and collected the dime.

The Thrills of 1924: Dorothy Day Encounters the "Underworld Denizens" of New Orleans

The New Orleans Item
Friday; March 14, 1924 (P. 28)

All Around New Orleans

Unsigned

The men who bring the vegetables to the French market get less sleep than debutantes during carnival week.[145]

It is not unusual for those who live furthest out in the truck-country to stay up all night loading their trucks, drive all day to the city, stay up all night selling their produce, and spend the second day driving home.

They take a sort of pride in their endurance. About three o'clock in the morning when the buying is just getting under way, they sit on the tail boards of their trucks and throw jibes at every nodding head. Men of all nations are there on the tail boards, their shoulders propped against the cabbages and potatoes.[146] By the glare of the electric lamps strung along the edge of the market one can see their faces; swarthy Italians with elaborate mustachios; paunch-bellied Spaniards; military-looking Poles; lithe, smooth-cheeked mulattos with skins of old ivory; a man with very

---

[145] Day had written about the French Market, in detail, in a previous article. See "All Around New Orleans," *The New Orleans Item*, December 18, 1923.

[146] The phrase "Men of all nations…" represents a recurring pattern in Day's writing. See Dorothy Day, "Dance Halls Flooded by Drink, Dope," *The New Orleans Item*, February 4, 1924 ("…men of all ages and occupations…"); Dorothy Day, "Danceland Girls Make Only 4 Cents but Manager Explains That It 'Isn't a Rough Joint,'" *The New Orleans Item*, February 6, 1924 ("…men of all description…"); Dorothy Day, "Girl Supplements Wages as Store Clerk at Dance Hall at Night," *The New Orleans Item*, February 9, 1924 ("…men of style and description…"); Dorothy Day, "Thrills of 1924," *The New Orleans Item*, February 26, 1924 ("…men of doubtful trades…").

dark skin and very high forehead who says he was born in Delhi and is called Dela Sarb; and a dwarf black man who claims to remember the dances in his village kampong back in Sumatra.

Their rest on the tail boards does not last long. More and more the stall keepers start walking up and down the line of trucks. The Dela Sarb, and the dwarf black man, and the mustachios and the military shoulders and all the others jump up, turn over the cabbages and potatoes and forget about having been awake two nights and a day.

––––––––––––

Anyone who will walk up and down Canal street, between Royal and Dauphine, at three o'clock every morning for a week, will certainly see a hunched-up old woman in a ground-sweeping black skirt, an engulfing white shawl, and a metallic turban, hobbling along with a green umbrella under her arm. The green umbrella is so short that it must have no spread at all; it is as much shorter than ordinary umbrellas as the old woman is shorter than ordinary women.

Some time after midnight the woman appears on Canal street, from Royal street. Usually she walks up and down several times, keeping her eyes on the pavement, and making defiant motions with her stunted umbrella. Occasionally she goes into Thompson's Canal street restaurant.[147]

One night the cashier of the restaurant told me all anyone seems to know about the woman.

She chased her son off. That was a long time ago. He went down to Honduras and got killed in one of them revolutions. They say she hears him pounding at the door on her home every night. I guess that's why she comes up here."

––––––––––––

[147] Thompson's Restaurant, different from the "one-armed" business on St. Charles Street, was located at 835 Canal Street, in New Orleans. See "Miscellaneous," *The Times-Picayune*, June 24, 1923.

The Thrills of 1924: Dorothy Day Encounters the "Underworld Denizens" of New Orleans

The New Orleans Item
Saturday; March 15, 1924 (P. 7)

All Around New Orleans

Unsigned

"Shall I wrap it, or will you carry it with you," said the salesgirl to the woman, referring to a handbag.

"I want to take it as it is," said the customer, "because I haven't my bag with me. But if the floorwalker or anybody sees me stuffing my things into it and walking out with it, I'm afraid they'll accuse me of shoplifting. So you must stand right by me while I'm doing it."

And while the salesgirl obligingly stood by, the woman extricated handkerchief, gloves, purse, pencil, shopping list and powder puff, et cetera, ad infinitum, from pocket, cuff, the front of her waist, et cetera, and sighed with comfort as she left the store.

What is woman without a handbag?

———————

Yesterday morning we saw a woman walking down Royal street, shuffling along miserably with a cane as though there were pains in every joint. Around her head was a strange scarf, wound round and round. In gaps and holes of the scarf here and there wisps of straggly hair stuck out. An indescribably old coat was clutched around her. Her face was as white as alabaster. We had never seen that particularly gleaming kind of powderless whiteness before. Her mouth was drawn down in misery.

This morning we saw the same woman, still with her cane, but although her step was infinitely slow and unhurried, she walked with lightness. She was dressed in the same peculiar way, but on her shoulder was a gorgeously colored parrot, turning this way and that to greet the passersby, and in her hand was an open jar of peanut butter and a sandwich. Her face in spite of its whiteness wore a look of beatific calm.

_____

On Magazine street, near the market, a well dressed man, about 60 years old, approached various persons and in a low, apologetic voice, told of many misfortunes and his unsuccessful search for work. His appearance, being so unusual for that profession, made it comparatively easy to collect many donations in the course of several blocks. At Magazine and Jackson streets he turned west and in the middle of the block got into a Ford touring car and drove away.

The Thrills of 1924: Dorothy Day Encounters the "Underworld Denizens" of New Orleans

The New Orleans Item
Monday; March 17, 1924 (P. 2)

All Around New Orleans

Unsigned

There was quite a crowd around one of Marks Isaacs windows the other day, but they weren't looking at anything for sale.[148] Neither was there a demonstration going on there. They were merely standing there gazing with wonder at a pair of graceful arms, curved languishly, seductively toward them. Doubtless the passersby had seen bare arms in such an artificially provocative gesture often enough in the movies and on figures of dressmakers' dummies, but what made them stand and stare was that the arms were lying detached in the showcase window, and the figure beside it, stood bare and alarmed in a long white shift, looking at her well-dressed and armed neighbors with envious eyes while she waited to be clothed. How animate inanimate objects can seem!

———

Recently a bootlegger, who maintained his "office" in a soft drink place on Burgundy street, decided his clientele had reached such proportions that he needed assistance. Accordingly, he hired office space, had a telephone installed and employed a "secretary" to answer phone calls and take "orders." This system has proved so successful that he now makes deliveries, without extra charge, to his customers.

Saturday night he was among a number of men arrested in a raid on a soft drink place.[149] He was charged by the police as being a "loiterer" and "having no visible means of support." After

———

[148] The Marks Isaacs Co. Men's Store was located at 711 to 725 Canal Street, in New Orleans. See "Our Semi-Annual Sale…," *The Times-Picayune*, January 10, 1924.

[149] A large raid had occurred, in March of 1924, in which dry agents had seized illegal alcohol at a grocery, a winery, two residences, and three soft drink stands. Among those men arrested, Mike Salvator had a soft drink

116

paying a fine Monday in police court he told his friends of his humiliation. "Just think," he stated, "how embarrassing it was to have them brand me, a successful business man, as a loafer, and warn me to get a job or be sent to the workhouse."

stand at 700 Burgundy Street; William T. Swan had a soft drink stand at 2117 Burgundy Street. See "Dry Raids Yield Variety of Liquor," *The Times-Picayune*, March 17, 1924.

The Thrills of 1924: Dorothy Day Encounters the "Underworld Denizens" of New Orleans

The New Orleans Item
Tuesday; March 18, 1924 (P. 22)

All Around New Orleans

Unsigned

This is merely a little scene on a back gallery of an old rooming house, where the robust landlady and decrepit little black servant were hanging up clothes. The little black woman comes from a small town in Mississippi and has worked for the last years for several dollars a week, and her dark and sunless room off the court yard. She says she is 40 years old, but she is dried up and jerky and wizened. In the coldest weather she goes about in her bare feet, widespread toes gripping the uneven pavement and she wears neither hat nor coat. Early in the morning she is often seen coming from the river with a load of driftwood on her head, which she carefully hides in her room in order that her mistress may not get hold of it. Around her neck are a half-dozen necklaces made of safety pins, nails, bits of leather, rabbits' feet, teeth, wisps of hair and other strange twisted things. In her ears are twisted paper clips for earrings.[150]

Her mistress is a black-haired, impressive woman in spite of her soiled pink bathrobe, clutched together in front with safety pins. "Mary," she was saying, "Mrs. So-and-So wants a quarter for her gas meter.[151] Where is the quarter I gave you? Here! I'll give you five nickels for it."

---

[150] Day would later use this vivid description, of her landlady's African-American servant, in an unpublished manuscript, held by the Dorothy Day-Catholic Worker archives at the Raynor Memorial Libraries of Marquette University. Written circa 1940, the servant's name was Columbine. See Dorothy Day, Dorothy Day Papers: Manuscripts, Ca. 1914-1977, Undated; Series D-3; Box 5, Folder 19.

[151] The boarding house where Day and Gordon lived contained apartments, which had gas meters installed; quarters were a much-needed commodity, in order to cook in the kitchenette. Day had later lamented that, "The gas was apt to run out just when we had spent our last cent on a rabbit stew which took hours to boil." See Day, *The Long Loneliness*, 108.

There were mumbled protests.

"But five nickels are as good as a quarter." The fact was demonstrated several times. Mary was finally convinced that none was trying to take her quarter away from her. She gave a clicking gulp and produced the quarter from her mouth, and carefully wiping it off, handed it to her mistress.

"Mary!" sternly. "How often have I told you not to put things in your mouth?"

"Got no place else to put it!"

"Well, don't you put those nickels in. Don't you know you'll get 'lepercy'? Give them to me to take care of."

But Mary was more afraid of her mistress keeping the nickels than she was of 'lepercy,' and back all the nickels went into her mouth. Her mistress sighed and continued to take down the clothes.

The Thrills of 1924: Dorothy Day Encounters the "Underworld Denizens" of New Orleans

"Visiting Celebrities"

Dorothy Day was glad to be removed from the unsigned column, as it had taken her a great amount of time and effort to find material relating entirely to the happenings in New Orleans. Shortly thereafter, she was allowed to publish articles for the Sunday magazine section, and daily features, stating, "They [*The New Orleans Item*] don't mind working you like hell for very little money. However, the work is fun, and keeps me occupied so that I don't miss liquor and the bright lights."[152]

Day soon began to write hard-hitting articles similar to her work for the *New York Call* and *The Masses*, nearly a decade earlier. Her new assignments, which she later called "visiting celebrities,"[153] consisted of interviewing Italian tragedienne Eleonora Duse, future Governor of Louisiana Henry L. Fuqua, and his family, and heavyweight boxing champion Jack Dempsey, who had humorously referred to Day as "little girly."

The "Visiting Celebrities" section encompasses four articles (the Dempsey articles are analyzed here, but are included in the "Going Undercover in New Orleans" section), which clearly demonstrate that Day was a master reporter, in the sense that she had allowed her interviewees to tell their stories amidst the contrast of both humor and sadness. Although Day could seem brash at times, even brazen, the reader will find that she also had a deep respect for the history that was unfolding in the Crescent City.

Day never got the chance to interview Eleonora Duse, as the famed European actress had rarely granted interviews—and yet, Day brazenly attempted to reach Duse by visiting her suite at the Roosevelt Hotel, unannounced. Had Day but telephoned first, she would have learned that she had no story. However, evincing both a youthful exuberance, and a determination not to be foiled, Day extracted an excellent article (published on January 15) by interviewing one of Duse's traveling companions, Katherine Onslow.

Had Day been able to interview Duse, albeit through a translator, the two women would have found much in common in terms of literary preferences. Both were voracious readers, and the younger Day would have identified with Duse's passion for such authors as Charles Baudelaire, Max Beerbohm, Anatole France, Victor Hugo, Rudyard Kipling, Guy de Maupassant, Françoise Rabelais, and Charles Algernon Swinburne. Later on in her life, Day would find great affinity with Duse's love of Julian of Norwich, especially her famous quotation: "All will be well, and all will be well, and every kind of thing will be well."[154]

There are several instances of humor in the "visiting celebrities" articles, related either by Day or by the figures she had interviewed. For example, in the first of three articles regarding future

---

[152] Day, "To Llewellyn Jones (January 2, 1924)," in *All the Way to Heaven*, 6.

[153] Day, "About Mary," 62-63.

[154] See Helen Sheehy, *Eleonora Duse: A Biography* (New York, NY: Alfred A. Knopf, 2003), 262-293; Anna Sica and Alison Wilson, *The Murray Edwards Duse Collection, Aesthetics*, No. 1 (Milan, Italy: Mimesis International, 2014), 130-258; Dorothy Day, "The Satan Bomb," *The Catholic Worker*, March 1950: 2; Dorothy Day, "On Pilgrimage," *The Catholic Worker*, October 1957: 8; Dorothy Day, "In Memory of Ed Willock," *Commonweal* 73, (February 24, 1961): 549-551; Dorothy Day, "On Pilgrimage," *The Catholic Worker*, March-April 1973: 2, 6; Dorothy Day, "On Pilgrimage," *The Catholic Worker*, January 1974: 1-2, 8.

Governor Henry L. Fuqua (published on January 27), Mrs. Fuqua narrated the events of a recent fight between her thirteen-year-old fox terrier, Nunky, and a dog at the receiving station of the Angola Prison. Mrs. Fuqua advised that Nunky had won the fight, but this could not be determined by the sight of the aged fox terrier alone. She added, humorously, that if the dog *could* talk, he would have said something like, "You should have seen what the other fellow looked like."

Day had chased Mrs. Fuqua around Baton Rouge for nearly thirty hours, failing to secure an interview. Learning a lesson from this failure, and the recent Duse fiasco, Day finally scored the interview by use of the telephone. Mrs. Fuqua had stated, with irony, that she hated to discuss politics. She had also admitted that, in an effort to avoid the brazen reporter, she and her son, Henry, Jr., had run off to see a motion picture show.

In the same article, Mrs. Fuqua told of the inseparable relationship her husband had with his grandson, four-year-old Walter M. Scott, Jr. Mrs. Fuqua explained that, on a recent visit, young Walter had pulled his grandfather into another room, exclaiming, "Let's go out here away from the women folks!"

Before Day and Henry, Jr. departed for the train station in order to meet Henry, Sr., they were both chastised by Mrs. Fuqua, who scolded, "Don't you make my husband late for lunch." Day had responded to this scolding by ending the article (January 27) on a sweet note. She concluded that Mrs. Fuqua's wrath was not the kind that could intimidate anyone, adding, "Besides they've been in love since they were twelve years old."

In the second Fuqua article, published on January 29, Day had asked Henry, Sr. for one of his baby pictures—presumably in a state of nakedness. After he had begun blushing, Fuqua comically replied, "If there are any pictures of me in that state—and I don't know of any—my wife has them—and I know you won't get them from her." Fuqua later gave Day a picture of himself and a hunting dog named Jack. Curiously, the picture was not used in any of the published Fuqua family articles.

The third and final article regarding Henry L. Fuqua, published on January 31, contained an amusing incident that had occurred during the near-catastrophic flooding of the Angola Prison, in May of 1922. Fuqua had had to be away from home for a month, in order to supervise the evacuation and rebuilding of the prison and adjacent farms. He had tried to allay his wife's fears concerning his health by telling her of the sight of "...an old mother pig, and her entire litter, floating unconcernedly down the river to their new home, grunting, happy and comfortable. Floods were nothing in their lives. Chickens and mules and pigs and cows, everything was saved."

Of particular interest is Day's schoolgirl crush on Jack Dempsey, seen in the article published on February 11. Day had met Dempsey at Union Station in New Orleans, and she had barraged the heavyweight champion with several telling questions: "Do you get mash notes from women?" "Are you engaged to be married?" "Do women ever propose to you?" and "Do you think women ought to go to prize fights?" Dempsey quickly answered all of Day's questions, except the latter. Regardless of Dempsey's opinion on the subject, Day had attended Dempsey's exhibition bouts the next evening, recording the results of a full boxing card from a unique, woman's perspective (published February 12).

The humorous anecdotes mentioned above are contrasted with a degree of sadness, in looking back with historical hindsight. Both Onslow and Mrs. Fuqua had rightful concerns regarding the health of their loved ones. Duse would die in April of 1924, barely three months after Day's article was published in *The New Orleans Item*. Ironically, Duse had died of pneumonia, the same cause that had concerned Onslow in New Orleans. Mrs. Fuqua's fears about her husband's exhaustion would also be realized with the death of Henry Fuqua, Sr. He died after a brief illness in October of 1926, a mere two-and-a-half years after assuming the governorship of the state of Louisiana.

Day may have "visited celebrities," but she also revisited history, and the discerning reader will sense the unfolding of the past in these articles. Prevalent landmarks mentioned include the Jerusalem Temple, and Roosevelt Hotel in New Orleans, and Fuqua Hardware, and the campanile of the Louisiana State University in Baton Rouge. Historical figures mentioned include President Zachary Taylor, Jefferson Davis, authors George Bernard Shaw, and Henrik Ibsen, and several governors of Louisiana (John M. Parker, and Ruffin G. Pleasant). Events that shaped both Louisiana and the United States include the Mexican War, the Civil War, and the Angola floods of 1922.

LEANS ITEM   **NEW ORLEANS IS THE**

Mme. Duse Here As Recluse; Even Sleuth Tactics Fail To Break Actress' Privacy

By DOROTHY DAY

Unlike most women of temperament and genius,. Eleanor Duse,

know, and a cold would be fatal to
her tour—but if your City park is
not too far away, we will go out

The New Orleans Item
Tuesday; January 15, 1924 (P. 21)[155]

Mme. Duse Here As Recluse; Even Sleuth Tactics Fail To Break Actress' Privacy

By DOROTHY DAY

Unlike most women of temperament and genius, Eleonora Duse, Italian tragedienne who arrived in New Orleans Sunday noon for a week's holiday before her appearance at Jerusalem Temple, resolutely refuses to be interviewed.[156]

Figure 5-Jerusalem Temple, A. A. O. N. M. S., New Orleans, LA, circa 1920s.

Not knowing that the New York press had respected her wish for uninterrupted privacy and had not set a single reporter on her trail, we blundered over to Hotel Roosevelt, where Madame Duse is registered, learned the number of her suite, and without waiting to telephone to find out whether admittance would be obtained went to the sixth floor and knocked on her door.

The most shocked face of a most French maid immediately peered from the next door. In broken English, French and Italian, she tried to make us understand that madame was sleeping and was not to be disturbed, was never to be disturbed. If we hadn't with blind faith hoped eventually to understand her and make ourselves understood, and continued the argument, we would have missed a very pleasant hour.

---

[155] This article was listed as appearing on January 14, 1924 (P. 17), in the Anne and Alice Klejment database of Day authored articles. A variation of this article, minus one interior headline, appeared either on January 14 or in an earlier edition of *The New Orleans Item* on January 15. See Anne and Alice Klejment, *Dorothy Day and the Catholic Worker: A Bibliography and Index* (New York, NY: Garland Publishing, Inc., 1986), 11.

[156] The Shriners' Jerusalem Temple was located on St. Charles Avenue. Although no longer open to the public, the building is still extant. See Kezia Kamenetz, "What Lies Past the Doors of This Historic New Orleans Building Will Astound You," http://www.onlyinyourstate.com/louisiana/new-orleans/historic-building-new-orleans/ (accessed November 6, 2017).

Fortunately our conversation disturbed Miss Katherine Onslow, a personal friend of Madame Duse, who is accompanying her on her last American tour.[157]

Friend Seeks Information

"If I didn't want to find out something about this very mysterious city of yours, I wouldn't talk to you," she told us frankly. "Whatever stories the papers get are given out by Mr. Gest or the Messrs. Selwyn or whoever it is that arranges the tour.[158]

Figure 6-The new Roosevelt Hotel, fronting Baronne Street, near Canal and extending to University Place, New Orleans, LA, circa 1920s.

"But I must find out whether there is a park or a drive of some kind so that I can take Madame Duse motoring. She hates traffic of every kind and has to take tremendous care of herself—she is 64, you know, and a cold would be fatal to her tour—but if your City park is not too far away, we will go out there.[159] We must see these cypress trees and the dripping moss you speak of.

"Madame Duse seldom leaves her room, as a matter of fact. I go out to walk and explore and then return to tell her about these American cities. No, I am not her secretary, but a friend of hers and it's because of my love and admiration for her that I wouldn't let her make this last tour alone. Nothing else would have dragged me from my relatives and friends, and most of all, the elections. When I was admitted to this country, however, and they wanted to know who I was and what I was doing here, whether I was an anarchist or a bigamist, I had to stop their questions so put myself down as Madame Duse's secretary.

Tour of Royal Street

"But tell me, I wandered down Royal street yesterday afternoon, and is this all there is to your city. We heard it was a quaint old French city, but do all the people live that way? Are there no rich people in town who have fine homes as in other American cities?"

Miss Onslow was assured that if she walked along some other streets, she would find homes and gardens in abundance. She was entranced at the idea of Lake Pontchartrain and the French market.

---

[157] Katherine Onslow was a wealthy Englishwoman, and a long-time admirer of Duse. In 1923, Onslow had loaned Duse money to pay off her debts, and the salaries of her acting troupe. See Sheehy, *Eleonora Duse*, 306-307; William Weaver, *Duse: A Biography* (San Diego, CA: Harcourt Brace Jovanovich, 1984), 346.

[158] Duse's farewell tour was produced by F. Ray Comstock and Morris Gest. See "Today Matinee at 2:15," *Chicago Daily Tribune*, December 31, 1923.

[159] Sadly, Miss Onslow's concern for her friend's health was duly warranted. Eleonora Duse died of pneumonia in Pittsburgh, PA on April 21, 1924, barely three months after Day's article was published. See "Eleanora Duse and Marie Corelli Die on Same Day," *Brooklyn Daily Eagle*, April 21, 1924; Arthur Brisbane, "Duse is Dead," *The Shreveport Times*, April 22, 1924.

"I shall visit all these places, but Madame Duse will hardly leave her room. She lives very much alone and to herself, spending all her time in her room reading—she is an extremely well read woman—and writing.

"No, indeed, not memoirs nor articles about herself.[160] She is exceptionally reticent and no doubt part of her force lies in her reserve. She studies, she reads, she lives within herself. She has seen few people since she came to America this time."

According to Miss Onslow, this is the first time her friend has been in America for 20 years.

"Of course she did no acting during the war, but she hasn't even appeared in London since 1906 until this last trip. Then she received a tremendous ovation."

Since her arrival in New York in October, Madame Duse has appeared in New York, Philadelphia, Boston, Washington and Chicago. With her is a company of 12.[161] All of her supporting cast are Italians. Her repertoire consist[s] of two of Ibsen's plays, "Ghosts" and "The Lady of the Sea," which are given in Italian, and several Italian plays.[162] It is not yet decided which will be given a week from Tuesday night.[163]

Plays to Huge Houses

"Just between you and me, I think that it rather unfair to Madame Duse's talent to make her appear before such tremendous houses. Of course you have to take into consideration the tremendous, theatre-going public of this country. But Madame Duse played in Chicago in the Auditorium,[164] a hall which is twice as big as the Metropolitan Opera house in New York.[165] It

---

[160] Onslow may not have known that Duse had attempted to write her autobiography in 1918, of which thirty-five pages still survive. See Sheehy, *Eleonora Duse*, 6.

[161] Members of Duse's supporting cast included Memo Benassi, Gino Fantoni, Ciro Galvani, Mario Gatti, Ione Morino, Maria Morino, Leo Orlandini, Alfredo Robert, and Enif Robert. See Ashton Stevens, "Duse Not Faded, But Electrical, Says Stevens," *Chicago Herald and Examiner*, January 1, 1924; Frederick Donaghey, "Duse Returns to the Poetry of D'Annunzio" *Chicago Daily Tribune*, January 4, 1924; Frederick Donaghey, "Duse is an Errant Wife in This One," *Chicago Daily Tribune*, January 8, 1924.

[162] Italian plays performed by Duse, during this period, included Marco Praga's "La Porta Chiusa" ("The Closed Door"), and Gabriele D'Annunzio's "La Citta Morta" ("The Dead City"). Tommaso Gallarti-Scotti's play, "Così Sia" ("Thy Will Be Done"), was also performed during Duse's farewell American tour (at the Century Theatre in New York). See Sheehy, *Eleonora Duse*, 301-302.

[163] Duse appeared at the Jerusalem Temple on January 22, 1924, performing Praga's "La Porta Chiusa." See Weaver, *Duse*, 355; Sheehy, *Eleonora Duse*, 316. The performance was underwritten by a Captain J. Eugene Pearce, and was witnessed by a capacity crowd. See "Eleanora Duse Plays in N. O. Wins Plaudits," *The New Orleans Item*, January 13, 1924; "Eleanor Duse to be Greeted by Throng at Shrine Mosque," *The New Orleans Item*, January 22, 1924; "Duse Sways Her First New Orleans Audience in Role of Tragic Mother," *The New Orleans Item*, January 23, 1924.

[164] The Auditorium Theatre is located at 50 East Congress Parkway, Chicago, IL. Duse's itinerary for the Chicago leg of her tour included Henrik Ibsen's "Spettri" ("Ghosts") on Monday, December 31, 1923, and on Thursday, January 10, 1924; D'Annunzio's "La Citta Morta" on Thursday, January 3, 1924; and Praga's "La Porta Chiusa" on Monday, January 7, 1924. See "Special—Auditorium Theatre," *Chicago Daily Tribune*, December 29, 1923; Frederick Donaghey, "Duse Begins Final Visit in 'Ghosts,'" *Chicago Daily Tribune*, January 1, 1924; "Auditorium Theatre," *Chicago Daily Tribune*, January 3, 1924.

shows how tremendous is her personal magnetism to sway a house like that. From the top gallery you could not see her face, not even with opera glasses, and yet the audience went wild.

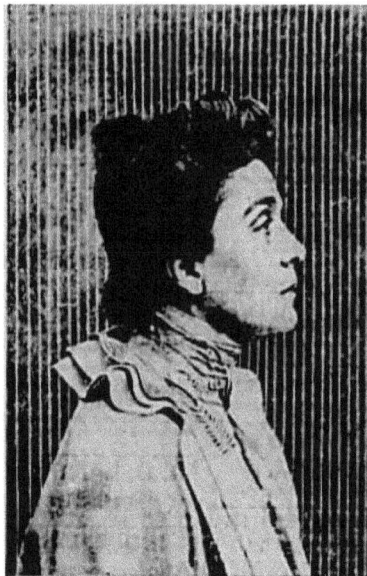

Figure 7-Eleonora Duse, *The Shreveport Times*, November 14, 1900.

"Madame was very much amused by the criticism, or rather appreciation of her work which appeared in some American papers. Mr. Ashton Stevens, for instance, said that Madame Duse in "Ghosts" made his spine jell.[166] And since she doesn't speak or read any English, I had a very difficult time translating it for her. She says she is inspired by America—she loves the country. It thrilled her to play before these audiences, which were so huge and so appreciative.

"Yes, Madame Duse was married. Her husband is dead.[167] She has a daughter who is married in England and lives at Cambridge.[168] Madame herself lives in retirement in a villa just outside of Venice.[169] Even if you have not seen her, you have read, of course, how beautiful her eyes are, how expressive her hands. Her hair is quite grey now. Even on the stage, she makes no attempt to hide her age, but appears without makeup of any kind. It's the tremendous inner force, her genius on which she depends."

From New Orleans, Madame Duse and her company will go to Los Angeles and San Francisco.

---

[165] Duse's first performance of "Ghosts" in Chicago was not a sellout, probably due to its being performed on New Year's Eve. Conversely, Duse's performance at the Metropolitan Opera House (Ibsen's "Lady from the Sea") on October 29, 1923 drew 3,800 patrons, with a gate of $30,000. See Burns Mantle, "Metropolitan Throng Pays Tribute to Duse Artistry," *Chicago Daily Tribune*, November 4, 1923; Donaghey, "Duse Begins Final Visit in 'Ghosts,'" January 1, 1924.
[166] Ashton P. Stevens was a noted journalist and drama critic. His work appeared in many newspapers, including the *San Francisco Examiner*, the *Chicago Examiner*, and the *Chicago Herald and Examiner*. See Inventory of the Ashton Stevens Papers, CA. 1850-1952, Bulk 1920-1940, "Biography of Ashton Stevens," The Newberry, https://mms.newberry.org/xml/xml_files/Stevens.xml (accessed November 5, 2017). In Stevens' review of "Ghosts," he had stated "…that Duse really jelled the marrow in our spines." See Stevens, "Duse Not Faded, But Electrical, Says Stevens," January 1, 1924.
[167] In September of 1881, Duse married fellow actor Tebaldo Marchetti, who had used the stage name "Tebaldo Checci." The couple did not marry out of love, but because Duse was five-months pregnant. They were all but separated by January of 1885. Marchetti died in the fall of 1918. See Sheehy, *Eleonora Duse*, 38-40, 44, 65-66, 72, 287; Sica and Wilson, *The Murray Edwards Duse Collection*, 51; Weaver, *Duse*, 32.
[168] Enrichetta Angelica Marchetti was born on January 7, 1882. She later married Edward Bullough, Professor of modern languages at the University of Cambridge. She died in December of 1961. See Sheehy, *Eleonora Duse*, 14, 44, 247; Sica and Wilson, *The Murray Edwards Duse Collection*, 57.
[169] Toward the end of her life, Duse lived in the village of Asolo, in northwest Venice. Her house was known as *Casa dell' Arco*. She was buried at the cemetery of Santa Anna, within sight of Monte Grappa, in May of 1924. See Marchesa Selvatica Estense, "Immortal Duse is Laid to Rest at Monte Groppa," *The Shreveport Times*, August 24, 1924; Sica and Wilson, *The Murray Edwards Duse Collection*, 7; Sheehy, *Eleonora Duse*, 326.

Mrs. Fuqua Gives First Interview

Evidences Pride In Telling of Her Family

Reared Together

Too Busy in Home To Learn Bridge, Mah-Jongg

The following article, upon Henry Fuqua, his home life and his family, is the first of a series of three stories by a member of The Item's editorial staff. The other two will appear during the week.

BY DOROTHY DAY

The New Orleans Item
Sunday; January 27, 1924 (Pp. 1, 3; Section 2)

Fuqua's Shown to be Real Home-Loving Family

Mrs. Fuqua Gives First Interview

————

Evidences Pride In Telling of Her Family

————

Reared Together

————

Too Busy in Home To Learn Bridge, Mah-Jongg

————

The following article, upon Henry Fuqua, his home life and his family, is the first of a series of three stories by a member of The Item's editorial staff. The other two will appear during the week.

————

BY DOROTHY DAY

"Mr. Fuqua and I have known each other ever since we were born right around the corner from each other in this neighborhood. And we've loved each other all the time although I don't suppose we knew it till we were twelve—anyway," and Mrs. Henry L. Fuqua, of Baton Rouge, laughed and blushed as she spoke.[170]

Figure 8-Mrs. Henry Fuqua, *The New Orleans Item*, January 27, 1924.

She blushes delightfully. That was one of the first things we noticed about her, after we had chased her around for almost 30 hours. She did her best to avoid being interviewed and she didn't tell us this about herself and her husband until we had talked with her for three hours.

She didn't want to be interviewed she said, first because the election hadn't been decided yet, although she admitted on pressure that of course she knew the outcome was sure.[171] Second, because she was a busy woman and had so many engagements, —and then she hastened to contradict herself, saying that she was indeed busy, but it was about her household affairs, and that she wasn't a giddy-gaddy woman.[172] Third, because it wasn't seemly to talk to a newspaper reporter until her husband had told her she should.

Finally, when we had reached the ear of Mr. Fuqua and he had laughingly persuaded his wife to help us out, she admitted that she didn't like the idea of talking to the press—"not nervous exactly, but just sort of fluttery."

Mutual Confidence Established

When eighteen-year-old Henry junior, who had come out to the porch with his mother to see if the mail had come, squeezed her arm and assured her of his own nervousness when called upon to face the dean, for instance and we assured her that we were not quite so brazen as we seemed, what with telephoning her and pursuing her all around town, mutual sympathy and confidence was established all around.

---

[170] Mrs. Henry L. Fuqua was born Marie Laure "Laura" Matta on February 26, 1866, in Baton Rouge, LA. She lived to be 102-years-old, dying on June 13, 1968. See "Ex-Governor's Widow Dies," *The Shreveport Times*, June 14, 1968; "Louisiana Governors," http://www.la-cemeteries.com/Governors/Fuqua,%20Henry%20Luse/Fuqua,%20Henry%20Luse.shtml (accessed November 6, 2017).

[171] Mrs. Fuqua was referring to her husband's victory in the first Democratic primary election, held on January 15, 1924. Fellow Democrat Hewitt Bouanchaud received 35.14% of the votes, Fuqua 33.98%, and Huey Long 30.89%. On February 19, 1924, Fuqua defeated Bouanchaud in the second Democratic primary election, 57.77% to 42.23%. Fuqua was elected Governor of Louisiana in the general election held on April 22, 1924, defeating his Republican opponent (James S. Millikin) by an overwhelming margin of 97.90% to 2.10%. See "Fuqua Leads in Race for Governor," *The Shreveport Times*, January 16, 1924; "Fuqua Winner in Run-off Primary," *The Shreveport Times*, February 20, 1924; "Light Ballot Cast in State," *The Shreveport Times*, April 23, 1924.

[172] The reference to being a "giddy-gaddy" woman meant that Mrs. Fuqua was not playing games with Day, by trying to avoid the interview. However, the statement is paradoxical, given that Mrs. Fuqua later stated that she *had* tried to evade Day by going to a motion picture show.

Nunky, a horribly scarred and brazen fox terrier was not so sure about the confidence, however. He sniffed around suspiciously and then leering out of his rheumy old eyes, turned and scampered into the house at the heels of his young master.

"You really must excuse Nunky's appearance," apologized Mrs. Fuqua. "He's thirteen years and he will fight, and not long ago while we were at the receiving station of the penitentiary with Mr. Fuqua, he got into an awful battle, although it was Sunday, and he won although he doesn't look it, does he? He'd like to say 'you should have seen the other fellow'" she laughed.

Mrs. Fuqua is a middle-sized woman, chubby, but not stout, she was neatly dressed in a black and white sport skirt, grey sport sweater with pale yellow embroidered collar and cuffs. Her feet were neatly shod in black patent leather, and her silk-clad ankles are slim.

"Be sure and say that my eyes are grey and that I'm an old lady—not a middle-aged one, or anything like that." She twinkled at us. "Because you know I'm fifty-eight years old, and Mr. Fuqua is only three months older than I am.

"He was born right down the street here and he had one brother and one sister. His brother is in the army, stationed in Hawaii and has been away for years, but it's expected that he is coming back to the states soon.[173] His sister married Thomas D. Boyd, president of Louisiana State University.[174] Her daughter and my daughter were the first women to register at the University when it became co-educational.[175]

Childhood Sweethearts

"As I said, I was born around the corner from him and my name was Laura Matta then. I had two brothers and five sisters. Henry's mother was born in Mississippi and his father in Baton Rouge.[176] The name Fuqua is a Scotch one and is pronounced with a long final vowel.

"My mother used to play with the daughters of Zachary Taylor who was afterwards president.[177] That was right after the Mexican war, and army officers weren't in very good standing with the mothers and fathers of marriageable daughters.[178] Mother often tells us how opposed Mr. Taylor was to his daughter's association with young army officers. One of his girls fell so much in love

---

[173] Major General Stephen Ogden Fuqua (born, December 25, 1878; died, May 11, 1943) spent his career in the United States Army. He served in the infantry during World War One, and was later awarded the Distinguished Service Medal. See "Maj. Gen. Fuqua of Louisiana Dies," *The Town Talk (Alexandria, LA)*, May 13, 1943.

[174] Thomas Duckett Boyd served as president and president emeritus of Louisiana State University (L.S.U.) for more than thirty-five years. He was married to Henry Fuqua, Sr.'s sister, Annie F. Fuqua. Boyd died in November of 1932. See "Former L.S.U. Head Dies at Baton Rouge," *The Shreveport Times*, November 3, 1932.

[175] L.S.U. became co-educational in 1906. See "Lady to Study Law," *The Daily Town Talk (Alexandria, LA)*, August 2, 1906. Boyd's daughter, who enrolled in the first co-educational class at L.S.U., was Minerva French Boyd. See "Former L.S.U. Head Dies at Baton Rouge," November 3, 1932.

[176] Henry's mother was Jeannette M. Foules. His father, James Overton Fuqua, was a veteran of both the Mexican and Civil Wars, having been wounded at the Battle of Shiloh. See "Kingston," *Natchez Democrat (Natchez, MS)*, May 27, 1900; "Career of Henry L. Fuqua," *The Shreveport Times*, October 12, 1926.

[177] Zachary Taylor was the twelfth President of the United States. He died while in office, on July 9, 1850.

[178] The Mexican-American War began on April 25, 1846, and ended on February 3, 1848.

with one, Jefferson Davis it was, that she made some excuse to visit her relatives in Kentucky and he joined her there and they were married. It wasn't an elopement, or anything like that. It was just a secret marriage and they started out immediately to travel by stage back to Baton Rouge to inform Mr. and Mrs. Taylor about it. It was a long and tedious journey then, and they had to put up at night in the small towns along the river. And when they reached one town where there was yellow fever, young Mrs. Davis caught it and died on her honeymoon. Her grave is still there.[179]

"Just a few months after I was born, my father was made manager of the state penitentiary which was in a huge building here in town where the Community Club now stands and from that time until I got married to Mr. Fuqua, my home was really in the penitentiary, although of course I was away at school a good part of the time.[180]

"It's strange how that state penitentiary has been bound up in my life. My mother's father was superintendent of it,[181] then my own father, and now for the last seven years, Mr. Fuqua has been manager of it. So you see I'm in a position to know all the good Mr. Fuqua has done while he has held the position of manager.[182]

Lives Closely Connected

"As I said, I was away at school a good part of the time and an aunt of Mr. Fuqua's was one of my teachers. From the very beginning, you see, our lives were closely connected. We played together, fought together, went to parties together all through our childhood. And then when I was twelve years old, I knew that I was in love with him. I don't know about him. He has said since that he fell in love with me before I fell in love with him, but of course I didn't know then.

"We got married thirty-five years ago, and Mr. Fuqua brought me here to live in this house with his mother. He had lived here since his early boyhood, and his mother handed it over to him when she died. When we started housekeeping together, she moved into a wing and we had the rest of the house. But the place wasn't then as it is now. There were servant's quarters out at the end of the block where the lawn and bushes are now, and the house itself was a long, low rambling affair, huge rooms that you couldn't keep warm. We had it done over just before my last baby was born, and now the rooms are smaller and there is a hall between the rooms on each side."

---

[179] Sarah Knox Taylor married Jefferson Davis on June 17, 1835. She died from yellow fever on September 15, 1835. See William C. Davis, *Jefferson Davis: The Man And His Hour; A Biography* (New York, NY: Harper Collins Publishers, 1991), 72, 75.

[180] John Harmon Matta, Mrs. Fuqua's father, was employed for many years at the Penitentiary, in the mid-to-late 1800s. See "A Plea for Justice," *New Orleans Republican*, February 19, 1876; "Von Phul," *The Times-Picayune*, July 5, 1931.

[181] Mrs. Fuqua's maternal grandfather, H. LaNoue, was Warden of the Penitentiary in the 1840s. See "Louisiana Penitentiary," *Baton-Rouge Gazette*, February 22, 1840.

[182] The Louisiana State Penitentiary, also known as Angola Prison, is located in the Parish of West Feliciana. Henry L. Fuqua was appointed as manager of the penitentiary by Governor Pleasant in 1916, a position he held until October 1, 1923. See "Wilkinson Takes Charge as Penitentiary Manager," *The Weekly Town Talk (Alexandria, LA)*, October 6, 1923.

The house in which Henry Fuqua has lived since he began to walk is a white frame house of a story and a half. There is a veranda across the front of it, pillared to the top of the building and there are green shutters at the long windows. Swinging chairs and rockers give the porch, which was fresh scrubbed, a most habitable appearance.

The house stands on a triangular block of property and has wide lawns and a noble grove of elms extending the length of the block.

"If you had only been here before the cold spell so that you could have seen how green and pretty everything was," Mrs. Fuqua mourned. "My poor flowers! And there were such gorgeous poinsettas along the side of the house!"

Home Modest and Retiring

To get to the Fuqua home from the center of town, you must walk up North Boulevard which dips, then rises again in a hilly manner most pleasing to one used to the flatness of the country around New Orleans. Napoleon street, where the Fuqua home stands is about ten blocks up from the river, then south from North boulevard and up another hill which rises slowly for three blocks.[183] The house is in a pleasant neighborhood where the homes are modest and retiring, some of them even a little battered. They have none of the sleek look of wealth common to the mansions along North boulevard. The Fuqua house is indeed more imposing than others in the neighborhood, but is not to be compared to the big white houses along the boulevard. For Henry Fuqua is not a wealthy man, as wealth goes.

Figure 9-The Fuqua family home on Napoleon Street, Baton Rouge, LA, *The New Orleans Item*, January 27, 1924.

"When I was going to school," Mrs. Fuqua went on with her story "Henry was going to the state university but he left there to work for the railroad with a surveying outfit which was laying tracks between Baton Rouge and Vicksburg.[184] At the end of that job, he went into the hardware business with a firm which was right across the street from where his store is now and when he had risen as far as he could there, he organized a stock company in which he had the principal stock and made himself manager of the Fuqua Hardware

---

[183] The Fuqua family home was located at 301 Napoleon Street in Baton Rouge. See "Thieves Attempt to Rob Home of Henry L. Fuqua," *The Weekly Town Talk (Alexandria, LA)*, February 16, 1924.

[184] During his teenage years, Henry L. Fuqua had attended Magruder's Collegiate Institute. He was later a student at L.S.U., but had left before he was twenty, to accept employment as an assistant with the corps of civil engineers (Yahoo and Mississippi Valley Railroad). See "Career of Henry L. Fuqua Ends; State Mourns Death," *The Weekly Town Talk (Alexandria, LA)*, October 16, 1926.

company.[185] Of course he isn't manager of it any more. He's got too much on his hands for that, and has had for the last seven years. But he still owns a large part of the stock and still spends time there with his friend, Frank Jones who is now manager and who went into business with my husband when he started over 30 years ago. Mr. Jones is one of his best friends and every year they go hunting or fishing together. Neither of them have had a chance at it this year, but as soon as Mr. Fuqua can settle down and get a little rest the two of them will be in the saddle and out shooting quail for days on end. And goodness knows he needs the rest."[186]

Three Children Born

Henry Fuqua has two children, a married daughter, Mrs. Walter M. Scott who lives with her husband and baby boy at Tallulah, Louisiana, where they have several cotton plantations, and an eighteen year old son Henry Fuqua Jr., who will enter the state university next fall.[187] There was another boy, born a few years after the daughter, who died at the age of eight.[188] It was when talking of her children that Mrs. Fuqua became really expansive.

"I don't know what I'd do without my boy," she smiled, "with Mr. Fuqua away so much as he has been these last years while going to one or another of the three plantations which make up the State penitentiary. During the flood two years ago at Angola, he was away for an entire month![189] And of course this campaign has taken him all over the state, so that I would have been entirely alone here if it hadn't been for [my] son and my brother who lives here with us.[190]

"Henry takes me out as though I were his best girl," she laughed. And then blushed as she admitted that the evening before when she was trying to avoid the representative of the press, the two of them had run away to a moving picture show.

"He's the baby of the family of course, born fifteen years after my girl, and she says I spoil him.

---

[185] The Fuqua Hardware Company was located at 358 Third Street, at the corner of Third and Laurel Streets in Baton Rouge. Erected in 1905, the building still bears the name Fuqua Hardware Company. See "Fuqua Hardware Company's Building, c. 1905," http://historicalbatonrouge.blogspot.com/2008/08/fuqua-hardware-company.html (accessed November 8, 2017).

[186] Henry L. Fuqua died on October 11, 1926, after a brief illness. He was the thirty-eighth Governor of the state of Louisiana, serving in that capacity for two-and-a-half years. See "Sudden Death Takes Governor Fuqua," *The Shreveport Times*, October 12, 1926.

[187] Walter M. Scott, Sr. owned several cotton plantations in Tallulah, LA. He later served as the president of the Tallulah State Bank and Trust Company. He died in January of 1954. See "Tallulah Planter Dies in Vicksburg," *The Shreveport Times*, January 4, 1954.

[188] James Overton Fuqua was born on February 17, 1893. He died at the age of seven, on December 24, 1900. See "Louisiana Governors," http://www.la-cemeteries.com/Governors/Fuqua,%20Henry%20Luse/Fuqua,%20Henry%20Luse.shtml (accessed November 6, 2017).

[189] In May of 1922, a levee broke at Bob's Bayou in Baton Rouge, causing the 6,000-acre farm adjacent to the Angola prison to be flooded with eight to twenty feet of water. Over 1,000 convicts had to be transported, on barges, to safety. It was estimated that the damages to sugarcane, corn, and other crops was in excess of $1,000,000. See "Break on Bob's Bayou Levee Flooding Angola, State's Loss a Million," *The Town Talk (Alexandria, LA)*, May 17, 1922; "Barges Remove Convicts from Angola's Farm," *The Monroe News-Star (Monroe, LA)*, May 19, 1922.

[190] Mrs. Fuqua's brother was Randolph Matta (May 27, 1874 – May 16, 1950). See "Randolph Matta," https://www.findagrave.com/memorial/141877382/randolph-matta (accessed March 7, 2018).

At least she used to until she had a boy of her own, and I tell her that he's the most domineering morsel that ever lived. But we're all so crazy about that baby that he can't help bossing us around. He and my husband are inseparable of course, whenever my daughter is visiting us. Last time they were here that little 'imp' pulled his grandfather out into the other room and said, 'Let's go out here away from the women folks!' And he's only four years old."[191]

Her daughter, Mrs. Fuqua said, had graduated from the teachers' course at the state university, although she had never taught school, nor intended to. Soon after graduating, she married and went to live on her husband's plantation.[192]

Figure 10-Mrs. Walter M. Scott, *The New Orleans Item*, January 27, 1924.

"You can't imagine what a good housekeeper she is. I had never taught her to do anything but sew—although I suppose I shouldn't say it. But I felt that young girls should have their good time and that it was time enough for them to take up the serious things of life when they got married. And as soon as she married, she showed herself to be as good a cook and housekeeper as her mother. Of course I pride myself on being a good cook and housekeeper!" Mrs. Fuqua boasted. "In this day when you can't get good help and are liable to be without a cook any time, a woman just has to be able to do anything. In Henry's mother's time, there were plenty of colored folk within calling distance so that in case of emergency you could get extra help. And the girls were far better then than they are now. All she had to do was to sit on her balcony and superintend the management of her house. But now I've got to start right in every morning and help. Very often servants don't know how to dust, or straighten up a room and when they get through with anything, they're just half done. Sometimes I have to go after them and finish up.

Daughter Good Housekeeper

"Yes, I'm glad my girl is a good housekeeper. I don't think much of a woman who isn't. We take turns spending Christmas and Thanksgiving with each other and last Christmas we spent with my daughter. And just before the holiday, she was suddenly without help, but she didn't write us a thing about it, but had us just the same, doing everything herself. And she might just as well have come here." And Mrs. Fuqua looked around the neat parlors we were sitting in, out into the spotless hall where school books and a boy's cap graced the hat stand, and her face was lighted with justifiable pride. "I don't know how to play bridge or Mah Jong and I don't think I'll ever learn," she added. "I've got enough to do."

---

[191] Walter M. Scott, Jr. continued in the plantation business after his father's death. See "Tidelands Board Adds 4 Members," *The Town Talk (Alexandria, LA)*, February 26, 1957.

[192] Adele Matta Fuqua Scott was born on May 19, 1891. In 1906, she was one of the first seventeen women to enroll at L.S.U. In 1939, Scott was the first woman elected to L.S.U.'s board of supervisors. She died on July 10, 1980. See "Woman Named on LSU Board," *The Daily Town Talk (Alexandria, LA)*, August 8, 1939; "Ex-LSU Supervisor Dies," *The Shreveport Times*, July 13, 1980.

And as for Henry the younger, a great big brown eyed fellow with long, lank hair, he met us at the Union station that afternoon and while we walked up and down the platform, waiting for the train which was to bring his father home from New Orleans he told us a little about himself.

"Don't you make my husband late for lunch," Mrs. Fuqua had scolded. "He's always late for meals now, when he's in Baton Rouge at all. He just won't take care of himself, and he's lost pounds and pounds campaigning."

Henry, Jr., Real Boy

Figure 11-Henry L. Fuqua, Jr., *The New Orleans Item*, January 27, 1924.

Henry, Jr., had the same eagerness for his father that his mother had, but he didn't show it in the same way, not being a housewife. He was filled with a youthful eagerness and excitement which made it hard to elicit from him facts about himself.

"I've been going down to Gulf Coast Military Academy for the last three years," he said.[193] "Mother didn't much want me to go, but she thinks I should use my own judgment about things so she never interferes with me—at least in big things like that. But I'm glad I'm home again and going to the university in the fall.[194] You never get enough to eat when you're away from home.

"I would have entered the university last fall except that I had to make up some courses tha[t] I missed out in at the academy—English for instance. My sister entered when she was fifteen," he added.

The train which was coming in that noon was the Frisco, bound for Mexico City. Mention of it brought out the fact that Henry, Jr., is a lover of travel and a collector of time tables than which no collection is more fascinating.

But as to his ambition in life, "I want to be an engineer and am going to take the course in engineering at the State U. Mother says I probably don't know yet what I want to do, and that I shouldn't hesitate to change my mind and change my course as many times as I want. She say[s] it's better to really find out what you want to do when you're young. She's a peach, isn't she," he added boyishly.

---

[193] The Gulf Coast Military Academy was located in Gulfport, MS.

[194] Henry Luse Fuqua, Jr. was born on August 7, 1905. He attended the University Demonstration School in Baton Rouge, graduating in 1924, and L.S.U. from 1925 to 1927. Fuqua also worked as a salesman at Fuqua Hardware; he served as technician fifth grade in the Pacific theater during World War Two. He died on July 19, 1992. See "Henry L. Fuqua, Jr., Lytle Photograph Collection and Papers, circa 1863-1978," L.S.U. Libraries Special Collections, www.lib.lsu.edu/sites/default/files/sc/findaid/1898.pdf (accessed November 20, 2017); "Louisiana Governors," http://www.la-cemeteries.com/Governors/Fuqua,%20Henry%20Luse/Fuqua,%20Henry%20Luse.shtml (accessed November 20, 2017) .

The minutes passed and the train came in, but Mr. Fuqua wasn't on it. "Darn!," said Henry, Jr. "Won't mother be sore!"

But Mrs. Henry L. Fuqua, with her curly greying hair, twinkling blue grey eyes and girlish blushes, doesn't look as though her wrath is of a kind which could intim[id]ate. Besides they've been in love since they were twelve years old.

Figure 12-Henry L. Fuqua, *The New Orleans Item*, **January 27, 1924.**

Henry Fuqua's Fri[...]

Life As Penitentiary Manager and Hardware Store Owner Related

This is the second of a series of three intimate stories of Henry L. Fuqua, written by a member of The Item staff. The third will appear during the week.

By DOROTHY DAY

Nashville tracks between Baton Rouge and Vicksburg, and he had left surveying to enter a hardware store. He loved the town and he loved his wife and the little baby girl, and he dreamed of building up a business in the heart of Baton Rouge.

The company which he organized as soon as he had learned all there

The New Orleans Item
Tuesday; January 29, 1924 (P. 4)

Henry Fuqua's Friends in Baton Rouge Recall Deeds of Life of Achievement

Life As Penitentiary Manager and Hardware Store Owner Related

This is the second of a series of three intimate stories of Henry L. Fuqua, written by a member of The Item staff. The third will appear during the week.

By DOROTHY DAY

In the center of Baton Rouge on Third street, which is the main street of the town, is the Fuqua Hardware company, organized by Henry L. Fuqua 30 years ago. He was then 28 years old and he had a wife and child and home.

He had left the state university to try his hand at surveying with a gang which was laying the Louisville & Nashville tracks between Baton Rouge and Vicksburg, and he had left surveying to enter a hardware store. He loved the town and he loved his wife and the little baby girl, and he dreamed of building up a business in the heart of Baton Rouge.

The company which he organized as soon as he had learned all there was to learn about his business was a stock company in which he held the most shares and the position of manager of the company. With him for the last 30 years has been Frank Jones, who started in at the bottom, rose to a clerk, accountant, salesman—went on the road for the company, and now for the last seven years has held the position of manager.[195] He took over this job when Henry Fuqua was appointed by Governor Pleasant to the post of manager of the state penitentiary.[196]

---

[195] Frank B. Jones was born on June 16, 1874. He rose to the position of Vice President of the Fuqua Hardware Company, dying on January 11, 1936. See "Necrology: Frank B. Jones." *The Daily Town Talk*

Knows Him Well

"I think I can say that I know Henry Fuqua better than anybody else in the world," said Mr. Jones. "Yes, even better than his own wife knows him. A woman can never know a man as his best friend does. And Henry Fuqua has been my best friend for the last 30 years. We've not only worked together but we've spent our vacations together, hunting and fishing.

"See that picture"—and the gray-haired manager indicated a large framed photograph hanging over his desk. It was a picture of Mr. Fuqua standing in a swampy field, dressed in a rough corduroy suit. The tall, reedy grasses brushed against his legs, the sky looked overhanging. There was a gun in his hand and a dog by his side.

"I don't know which one of those creatures I love the most," Mr. Jones laughed. "Jack, the bird dog, is dead now and I'll never find another to replace him. That dog had a human heart and he understood every word you said to him. And it wasn't by intonation either. I'd just say in an ordinary conventional tone of voice, 'Go get in the car and wait for me, Jack.' and he'd walk out of the room and do as I said.

Another Trip Promised

"Every year Fuqua and I would go out shooting quail and Jack enjoyed himself as much as we did. But we haven't had any shooting or fishing yet this year. As soon as we had persuaded Fuqua to enter the race for governor I gave up everything else, summer vacation, fishing and hunting, and have been working night and day for him. But our time is coming. As soon as this thing is over we'll be out in the saddle." And Mr. Jones sighed and seemed to luxuriate in the thought.

There were other pictures around the walls of woods and fields and dogs and baseball teams. "Fuqua always was a man who was great for outdoor life," said his friend. "He likes sports of all kinds and played on the baseball team of the university when he was a kid. Baseball wasn't the national game then as it is now and there were no big games. No, that isn't his team which you're looking at. They didn't even have uniforms."

Recalls Old Furniture

The office in which we were sitting was not a spick and span, up-to-date business office. The furniture was old and battered and crowded into the glass-enclosed office. The room had more the look of a man's den than an office.

Outside of the office stretched the store, which fronts two streets. There was a smell of leather and a general gleam of many sharp, shining things.

(Alexandria, LA), January 11, 1936; "Frank B. Jones (1874-1936)," https://www.findagrave.com/memorial/145084363 (accessed November 9, 2017).
[196] Ruffin G. Pleasant was the thirty-sixth Governor of the state of Louisiana (May 9, 1916 – May 11, 1920).

Frank Jones isn't the only man who misses the daily companionship of Henry Fuqua. With him for the last seven years has been Judge G. A. Killgore, who has been connected with the penitentiary for the last quarter of a century and has held the position of secretary to the manager ever since the manager replaced the old board of three.[197] Since October of last year, Horace Wilkinson Sr., has held the position which Fuqua resigned to run for governor.[198]

Tells Story of Flood

"I've known Fuqua ever since he was a youngster, and I've been his secretary for seven years, and I can't say that there is another man in the world whom I love and admire more. Everybody who comes in contact with him feels the same way."

Judge Killgore told again the story of the flood, told with pride for his friend, how, when the men were being taken off the steamer which rescued them from the flooded country, each one of them had some cheerful, hearty word for the manager of the state penitentiary.

"It wasn't only him encouraging and exhorting them," said Judge Killgore. "They were showing him how much they liked him and how they meant to stand by him and do all that they could to help him in this misfortune. Fuqua was never a man to show off his authority. The prisoners felt it, but they did not feel it necessary to ingratiate themselves or do any bootlicking around him. He was a man who brought out their manhood, and he made them feel that he was a man working among men, and not just a penitentiary superintendent, bossing them around."

Given Medical Care

Other things Judge Killgore told. For the first time in the history of the penitentiary men were given adequate medical attention, he said. "I don't suppose I should tell this because it might establish a precedent, which other released prisoners would like to follow. But anyway, it shows you what sort of a man Fuqua is. There was a prisoner who was paroled and, after leaving the penitentiary and taking a job which we got for him, he fell sick and a major operation was necessary. When Fuqua learned that the employers couldn't see the man through, he readmitted him to the penitentiary—that's a funny way of putting it, isn't it?—and called in the best specialist in the state who had volunteered his work whenever it was found necessary for the convicts. That man would have had to pay three or four hundred dollars for doctor's bills alone if he had been a free man. But of course he wouldn't have been able to pay it and he would have died. It's a good many lives which Governor Fuqua has saved."

---

[197] G. A. Killgore was a former district judge in Union parish. From 1900 to 1943, Killgore served as secretary-treasurer of the penitentiary board in Baton Rouge. See "Judge Killgore Dies Wednesday," *The Shreveport Times*, February 19, 1948.

[198] Horace Wilkinson, Sr. was a former state representative and plantation owner. Wilkinson also served as the manager of the state penitentiary at Angola, under the governorship of James M. Parker. See "Death Takes Two Former Legislators," *The Shreveport Times*, December 27, 1941.

The Honor System

With the honor system which was instituted by Henry Fuqua, terms are greatly shortened, according to Judge Killgore. Prisoners who are sentenced to a life term can be released at the end of 10 years for good behavior. Twenty year sentences are reduced to seven or eight years, fifteen years to three.

"You can ask any one of them how long he has to serve," said the judge, "and he will tell you not only the number of years, but the months and the days left of his sentence. Naturally the greatest desire in the heart of every prisoner is for freedom."

Fuqua accomplished more by his abolition of the stripes than the mere bolstering up of the prisoners' self-respect, Judge Killgore pointed out. He provided occupation and a trade for prisoners in making the new khaki outfits, which provided them with the means of earning a living when they left the penitentiary. And not only are the men provided with an entire outfit on leaving prison, but they are given $10 to face the world on. $5 more than any other state provides.

Rupture With Parker

In the course of the conversation, the judge went on to say that not only the Fuqua family but the town itself was grieved at the rupture between John Parker and Fuqua.[199]

"They were personal friends for 20 years, but Parker has created a breach and it's hard to understand why he did it.[200] We all have our surmises, of course, as to why Parker sponsored his lieutenant governor and didn't want Fuqua in the race. He seemed to think that Fuqua owed his position as manager of the state penitentiary to him, forgetting that Mr. Fuqua had held the office for four years before Parker reappointed him."

The subject was mentioned but indirectly to the retiring governor.

In the governor's office of the old state house, which was built in 1847, destroyed by fire during the Civil War when it was occupied by federal troops who used it as a barracks and prison, rebuilt, and used as the seat of government since 1882, Governor Parker sat alone.[201] A fire burned quietly in the grate and cast a soft glow over the heavy carpet and fine old gleaming furniture. From the long windows you could look down over the terraced lawn which was sere

---

[199] John M. Parker was the thirty-seventh Governor of Louisiana. He held office from May 11, 1920 to May 13, 1924.

[200] An underlying source of friction between Fuqua and Governor Parker may have concerned their opposing views of the Ku Klux Klan. Fuqua claimed that Parker's adjutant general, a Mr. Toombs, was a Klansman. Fuqua further vowed that his administration would enact legislation to eliminate the secrecy of such membership. See "Long Opens Campaign for Governor; Fuqua Strongly Scores Klan," *The Shreveport Times*, September 2, 1923; "Bouanchaud Will Answer Fuqua Monday," *The Shreveport Times*, November 19, 1923.

[201] The old state house was located at 100 North Boulevard in Baton Rouge. On December 28, 1862, a portion of the state house burned down, seemingly by accident. See "Burning of the Capitol at Baton Rouge," *The Times-Picayune*, December 31, 1862.

and withered. You could look far down the river, which gleamed cold and impassive in the fading sunlight, conscious of its own greatness and indifferent to the fading fortunes of the old man who sat at his desk in the state house. Probably the same age as the new governor, yet his head seemed bent and there was no spring in his step nor light in his fine old eyes.

Dreams of Campanile

He had said that he was very busy with only time for a few moments' talk, but before him on the mahogany desk were only many catalogues of chimes over which he was poring, comforting himself with the thought of the campanile of the new university in which the chimes will play, morning and evening through the reign of many governors.

Figure 13-Campanile, Louisiana State University, Baton Rouge, LA. Photograph by Francis Fuller, circa 1920s.

"It is my dream," he confessed. "We must have dreams. The most beautiful part of this dream of a greater state university is this plan for the campanile, a dream which is being shared by the thousands of donors from every section of the state. It is to be 174 feet high and in it there will be tablets bearing the names of all the soldiers and sailors of the state who lost their lives in the war.[202] There will be a clock to strike the hour and chimes to play morning and evening simple and homely tunes like 'Over There' and 'Tipperary,' which are great in their associations.[203]

"Yes, it is my dream which I am dreaming for the young men and women of the state. And now I am being reviled by the press and every hand is turned against me," he said bitterly. "Friends that I had are no longer my friends," and probably he was thinking of Henry L. Fuqua.

Adores Grandchildren

"But I'll show you whom I'm working for," he added, handing us a paper weight under the glass of which laughed the faces of three youngsters. "My grandchildren," he said proudly. "I've worked for them and for the young people of the state, so I do not care what they are saying about me."

---

[202] On May 1, 1926 the campanile was dedicated as part of the new L.S.U. campus. Known as the Memorial Tower, the campanile paid tribute to the fallen soldiers and sailors of Louisiana, who had perished in battle during World War One. Curiously, although former Governor Ruffin G. Pleasant made a speech on the day of the dedication, neither Governor Henry L. Fuqua, nor former Governor John M. Parker, were in attendance. See "Inspect New L. S. U. Grounds and Buildings," *The Weekly Town Talk (Alexandria, LA)*, May 8, 1926.

[203] "Over There" was composed by George M. Cohan in 1917; "It's A Long Way to Tipperary" was composed by Jack Judge in 1912.

And as we left, he bent again over the catalogues on his desk and the rays of the setting sun crept in over river and valley and lit up his white hair and the furrows on his cheeks.

Mr. Fuqua came into the hotel that evening with swinging step. The fight was on and he looked as though he was enjoying it. During our brief talk he was interrupted by men who came up to shake him by the hand, to grab him affectionately by the shoulder. Invitations by the archbishop to attend a meeting at Knights of Columbus hall—invitation to attend the ceremony at St. Joseph's church the next day.[204] "Sure. I'll be there" he said to all of them.

Wife Hates Politics

"How do you like my wife?" he said boastfully. "No, she didn't want me to run for office—just like a woman, worrying for fear I'll wear out. She doesn't like politics anyway—I just have to force her to go and vote—and the idea of a long and bitter political fight distressed her.[205] But she stands by like a brick always, ready to do anything in the world for me.

"What is it you wanted? Pictures of me when I was a baby?" and Mr. Fuqua looked startled and blushed. "If there are any pictures of me in that state—and I don't know of any—my wife has them—and I know you won't get them from her. But sure, you can have the one of me and Jack out hunting. It's just after six o'clock and the store is probably locked, but I've a key, so we'll go down there and rifle the place."

All the way down Third street Mr. Fuqua was stopped and congratulated and beamed at. Baton Rouge has known him for 58 years and what they know and think of him can be seen by the light on their faces when they speak to him.[206]

Hold On to Picture!

Frank Jones was still in his office and shouted heartily at his friend as he came in. "If anything happens to that picture!"—he warned as he took it down from the wall and dusted it affectionately. "Remember when that was taken, Henry. That was a great day, all right. I wonder when we'll get a chance to have another like it."

Governor Fuqua looked at the picture of the baseball team on the wall and laughed.[207] "Say, Frank, do you remember my pitcher—you know the chap, but I can't think of his name. At every

---

[204] St. Joseph parish, now a cathedral, is located on Main and Fourth Streets in Baton Rouge.

[205] Ironically, Laura Fuqua's obituary made a point of stating that, "She had little interest in politics, except as it affected her husband." See "Ex-Governor's Widow Dies," June 14, 1968.

[206] Both Day and Fuqua were born on the same day. Day was born on November 8, 1897 in Bath Beach, NY; Fuqua on November 8, 1865 in Baton Rouge. See Day, *The Long Loneliness*, 19; "Career of Henry L. Fuqua," October 12, 1926.

[207] Although it seemed presumptuous for Day to refer to Fuqua as "Governor" at this point in the election process (see Footnote no. 171), newspapers had reported that Fuqua was heavily favored in Louisiana. See "Thomas Raps Bouanchaud and Long In Talk Which Boosts Fuqua Candidacy," *The Shreveport Times*, January 5, 1924; "Fuqua Draws Biggest Crowd to Last Rally," *The Shreveport Times*, January 14, 1924; "Bouanchaud is Expected to Quit Race," *The Shreveport Times*, January 22, 1924.

meeting down in New Orleans, there he was grinning at me from the end of the hall. When I first saw him, I was so tickled that I just shouted out at him.

"I'm new to the political platform—never did much speech-making," he turned to us, "so whenever I see my friends in the audience, I'm delighted."

Wrapping up the picture, the governor carried it back to the hotel, although he was so jostled by friends whom he met on the street that he almost dropped it once or twice.

"Your wife telephoned and says you're to come right home and get your dinner," the hotel clerk told him, and looking as hungry as his own growing son could look, and as anxious to see his wife as though he had been away from her four months instead of four days, Mr. Fuqua slipped from the detaining hands of his friends and hurried away.

Fuqua Liked by Convicts
For Making Prison Life
Comfortable As Possible

This is the third of a series of
three intimate stories about Henry
L. Fuqua, his life and his home,
by a member of The Item Staff.

BY DOROTHY DAY

work is, too, and can pitch in with
the rest of them.

"Just look at the way he had to
meet the crisis that the flood made
in the affairs of the penitentiary! Out
there working night and day with the

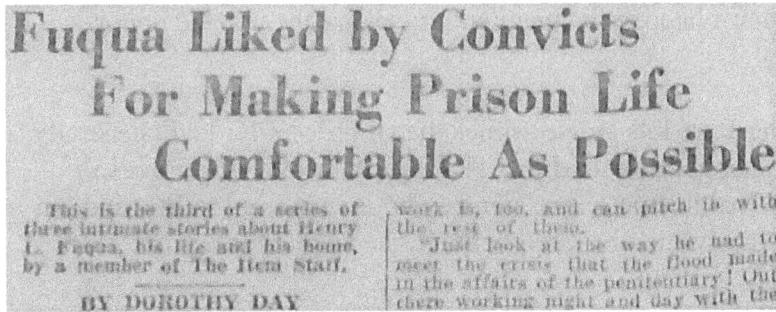

The New Orleans Item
Thursday; January 31, 1924 (P. 14)

Fuqua Liked by Convicts For Making Prison Life Comfortable As Possible

This is the third of a series of three intimate stories about Henry L. Fuqua, his life and his home, by a member of The Item Staff.

BY DOROTHY DAY

"Yes, my life has been pretty well bound up with the state penitentiary, with my grandfather, my father and my husband all holding positions as manager of it," said Mrs. Henry L. Fuqua as she sat in the comfortable little sitting room of the Fuqua family home on St. Napoleon street, Baton Rouge, La. There was a grate fire burning cheerily, although the window facing the sun was open and a soft breeze stirred the curtains. Bookcases, filled with well-worn volumes, were there, and Mrs. Fuqua's work basket, and Nunky, the old fox terrier, curled up on a cushion.

"I'll tell you as much as I can about the penitentiary and my husband's work there. Just as long as you don't puzzle me with questions about politics and the issues of the election. I am glad to answer you. But I don't know anything about politics and I'm not ashamed of not knowing. I'm not one of these women who think they know as much about running the state as the men. I'm a wife and mother and I'll help my husband all I can without taking any active part in politics.

Abolished The Stripe

"As to the penitentiary, one of the first things Mr. Fuqua did when he was appointed to office by Governor Pleasant in 1916 was to abolish the stripe and adopt an ordinary khaki uniform. Then he established the honor system and by that the sentences are shortened and a better spirit prevails among the men.

"Just think of all the stories you read in the papers, of mutinies among convicts in other states. You'll find them tunneling their way out and making their escape. In Kentucky, only a few months ago, prisoners barricaded themselves in the dining room of the jail and fought off the guards for days.[208] Things like that don't happen in a penitentiary where there is the honor system.

"You see, Mr. Fuqua believes that there are lots worse crimes than murder. Murder is generally committed when a man is insane with anger or with drink. Having a horrible temper doesn't necessarily mean that a man has criminal instincts. And a man who is sentenced to life, and put on his honor in the penitentiary, and knows that by good behavior he is going to get out years earlier, will act like a man, honorably.

Clean Clothes and Baths

"And Mr. Fuqua believes too, that clean clothes and baths and good food are going to make a convict feel more like a man and less like a criminal, so he started in to work for these things.

"As soon as he was appointed to office, and orders came to scrap the old penitentiary, which stood in the city here, where the Community club now stands, Mr. Fuqua was told that he could have all the brick and materials which he could obtain and carry away within a year.

"This saved him lots of expense in building the receiving station on the 40 acres of land outside of the city. He had plenty of convict labor, and, with the bricks saved from the old penitentiary, the building of the new receiving station was constructed. They were able to use all the slate, the iron bars, and lots of other materials."

But the period which Mrs. Fuqua remembers most vividly in connection with her husband's work is the time of the flood at Angola two years ago.

Strain Terrific

"From the very first moment of danger, Mr. Fuqua was on the job at Angola, fighting with all the men and materials at his disposal to keep back the river. The penitentiary had had a large debt, and he had decreased that, but he knew that, in case of flood, there would be a tremendous loss, and more money would have to be raised to rebuild and replant the plantation. He was away from home for a month, fighting night and day, and the strain was terrific. But it was a losing fight. When he finally came home, he looked broken, and my heart ached for him."

Angola, one of the three plantations which make up the state penitentiary, and which is 60 miles north of Baton Rouge, is the only one of the three which takes care of both men and women. It was originally purchased by the board of control, which took the place of the office of manager in 1901, as a cotton plantation, but, owing to the boll weevil invasion, it was necessary to change

---

[208] On October 3, 1923, Monte "Tex" Walters, and two other prisoners (Harry Ferland and Lawrence Griffith) of the Kentucky State Penitentiary (266 Waters Street, Eddyville, KY), murdered three prison guards (Hodge Cunningham, William Gilbert, and V. B. Mattingly) in a failed attempt to escape. It was later determined that Walters' wife, Mrs. Lillian Walters, had aided in the crimes by smuggling weapons and ammunition into the prison. See "Gas Bombs Are Ordered for Drive to Kill Convicts Who Shot 4 Eddyville Guards," *The Courier-Journal (Louisville, KY)*, October 4, 1923; Russell Briney, "Convicts Still Hold Retreat," *The Courier-Journal*, October 4, 1923; "Sparks Remanded to Eddyville Jail," *The Courier-Journal*, October 25, 1923.

it from cotton to cane.[209] In 1911 a huge sugar house was built, with a capacity for grinding and manufacturing from 1,000 to 1,200 tons of cane a day. It is one of the largest and most modern plants of its size in the state.

Knows How To Work

"But doesn't Mr. Fuqua have to know a tremendous lot about plantation work and chemistry and market conditions to run three huge plantations and make them pay?" Mrs. Fuqua was asked.

"Of course he does," his wife said proudly, "but what especially fits him for the job is the fact that he's a first class business man and has a tremendous knowledge of human psychology, although he would call it human nature. And he knows what work is, too, and can pitch in with the rest of them.

"Just look at the way he had to meet the crisis that the flood made in the affairs of the penitentiary! Out there working night and day with the waters of the flood creeping up on them hour by hour. And when they saw that their fight was hopeless and that they would have to desert the plantation, he gave up in time to get a steamship there to take the convicts down the river and to save the stock and the equipment. Of course, a great deal was lost. Tools had been left in the cane where the laborers had dropped them, and, of course, all the crops were lost.

"The furnishings of the houses were strung up to the ceilings or roofs of the buildings, so they were saved.

Flood Subsides

"When the flood finally subsided and the work of rebuilding was begun, it was found that most of the houses, aside from being muddy and water-soaked, were intact.

"Mr. Fuqua, in spite of the nerve-racking toil he had been through, even found something to laugh about. But he laughed more to keep me from despairing about him than anything else. I remember he told me about an old mother pig, and her entire litter, floating unconcernedly down the river to their new home, grunting, happy and comfortable. Floods were nothing in their lives. Chickens and mules and pigs and cows, everything was saved. And the convicts all helped with a will, and not one of them escaped or tried to.

"The entire camp was moved to the property where the new university now is being built, and the men were put to work there, building new quarters. The women were removed to the

---

[209] The boll weevil crisis was a great danger to all of the southern states raising cotton. In 1906, a symposium held in New Orleans by the Association of Economic Entomologists came to three distinct conclusions: "1. The boll weevil has not been exterminated, except in limited regions. 2. This local extermination was due to a combination of influences [such as unseasonably cold temperatures] which may not occur again for a long time. 3. The pest continues to spread and is reaching regions where the environment will certainly change its habits." In 1909, the Pointe Coupee Parish in Louisiana estimated that their cotton crop would be shortened by 50,000 bales, due to the rampant spread of the weevil. See "Invasion of the Pest Can Hardly Be Stayed," *The Semi-Weekly Times-Democrat (New Orleans, LA)*, January 5, 1906; "News of the State Culled in Day," *The Shreveport Times*, August 12, 1909.

receiving station so that they would have shelter and would not have to undergo the hardships of the men."

How tents were thrown up, how land was cleared, food and shelter found for the stock as well as the men, how all the farmers from the neighborhood gladly contributed everything they could in the way of machinery and help for the planting of new crops, not of cane, but of vegetables and sweet potatoes for the men—this was an engrossing story.

Can't Drive Auto

We visited the receiving station that afternoon to see with our own eyes the work which had been done. "I'd be glad to take you out there myself," Mrs. Fuqua told us, "but I don't know how to drive—that's old-fashioned of me too, isn't it?—and the boy is off today. I've visited the place often with my husband, and I find the work engrossing."

It was with much interest that we took a cab and drove over roads, which were yellow in the sun, and dappled along those stretches where magnolia trees spread their shade.

The receiving station, situated three miles east of the city limits, has one long building in the shape of an ell. In the bend of the ell is the office, like a light house with windows on all sides. It is fitted with several high old desks at which it would be impossible to sit except on the very highest stools, and several old cupboards which any collector of antiques would appreciate.

Captain M. E. Garrison, who has charge of the station, met us at the huge iron gate and took us through the garden into his office.[210] He mourned the loss of his flowers through the cold spell several weeks before and assured us that our visit should have been in the spring.

Captain Garrison is a young man with a lean tanned face and steady eyes. He lives in a little cottage to the south of the station with his wife and child. At the time of our visit there were 49 white men at the station and 48 negroes.

Captain Likes Work

Captain Garrison likes his work and is proud to have served under Mr. Fuqua. "Since I've been here I've had 289 men pass through my hands to the various plantations and I have never lost a man. All the other captains of the various camps—that's what we call the penitentiary plantations—can say the same thing, and it's all because of the honor system."

As soon as a prisoner is brought to the receiving station, he is put in the hospital for a thorough physical examination. All the camps have hospitals attached to them, but the one at the receiving station is fitted with operating room, X-ray machines, sterilizing apparatus, drugs and beds. Only emergency cases are taken care of at the camp hospitals: patients with serious ailments are sent to the receiving station. Many patients whose condition does not allow them to work in the fields or about the plantations are kept at the receiving station during their entire term.

---

[210] M. E. Garrison was a long-time employee of the penitentiary, resigning after nineteen years, in 1928. See "Garrison Resigns Penitentiary Post," *The Shreveport Times*, August 2, 1928.

Mere Boy In Prison

There's 16-year-old Jimmy, for instance (that isn't his name but we'll call him that) who was sentenced to 15 years for manslaughter. Under the honor system, he will be out in two and a half years. Captain Garrison pointed him out proudly.

"When that boy came in here he wasn't able to read or write, and now he spends all his spare time over his books and writes a letter home every week. He'll have learned a trade by the time he gets out."

The boy of whom he was talking was dressed in a clean khaki suit, with a jockey cap pulled down over his eyes. His was a position as trusty, and he was perched in a little tower which overlooked a vegetable patch, lazily playing with a puppy. Down in the garden men were at work, and in the yard below him half a dozen of the laundry squad were sitting on logs around a huge black cauldron, hung from sticks, in which they were boiling clothes. The men talked desultorily, and, aside from the occasional cackle of a hen or bark of a dog, a brooding silence hung over the place. It was like a day in spring, that makes men dream.

Uniforms In Stacks

We went through the sewing room, where there were a long line of machines. On the shelves in stacks were bright, clean uniforms, light one for summer, and heavy ones for winter.

"Everybody changes his clothes and bathes twice a week, and we have a barber shop which the men use three times a week," said the captain. "Men in the fields can take a shower every night.

Figure 14-Kitchen, State Penitentiary at Baton Rouge, circa 1900. Henry L. Fuqua, Jr. Lytle Photograph Collection and Papers, Mss. 1898, Louisiana and Lower Mississippi Valley Collections, LSU Libraries, Baton Rouge, LA.

"One rule was made and insisted on—that the inmates take off their work clothes and wear sleeping garments. They were provided with two sheets and pillow cases and towels. Things like these bolster up a man's self-respect. And its things like these that Mr. Fuqua has been doing for the men since he came into office.

"He was out here about three times a week, in between his visits to his other plantations. Sometimes you'd wonder how he managed to get all his work done, but he was always a man who made you think he could accomplish the impossible.

"The men all know him and love him, and he's a friend to all. We're missing him out here."

Then there was the supply room, where sugar and rice and coffee were kept in white wooden bins that looked clean enough to eat out of. Food was stacked on shelves and through the windows at each end of the room the afternoon sun poured. The library and rest room came next. One entire wall was lined with shelves of books and there were tables with magazines and a phonograph. In the next room was the chapel, where services are held every Sunday by various denominations.

One Prisoner a Druggist

The upstairs of this end of the ell was taken up by the hospital.

"We don't even need to have a resident doctor," the captain told us, "owing to the fact that one of our prisoners is a druggist and has studied medicine and surgery."

Figure 15-Inside view of hospital, Angola State Farm, circa 1900-1901. Henry L. Fuqua, Jr. Lytle Photograph Collection and Papers, Mss. 1898, Louisiana and Lower Mississippi Valley Collections, LSU Libraries, Baton Rouge, LA.

Three men in spotless white uniforms, looking like internes in a hospital, were working over a man with a broken leg when we came into the white ward, and the man whom Captain Garrison had pointed out as the druggist hastened to apologize for the plaster of paris and bandages strewn around the floor. We were glad to learn that the patient had been given morphine as soon as the accident occurred, and had also been given ether during the setting of the broken limb.

Other men lay around languidly reading, but none seemed very sick and the room had a cheerful look.

In the kitchen, the first room at the other end of the ell, a big black cook, dressed in a white apron and white hat, prepared us a cup of strong black coffee and welcomed our inspection of his cupboards and kitchen stove.

Kitchen is Spotless

The dining room was quite as spotless, and the unpainted wooden tables were as white as snow. What made for cheerfulness in all these rooms were the windows at each end. Next to the dining room was a room in which half a dozen boys were making shoes out of soft, pliable leather, and we thought of the stiff paper shoes which were put on us at Occoquan.[211]

Small, crisp loaves of white bread were being raked out of the oven in the bakery. The oven, Captain Garrison explained, was one of those which had been in use in the army, but which they had bricked and cemented over until it was as good as new. From the look of the deep brown loaf, we judged that there was no complaining as to the way that oven baked.

By now we had seen everything there was to be seen around the jail and had found everything spotless, and working smoothly in spite of the fact that our visit was totally unexpected. We could not help but think of the three above mentioned jails with their dirt and squalor and graft.

For the last seven years, Henry L. Fuqua has had the management of these plantations which make up the Louisiana state penitentiary.

"By their works you shall know them," Mrs. Fuqua had said simply, in talking of her husband.[212]

Figure 16-Bakery, State Penitentiary at Baton Rouge, Circa 1900. Henry L. Fuqua, Jr. Lytle Photograph Collection and Papers, Mss. 1898, Louisiana and Lower Mississippi Valley Collections, LSU Libraries, Baton Rouge, LA.

---

[211] On November 10, 1917, Day and forty suffragists were arrested for picketing in front of the White House. The women were ultimately sent to the Occoquan Workhouse where many of them, Day included, were brutalized by prison guards. Day had related the often-harrowing details of her prison experience in several sources. See Day, *The Eleventh Virgin*, 185-220; Day, *From Union Square to Rome*, 83-89; Day, *The Long Loneliness*, 72-83.

[212] A reference to Mt 7:16, "You will know them by their fruits" [NRSV].

The Thrills of 1924: Dorothy Day Encounters the "Underworld Denizens" of New Orleans

Going Undercover in New Orleans

Toward the end of her life, Dorothy Day recalled an ugly incident, which had occurred in a New Orleans tavern in 1924. She had been assaulted by a group of taxi-dancers, who must have recognized the young reporter as the girl who had exposed their industry in the pages of *The New Orleans Item*. Day had received a black eye in the fracas, from a heavy cup that had been thrown at her face by one of the girls. She further recalled that author John Dos Passos had been present during the incident of violence, which was but one of the many inherent dangers faced by the flappers of the Crescent City.[213]

Day had been asked by the editors of *The New Orleans Item* to go undercover, using an assumed name, and report upon the rampant vice found in the taxi-dancing industry. The newspaper had also tried to protect her, by publishing her articles a month after they had been written. In further describing the assignment to Chicago editor Llewellyn Jones, Day had explained that, "These dens of vice cater only to men, and many girls are hired to dance with them. They pay ten cents a dance, and the girl gets four of it."[214]

In light of the act of violence committed against Day, several pertinent questions arise. Exactly who, if anyone, was present with Day during her week of dancing at the Arcadia, Danceland, and Roseland dance halls? What were the vices, or dangers that Day and other women faced as taxi-dancers? Finally, what impact did Day's articles have upon the dance hall industry in New Orleans?

Who was Present with Day?

Day had stated that she had traveled from Chicago to New Orleans in December of 1923, because she "was getting sick of cold northern winters."[215] Accompanying her on the journey were her younger sister, "Della" Day, and Mary Gordon, whom Day later described as "a big golden-haired, pink-cheeked girl with an irresistible sense of humor and a huge appetite for a 'good time.'"[216]

In Day's letter to Jones, which was previously proven to have been written on January 2, 1924 (see Footnote no. 14), Day had stated that her sister had been unable to find employment in New Orleans, and had recently returned to New York to live with her parents.[217] Therefore, Della was *not* present when her sister visited each of the three dance halls that same evening, in the hopes of gaining employment.

In *The Long Loneliness*, which was published in 1952, Day had recalled that she and Mary Gordon had encountered a pair of neighbors, "two other girls like ourselves, both of whom were

---

[213] Dorothy Day, "On Pilgrimage," *The Catholic Worker*, June 1979: 2, 6. Dos Passos was in New Orleans in mid-February 1924, where he worked on his novel, *Manhattan Transfer*. See John Dos Passos, *The Fourteenth Chronicle: Letters and Diaries of John Dos Passos*, edited by Townsend Ludington (Boston, MA: Gambit Incorporated, 1973), 337, 356.

[214] Day, "To Llewellyn Jones (January 2, 1924)," in *All the Way to Heaven*, 6.

[215] Ibid., 5.

[216] Day, *The Long Loneliness*, 108.

[217] Day, "To Llewellyn Jones (January 2, 1924)," in *All the Way to Heaven*, 6-7.

out of work and were only too anxious to go taxi-dancing with us."[218] Although Mary Gordon and the two, unnamed, female acquaintances may have been present at the dance halls, the internal evidence shows that Day had more than likely gone "undercover" alone.

As a young reporter for the *New York Call* (1916-1917), Day had learned a hard lesson regarding traveling the streets of New York City, alone at night, and in search of a story. An ugly incident had occurred, in which she was accosted by a taxi driver in the early hours of the morning. The taxi driver, whom Day described as a young street urchin, had driven her in the opposite direction of the subway station in order to have his way with her. Day had escaped, largely unharmed, after biting the driver's hand.[219] She had finally realized that she needed to protect herself as a journalist, and began using "we" personal pronouns instead of "I".[220] It can be inferred that by using "we" statements, Day's readers would have assumed that she did not travel alone, thereby lessening the risk of further incidents of violence.

In her first eighteen signed articles for the *New York Call*, Day had used "I" pronoun statements on 307 occasions. After the above-mentioned incident with the taxi driver, she began writing in the second person (e.g. "a *Call* reporter," and "a reporter for *The Call*"), and used more "we" pronoun statements. In her last nineteen articles for the *Call*, Day had only used "I" pronouns on four occasions.

Over the course of her twenty signed articles for *The New Orleans Item*, Day had used an "I" personal pronoun only on one occasion. She wrote in the second person (e.g. "the writer," and "the author"), and used 182 "we" pronoun statements. The indication that Day was alone while reporting on most of the articles, stems from the number of times that she wrote a "we" statement, which transitioned into the first person in the same, or next sentence. This slippage from the plural to the singular occurred on nearly two dozen occasions during the twenty articles, with eleven transitions written during the string of eight dance hall articles.

On several occasions, the plural pronoun usage led to awkward composition. For example, in the final Fuqua article ("Fuqua Liked by Convicts…," published on January 31), Day and Mrs. Fuqua had supposedly traveled together by taxi to tour the receiving station of the Angola Prison. While visiting the area where the prisoners were making leather shoes, Day had stated "…we thought of the stiff paper shoes which were put on us at Occoquan." Day had been arrested in 1917 with forty suffragists for picketing the White House, and all of the women were sent to the Occoquan Workhouse. Although Day's statement here was not a pronoun slippage, the incident is strange because neither Mrs. Fuqua, nor Mary Gordon were present with Day when she was arrested in 1917. This is just but one indication that Day was alone during the investigation of most of these articles.

---

[218] Day, *The Long Loneliness*, 108.

[219] Dorothy Day, "Does Heaven Protect Working Girl? Taxi, Cop, Matron, Answer," *New York Call*, January 28, 1917.

[220] In 1979, Day had addressed this issue by stating, "Writing personally means the reader identifies with the writer. Writing 'I' the reader reads 'I.' In newspaper work, women were almost forced into it." See Day, "On Pilgrimage," June 1979: 2, 6.

The Thrills of 1924: Dorothy Day Encounters the "Underworld Denizens" of New Orleans

The Dempsey interview article ("Dempsey Scores Another Knockout...," published on February 11) contains three telling instances of pronoun transitioning. In the article, Day had stated:

> And then we elbowed our way through the crowd and fell brazenly into step beside him, he knocked all the questions out of our head by calling us "little girly" (in spite of 5 feet 10 1-2 inches) and helping us through the station by clutching our shoulder, the elbow being too far below him.

First, if Day were not alone upon meeting Dempsey at the Union train station in New Orleans, should she not have written "...he knocked all the questions out of our *heads*"? In addition, Day was five feet, ten and a half inches in height, and if she were present with Mary Gordon, why would Dempsey call her "little girly," as opposed to "little *girlies*"? Finally, it would have been extremely awkward for Dempsey to grab more than one woman's shoulder at the same time, and walk unhindered on the crowded train station platform.

In the later series of articles, which exposed women's gambling ("The Thrills of 1924," specifically the article published on February 25), Day had recounted the experience of losing money at the roulette wheel. She stated, "We had to go on, trying other fascinating combinations until we relinquished our seat, a ruined woman." If Day were with another female, as she had purported, should not the sentence have ended with "ruined *women*"?

The dance hall articles also contain numerous examples of pronoun slippage, and several inconsistent statements that do not gibe with the notion of Day being part of a group. For example, in the first article of the series ("Dance Hall Life of City...," published on February 3), Day was hired on as a taxi-dancer. She had stated, "We expressed ourselves as hopeful of amassing a fortune." This statement is also strange because, if Day were with someone else, she would have said something like "We were hopeful of amassing *our fortunes*."

A similar pronoun slippage occurred in the second article of the series ("Dance Halls Flooded by Drink, Dope," published on February 4). In describing the Arcadia Dance Hall, Day had stated "There was drink in abundance, that second night when we came to take the job of dancing given us by the manager... ." If there were more than just one dancer hired, the statement should have been "...when we came to take the *dancing jobs* given us... ." It should also be pointed out that women, who were not employed as dancers, were not normally allowed on the premises in the evening. Day had snuck into the Arcadia dressed as a flapper, and it was probably assumed that she was already employed there as a dancer.

Finally, in the article where Day is forced to sample marijuana, by an escort who had driven her against her will to City Park ("Hangers-On Scramble...," published on February 5), there is a passage which contains a number of transitional errors. Day had written that:

> As we pretended to sip the whiskey, we puffed at the cigarets, careful not to inhale, and trying to let the cigaret burn itself out as fast as it could. When ours was down to a stub, we put it out against the side of the car, and in an effort to save the "snipe" for evidence, if necessary, secreted it in the top of our stocking, which after the manner of young women was rolled.

The passage is strange because, if Day were with another female, the final sentence should have read, "...secreted it in the top of *our stockings*." It is also beyond coincidence that both women performed the exact same actions (putting the cigarette out against the side of the car, and hiding it in a stocking), at exactly the same time.

The notion that Day was alone during her week of employment as a taxi-dancer, merely accentuates the inherent dangers faced by her, and the dancers of New Orleans. These dangers are elaborated upon in the next section.

The Dangers of Taxi-Dancing

In addition to being exposed to vulgar language, petty jealousy, and the theft of personal property, the flappers of New Orleans experienced several potential dangers. These included being plied with drugs and alcohol, physical altercations with other dancers, and deviant sexual behavior (i.e. lesbianism).

Day had written about a fellow taxi-dancer ("Woman with Knife…," published on February 8), who had accepted a date after work. The dancer's suitor had given her apricot brandy, and she had become so drunk that she experienced memory loss. She *did* remember the harrowing events of going to a speakeasy, wherein she got into an altercation with a woman who had a small knife. After being chased in the street by the woman and two strange men, the dancer safely made her way home.

The article in the next issue of *The New Orleans Item* ("Girl Supplements Wages…," published on February 9), contained the dangers of deviant sexual behavior and harassment. Day had reported that an older taxi-dancer had constantly kept asking younger dancers to become her roommates. Although she did not define it as lesbianism, Day had asked inquisitively:

> What is the basis of these overtures from a woman well over thirty, to this girl of eighteen, is the question which arises. It is not often that a woman of her age desires close companionship with a girl twelve years her junior. The contrast between the two reacts against the older. But she continues her questioning, "Why don't you come and live with me, girlie?"

The last article in the dance hall series ("Dance Hall Girl…," published on February 10) contains an additional incident arising from too much alcohol consumption. Day related the details as told by a fellow dancer, who had drank so much alcohol that she also experienced memory loss. The young dancer awoke in a strange hotel room the next morning, in a state of partial undress. Although she had not been victimized by her escort, she could have potentially been raped or murdered.

Day had also experienced many of the dangers of taxi-dancing, including having to fend off "importunate advances," and being accosted by strange men. In the article mentioned above ("Hangers-On Scramble…"), Day had accepted a ride home at the end of the evening, by an escort or escorts. Instead of taking her home, the man or men drove Day to City Park against her wishes, and forced her to drink alcohol and sample a marijuana cigarette.

When Day's escort had tried to grab her, she exited the vehicle, and began walking home. Day had lived in an apartment on the corner of St. Peter and Chartres Streets, overlooking the Spanish

Cabildo and St. Louis Cathedral.[221] Her arduous journey from City Park to her apartment would have amounted to a four-mile hike, possibly fraught with additional dangers (i.e. robbery, rape, or murder) considering the lateness of the evening.

The Effects of the Dance Hall Articles

What effect did Day's dance hall articles have upon the industry in New Orleans? The evidence shows that, although Day had received a beating in the tavern, some short-term improvements were in fact made. Day's exposé had also resulted in her receiving a severe upbraiding from representatives of the United States Navy.

Within days of the first few dance hall articles appearing in the pages of *The New Orleans Item*, the editors received glowing acclaim from the New Orleans Business and Professional Women's club. In an article published on February 6, 1924, members of the women's club thanked the newspaper for revealing the true conditions of the dance halls, which were considered "disgraceful and a menace to young girls."[222]

Members of the women's club had formed a separate committee, in order to keep the spotlight shining on the dangerous working conditions of the dance halls. The committee's ultimate goal was to shut down the halls, "freeing the city of 'a menace.'"[223] In the absence of immediate closure, the committee proposed either the appointment of several policewomen to supervise the halls, or working with a district attorney to initiate legal action.[224]

A follow-up article was published by *The New Orleans Item*, in which members of the New Orleans Federation of Clubs also thanked the newspaper for the dance hall series, claiming, "The recent expose of The Item must have resulted in a decided improvement." The article further stated that Mrs. Olivia Blanchard, a police matron, had been hired to oversee the working conditions of the cabarets.[225] Due to Mrs. Blanchard's presence, the laws of Prohibition were finally enforced at the dance halls, men and women were no longer permitted to smoke on the dance floor, and the dancers were allowed to leave earlier in the evening, in order to arrive home safely.[226]

Although the working conditions may have improved for a time, both the Arcadia and Danceland were closed on May 28, 1924 when the Commissioner of Public Safety, Stanley W. Ray, had the

---

[221] Day, *From Union Square to Rome*, 112.

[222] Oddly enough, Day is not mentioned by name in the article. See "Women's Club Favors War on Dance Halls; Item Reports Lauded," *The New Orleans Item*, February 6, 1924. The Housewives' League of New Orleans also called for a further investigation of dance hall conditions in light of Day's articles. See "League to Push Billboard Fight at Zoning Parley," *The Times-Picayune*, February 9, 1924.

[223] "Women's Club Favors War on Dance Halls; Item Reports Lauded," February 6, 1924.

[224] "Women to Ask Regulation of Dance Halls," *The New Orleans Item*, February 12, 1924.

[225] "Women Thank Item for Dance Hall Expose," *The New Orleans Item*, February 27, 1924.

[226] "Policewoman Named to Stop Dance 'Necking,'" *The Times-Picayune*, February 20, 1924; "Dancing Girls Find Champion in Policewoman," *The Times-Picayune*, February 24, 1924; "Right of Council to Close Dance Hall is Upheld," *The Times-Picayune*, June 10, 1924.

halls declared as fire hazards.[227] A week later, over 100 dancers were set to protest in front of the commission council (fifteen girls actually appeared), to stress that taxi-dancing was neither vulgar nor immoral. The young women also claimed that they would not be able to find equitable employment if the halls remained closed.[228]

The greater issue at hand was not the morality of dancing, but the potential danger to the people who had patronized the dance halls on a nightly basis (estimated at 300 at Danceland). Danceland, located on the third floor, had only a narrow stairway leading to the street, and a fire escape that ended at the second story. The council also debated over the sufficiency of newly erected fire escapes at both clubs. In the end, it was determined that the structures were sound, and that the dance halls could remain in operation.[229]

The next four years saw a dramatic increase in vice, and acts of violence surrounding the dance halls. These heinous acts included a girl of fifteen found employed as a dancer at the Roseland; a gang fight wherein five men were ejected from the Roseland—the fighting continued on the street, and two men were stabbed; a carbolic acid attack at the Arcadia by a jealous wife—at least six dancers suffered burns; an Arcadia dancer and her escort, who were murdered on the street by a male acquaintance from the dance hall; the arrest of four men for fighting, and violating the dry laws, at the Arcadia; two Arcadia dancers involved in a serious automobile accident; the robbing of the Arcadia's payroll ($534) at gunpoint; two Arcadia dancers among four people arrested for alcohol consumption—the dancers were charged as dangerous and suspicious characters with no visible means of support; and, five men arrested for brawling, after assaulting a police officer at the Arcadia.[230]

The dance halls ultimately fell out of fashion. The Arcadia had closed abruptly, in July of 1928, when the owner had run out of funds to pay the wages of the dancers, and police staff. When reached for comment regarding his finances, the owner of the hall had no solution, and exclaimed that he was "through with dance halls anyhow."[231]

The impact of Day's contributions to changes in the dance hall industry also seemed to be minimized. Perhaps this was because Day had written the dance hall articles in a humorous, light-hearted fashion. However, in addition to being physically assaulted in a local tavern by her

---

[227] "Council Orders Two Dance Halls to Close Doors," *The Times-Picayune*, May 28, 1924; "Dance Halls Closed," *The Shreveport Times*, May 29, 1924; "Women to Fight Dance Hall Law," *The Times-Picayune*, June 6, 1924; "Protest on Dance Hall Bill is Filed," *The Times-Picayune*, June 13, 1924.

[228] "Dancing Girls Will Protest Ray Ordinance," *The Shreveport Times*, June 6, 1924; "Council Hears Dancing Girls' Dramatic Plea," *The Times-Picayune*, June 25, 1924.

[229] "Explains Approval by Fire Marshal," *The Times-Picayune*, June 18, 1924; "Officials Disagree on Fire Escapes," *The Times-Picayune*, June 20, 1924.

[230] "Find Erring Girl in Dance Hall," *The Times-Picayune*, June 8, 1924; "Youth Wounded in Alleged 'Gang' Fight May Die," *The Times-Picayune*, August 25, 1924; "Girl Seriously Hurt as Jealous Wife Hurls Acid," *The Times-Picayune*, August 29, 1926; "Son of Murdered Dance Hall Girl to Have Chance," *The Times-Picayune*, October 17, 1926; "Four Are Arrested in Dance Hall Row," *The Times-Picayune*, September 4, 1927; "Dance Hall Girls Injured as Auto Spins Over Twice," *The Times-Picayune*, October 31, 1927; "Masked Bandit Robs Dance Hall of $534 Pay Roll," *The Times-Picayune*, February 21, 1928; "Speeder Taking Liquor to Party Caught by Police," *The Times-Picayune*, February 25, 1928; "Five Arrested as Friends Try to Save Prisoner," *The Times-Picayune*, April 22, 1928.

[231] "Employes Jolted by Dance Hall's Sudden Closing," *The Times-Picayune*, July 17, 1928.

fellow dancers, Day had also faced a severe reprimand from representatives of a United States Navy battleship, who visited the offices of the newspaper to deliver their missive.

One can only presume that Day was rebuked over an article ("Dance Halls Flooded by Drink, Dope," published on February 4), which had described the feeble attempts of a drunken sailor in learning how to dance.[232] Although it seems innocuous by today's standards, the idea of a drunken sailor frequenting a dance hall during Prohibition was indecorous. It is not known if the reprimand directly affected Day's employment with the newspaper. However, she was soon sent on a similar assignment: the exposé of women participating in the underworld of illegal gambling.

---

[232] Day, "About Mary," 62-63.

The New Orleans Item
Sunday; February 3, 1924 (Pp. 1-2)[233]

Dance Hall Life of City Is Revealed

Girl Reporter Is Employed As Dancer

Pep Brings Cash

Loiterers and Riff Raff Fill Places Nightly

This is the first of a series of articles on the "free" dance halls of New Orleans by a girl reporter for The Item who worked in them.

In writing these stories, the reporter has given the uncolored facts and conditions as they exist.

BY DOROTHY DAY

---

[233] Although this article was published on February 3, 1924, the events of this evening actually occurred on January 2, 1924. In the last paragraph, Day stated, "it was the night after New Year's."

off

157

The Thrills of 1924: Dorothy Day Encounters the "Underworld Denizens" of New Orleans

The moaning of saxophones, the short staccato notes of banjos, the barbaric rhythm of the drums and above all the sentimentally slow notes of the piano, interspersed with whimsical and rather ridiculous runs and trills—these are the sounds you will hear every night from eight until twelve thirty, if you are lingering on the corner of Burgundy and Canal streets. On this corner are situated two of the three dance halls in the city where admission is free, and where once admitted, you are lured by the music and the smiles of girls, to pay the cashier the small sum of ten cents for a dance which lasts a little over a minute. Loiterers on street corners, sailors on leave, all the riff raff of the city streets, find these dance halls noisy and vivacious places to spend an evening, and every night hundreds climb the stairs and finding that they do not have to dance if they don't want to, hang over the railing which surrounds the dance floor, and watch the dancers.

Figure 17-Floor of the Arcadia Dance Hall, *The Times-Picayune,* **August 13, 1922.**

The Arcadia, which began business a year ago, and was the first of the three to open, is situated on Burgundy street, just a few doors off Canal.[234] Danceland, a rival place of business, is on Canal. Women are not allowed in these halls, because girls are supplied by the house. There are thirty girls at the Arcadia, who are paid five cents for every dance they make, and twenty-five at the Danceland, who receive four cents a dance. These places never advertise for girls, for those who dance there are steady workers, and when new girls are needed they bring their friends.

New Hall Opens

Recently a new hall was opened by the manager of the Arcadia, called Roseland, situated at 318 St. Charles St. There are ten girls working here, and because of the fact that the place is new and off the main street, business is not so good.

The writer visited these halls; and then worked in them. Seven-thirty one evening found us heavily made up with rouge and powder, climbing the steps of the Arcadia. The music had not begun, but nevertheless there was a crowd of young men hanging around the stairs, shouting familiarly to the girls as they came to work.

---

[234] The Arcadia Dance Hall, which was located at Canal and Burgundy Streets, began operating on the evening of August 12, 1922. See "Dance Hall Aims to Set New Pace," *The Times-Picayune,* August 13, 1922.

"Hey, Redhead, save a dance for me, will yuh kid?" "See the little fat one—she's some stepper but you wouldn't think it. I danced ten with her last night and everybody was watchin' us." "Aw, I like the goil with the King Tut hair.[235] But she's got a guy what's jealous as h-ll."

The girls shouted back as familiarly. Upstairs the hall was half lit and cold, not yet warmed by the crush of human bodies, for there is no other method of heating. A few musicians were taking their instruments from their cases, and tuning them, and a man behind the soft drink stand was swabbing off his counter with red, chapped hands. A good-looking policeman sauntered around chatting with the musicians and the girls. From the dressing room, where the girls were taking off their coats and hats and applying more layers of rouge and powder, came the sound of shrill giggling.

"How much did you make last night, kid? Cheesus and Murry, *I* only made sixty dances. If this keeps up I'll have to go back to the beanery. Say, did you hear that Marie made a hundred and twenty. Gosh, if I danced the way that b— dances, I'd make it, too."

Given Employment

Finally, after we had waited for half an hour, a tall gaunt man with eye glasses, the owner and piano player of the Arcadia came in, and fortified by the fact that we had as much paint and lip stick and powder on our faces as the other girls, we asked him for a job.[236] "Need any more girls?" we said.

"How did you happen to hear I needed girls?" he asked, looking us over.

"Oh, I had a friend called Jackie who used to work up here and she said she made about three dollars a night. That's better than working in the store."

"Well, I don't know—I do need some girls over at the Roseland—there's only ten there, but of course if you want to take a chance here, you can. We've thirty already, but they all make pretty good money. You can stick around here for a couple of nights, and if you don't make out, you can go over to the other place."

Having taken us on, he became more genial and communicative. "There's pretty good money in it for the girls that have lots of pep. Of course if you stand around talking to the fellows all evening you don't get the dances. The only thing to do is to stick close to business. That skinny one there makes about three dollars a night and thinks she's doing well. Whereas if she talked less and were a little more spry she'd make five and more.

---

[235] The King Tut bob was a popular trend for women's hairstyles in 1924. Considered highly controversial, the hairstyle led to the indefinite suspension of at least sixteen New Orleans-area nurses. See "Suspension of Bobbed Haired Nurses Argued," *The Town Talk (Alexandria, LA)*, March 25, 1924; "3 More Nurses with Bobbed Locks Suspended," *The Town Talk*, March 28, 1924.

[236] The owner of the Arcadia was Dominick J. Tortorich. See "Employes Jolted by Dance Hall's Sudden Closing," July 17, 1928. Day may have mistaken Tortorich for the manager of the Arcadia, Edward Berg. In the second article of the dance hall series (February 4), Day affirmed that it was the manager, not the owner, who had offered her the job.

The Thrills of 1924: Dorothy Day Encounters the "Underworld Denizens" of New Orleans

"Do you see that little Wop with the frizzy hair. She danced for forty-eight hours in a marathon down in Texas and she makes six dollars a night most of the time.[237] She's got an eye for business.

"I can crowd about forty or fifty dances into an hour. That makes you see you can pick up quite a bit. Of course no girl dances all of them—she's gotta rest once in a while, but New Year's eve we didn't stop till three o'clock and all the girls were about ready to drop. But they earned a lot of money all during Christmas week."

We expressed ourselves as hopeful of amassing a fortune.

"I'll tell you what, though," he added, "don't wear your good shoes up here. The new ones always do, and they find out their mistake. The thing to do is to wear sneakers, or gym slippers and don't give a damn how your feet look. Lots of them bring three or four pairs of shoes up here with them and change during the evening to ease their feet. Every couple of weeks, I have to throw out a pile of old shoes that they've danced the soles off of. I oughtta start in the second hand shoe business."

Warned About Thefts

When the "lady manager" of the place arrived, we were introduced to her, and shown into the dressing room. "Don't leave your bags around here," she warned us, "because everybody swipes everything they can lay their hands on. Leave your bags outside where the men check their hats."

The girls treat the manager with an easy informality, but when Mrs. S., his associate, enters their dressing room, they quit their chatter and kill their surreptitious cigarets. During the course of the evening, some of them are running in and out of the dressing room, changing their shoes, eating sandwiches, drinking bottles of soft drinks from the fountain outside, and leaning out of the window, which looks down on Burgundy street, to take a few puffs of a cigaret. Down below, a gang of rowdy youths yell up at them, commenting on the details of their toilet.

Owing to the fact that it was the night after New Year's and business was expected to be dull, Mrs. S. after showing us around, told us we needn't start work until the next night, and adjured us to be there promptly at seven-thirty.

---

[237] This particular taxi dancer may have made an additional impression on Day. Housed in the Dorothy Day-Catholic Worker archives at the Raynor Memorial Libraries of Marquette University, is a fragment of an unpublished novel, written circa 1928. Part of the story concerned a dance marathon where a brother and sister team from Chicago competed for the grand prize. Day had written that the couple "…were short and handsome, and so used to hard work that marathon dancing was nothing to them. They had started dancing in marathons three years before and as fast as one contest had ended they had entered another. In that way they had traveled all over the United States. Going from Chicago to New Orleans and from New Orleans to Miami…" See Dorothy Day, Dorothy Day Papers: Manuscripts, Ca. 1914-1977, Undated; Series D-3; Box 1, Folder 1.

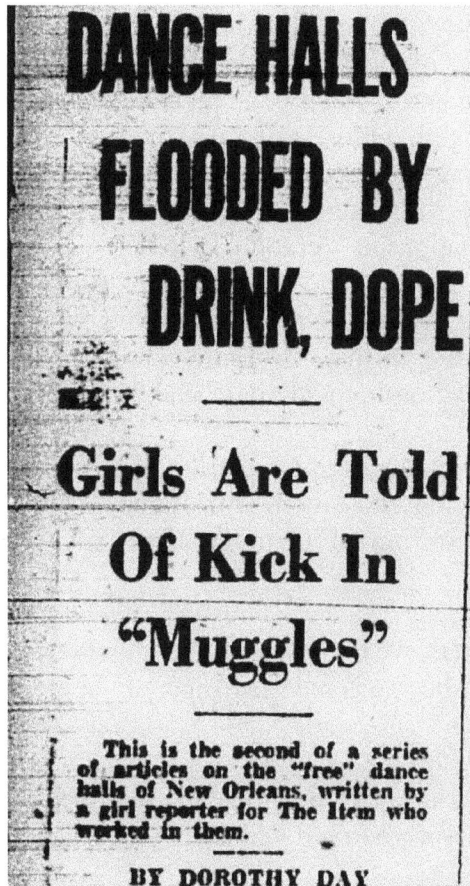

The New Orleans Item
Monday; February 4, 1924 (Pp. 1, 3)[238]
Evening Edition, (Pp. 1, 7)

DANCE HALLS FLOODED BY DRINK, DOPE[239]

———

Girls Are Told Of Kick In "Muggles"[240]

**This is the second of a series of articles on the "free" dance halls of New Orleans, written
by a girl reporter for The Item who worked in them.**

———

BY DOROTHY DAY

———————————

[238] The events of this evening occurred on January 3, 1924. Day mentioned an incident, involving herself, where she was forced to sample marijuana. She explained the incident in the article of February 5, leading one to believe that Day composed these articles either from notes or from memory, and well after her week of dancing was completed.

[239] This article was more than likely the one that caused Day to receive a stern rebuking from naval representatives of a nearby battleship. See Day, "About Mary," 62-63.

[240] The word "muggles" is slang for marijuana, or what Day called "Mary Warner." The term "muggles" actually originated in New Orleans in the 1920s. See "Thousands Addicted to Use of Marijuana," *The Town Talk (Alexandria, LA)*, September 7, 1926.

The Thrills of 1924: Dorothy Day Encounters the "Underworld Denizens" of New Orleans

Drink, dope and men of all ages and occupations—these are to be found night after night at the Arcadia dance hall, corner of Burgundy and Canal streets, one of the three "free" dance halls in which the writer worked for a week. There was drink in abundance, that second night when we came to take the job of dancing given us by the manager the night before—although nothing but soft drinks are sold on the premises. And drunken men, as long as they can toddle around the dance floor, are welcomed both by the management and the girls because the drunker they are, the more they suffer under the delusion that they are reincarnations of Vernon Castle.[241]

Dope came afterward, in the form of "Mary Warner" cigarets, which two young men who pressed their services on us as escorts home, offered us, assuring us that "they sure would give us a lift—much better than whiskey because you woke up in the morning without a head."

The girls who dance are glad to accept liquor from their acquaintances of the dance floor, needing a stimulant after two or three hours of continual dancing, most often with clumsy partners or drunken ones, who have to be held up to keep them from falling to the floor. Dancing for pleasure and dancing for a living are two different things.

As to whether the girls accept offers of "Mary Warner" cigarets, we don't know. We only know from our inquiries that all the girls had heard of them, all had been offered them, and all knew some girls who smoked them.

"But Cheesus, I'm scared to death of them—they make you crazy," seemed to be the sentiment of most of them. "And you get a habit from them. Give me some good old whisky any day. That has a real kick in it."

Drunken Nights Recalled

"Say kid, do you remember the night we were all so drunk that we couldn't dance, and gosh, wasn't Mrs. S. mad?"

"And do you remember the night that Sadie got so stewed she fell on the floor, and cut her face all up. Gee, I never laughed so much in my life."

Not that the girls openly accept bottles from the men and tilt them on the dance floor. After all, these are times of prohibition, and there is a policeman on the floor whose uniform causes even the most riotous to moderate his conduct.[242] But hip pockets bulge, and the men's room in the rear is next to the girls' dressing room, and bottles can be passed from the window of one into the other. The stuff is more palatable when poured into a bottle of limeade or such-like drink. Then, disguised by the innocent pop bottle, the girls can leave their drink on the shelf, and come in between dances every now and then and sip at it. "You need something to keep you going," they say.

---

[241] Born in Norwich, Norfolk, England, Vernon Castle was a well-known ballroom dancer, making his fame on Broadway with his wife Irene. Castle was killed in an airplane training accident in Fort Worth, TX on February 15, 1918. See "Vernon Castle Killed in Airplane Fall," *The Seattle Star*, February 15, 1918.

[242] Prohibition began in 1920 in the United States; it ended in 1933.

It is only the habitues who know that the policeman is after all a figurehead. Most of the customers are transients, salesmen, sailors and boys from the army and navy, high school boys out seeing life. But there is a goodly number of low-browed young men, dressed in the most dapper styles who hang about the dance hall every night as they would about a pool room. Some of these are the "steadies" of some of the girls, although one steady may have belonged to Marie last week, and Sadie the week before. Some of the girls have "husbands" who profess themselves to be very jealous of their wives. The fellows who look as though they made an occupation of "steadying" the girls, do little dancing, but lean over the railing, talk to the musicians, and escort their girls home. And woe unto the girl who dances, however innocently, with the steady of one of the others. Forthwith there will be a battle royal in the dressing room, and then the stream of filth and obscenity can be heard on the streets below. The girls of sixteen outdo the "girls" of thirty-five. The younger they look, the more hard-boiled they seem.

It was one of these steadies who gave us an inkling of the policeman's position in the dance hall. The steady had proved himself objectionable New Year's night, refusing to go home. The policeman shouted at him and he shouted back. They swore at each other, quite oblivious of their listeners.

"You're nothing but a louse," yelled the steady. "And what's more you're a d—d liar."

At this we expected to see him turned out, but the policeman retreated, vanquished by the superior shouting power of the other.

Jerry, New On the Job

Jerry, which seems to be the policeman's name, has been at the Arcadia only for the last six weeks. Before that he was required only on Saturday nights. "Oh, yes, I have lots to do," he replied to our inquiries. "They keep me pretty busy around here." And although he said nothing farther, he chuckled as though in reminiscence of some strenuous nights.

We were welcomed, that second night, with glances of hostility, by some of the girls, and with friendly overtures by the more assured and successful ones. However popular we might prove, the latter have a steady clientele, who come night after night and send their friends when they are out of town. For it goes without saying that only traveling men or soldiers and sailors spend their money in these places. The steady ones who hang over the railing know that you spend more in one of these dance halls than you can at a cabaret or a dance hall where they can bring a girl and where admission is charged. You can spend a dollar in exactly ten minutes, and if you are too drunk to realize that a hundred dances means a hundred times ten cents, you will wake up the next morning wondering where your money has all gone.

If the men complain of the shortness of the dances, the girls are instructed to say that they were late in starting to dance—they didn't get on the floor when the music started, and that's why the dance seemed so short.

If we had been dancing for our living we would have considered it our good fortune that second night, to have been picked on by an especially drunken sailor who was intent on learning to dance. With him was a tall, serious faced sailor lad, who explained to all who would listen, that he did not believe in dancing himself, but that he was going to see to it that his friend learned how. Time after time he went to the cashier's desk and bought a dollar's worth of tickets which he gave to his friend, one at a time. On the ticket is written the words, "Good for one lesson," and the girl tears off half which she keeps herself, and gives the other half to the keeper at the gate. The tickets which she collects, she keeps in the palm of her hand, held there by some elastic bands. Most of the men decline to pay for checking their hats, and the girl holds this for them while they dance. Sometimes, if she has been having nips from a bottle in the dressing room, she wears the hat herself.

Wild Scramble for Partners

When the dance is over, unless she thinks she can get another dance from her partner, each girl makes a mad dash towards the cashier's desk, and stands there, ready to be taken for the next. The bolder ones elbow their way to the front, shout at the lookers-on, taunt the men into dancing, grab hold of the more timid ones before they have a chance to express their choice of girls. If they don't get that dance, they stand at the gate swaying their shoulders and hips suggestively, looking with meaning eyes at the men around. Or if they have been standing around too long, they dance with each other exhibiting their various steps and movements, all the while with their eyes on the long line of men watching them.

The railing extends all the length of the dance floor, and from ten thirty to twelve, the crowd of onlookers increases until the men are standing, crowded three and four deep, peering over each other's shoulders, elbowing to get a point of vantage. On good nights there are probably three hundred or so men in the hall, and you would think that thirty girls would not find it hard to make a living. Only the girls themselves know what a scramble it is.

Hangers-On Scramble to Gain Dance Hall Girls, Then Offer Them Whisky, Dope Smokes

This is the third of a series of articles on the "free" dance halls of New Orleans, written by a girl reporter for The Item who worked in them.

BY DOROTHY DAY

The New Orleans Item
Tuesday; February 5, 1924 (Pp. 1, 4)[243]

Hangers-On Scramble to Gain Dance Hall Girls, Then Offer Them Whisky, Dope Smokes[244]

This is the third of a series of articles on the "free" dance halls of New Orleans, written by a girl reporter for The Item who worked in them.

BY DOROTHY DAY

Figure 18-Arcadia Dance Hall, Dauphine and Canal Street, circa 1921. Gift of Buzzy Williams, June 18, 1980. Tulane University Digital Library.

Whether it is the customary thing for the hangers-on around the dance halls in the business section to offer doped cigarets to the girls with whom they make dates, we will not say. We only know that the second evening we spent working at the Arcadia dance hall, on the corner of Burgundy and Canal street ended up by our finding ourselves stranded in the middle of City Park at one-thirty in the morning, not appreciating the whiskey, Marrawanna cigarets and other attentions which our escorts tried to force on us.

The long evening had finally come to an end. Owing to the fact that Danceland, another rival hall around the corner on Canal street, closes at twelve, the Arcadia keeps open until twelve-thirty or one every night to catch stray customers. The music becomes wilder and wilder, the drummer in a last spurt of enthusiasm becomes more and more entertaining to the onlookers, the piano player becomes more frenzied. The girls are tired out and keep shaking their heads at the manager.

---

[243] The events of this evening occurred on January 4, 1924.

[244] The Evening Edition of *The New Orleans Item* carried the alternate headline: "Hangers-On Scramble for Dance Girls; Escorts Offer Whisky and Dope."

"Make this the last one," they plead, their feet throbbing, their backs aching, their necks stiff from holding their heads up.

"Last Dance"

At last there is a shout, "Last dance," everybody rushes for the floor, the girls' faces light up, and there is a last abandoned fling. This last dance is perhaps the only joyous one of the evening. Everyone becomes gay and care free. Business is over until seven-thirty the next evening, and the girls are looking forward either to bed, or to regular hilarity and dancing, for which they are not paid, but for which someone else will pay.

The men crowd around the railing and entrance to the dance floor, trying to get a word with the girls. "Are you going home alone?" is the question, and if one already has an escort, it makes no difference, the question is again asked of the next one. "Can't I see you home?"

From the chatter of the girls in the dressing room, we have learned that if you haven't a steady, the place to find one is on the dance floor. If your regular "fellah" is not calling for you or waiting for you at the door downstairs it is customary to accept the offer of escort from anyone who asks you, provided he is young and passable looking. Then, too, there is always a chance to get a bite to eat, or to go cabareting. And if the fellah who asks to take you home says he has a car waiting downstairs, why all the better.

Would Be Very Nice

As we waited for our friend who had been grabbed for the last dance and left us standing by the railing, a young man leaned over and said, "Are you going home alone?"

"No," we replied. "We've got a girl friend here with us."

"Oh, that's fine then, because I've got a friend with me in the car downstairs." The tone implied that we had already accepted the offer. "What do you say we wait for you at the door and take you home?"

"That would be very nice of you," we reply, and proceed to the dressing room for our wraps.

"The dance halls in themselves might be all right," we had heard. "But it's what they lead to. Cabareting and drinking and all that sort of thing." So it was up to us to size up those who offered their escort. The two young men looked quiet and well mannered enough, we ruminated, and put on our things with no misgivings.

Down on Canal street a big car was parked. We gave our address and piled in, stiff and tired but nevertheless alert. Throwing in the clutch and shifting the gears, the driver started down Canal street, but in the wrong direction. A few block[s] passed, and we off-handedly reminded him that we lived in the other direction.

Need a Little Air

"Aw, that's all right, you girls need a little air after dancing for so long," they assured us. There was no mention made of having a bite to eat though it was now six hours since dinner time. We wondered what the girls did about it—whether they hinted delicately, "Say, what about something to eat out at the Moulin Rouge?"[245] Or perhaps a little more frankly, "Hey, you cheap skates, we get plenty of rides. What about grub?" Not knowing the technique, however, we chattered brightly as is the manner of flappers.

At least the boys were going in the direction of the cabarets, we thought and did not take it amiss when the car entered City Park. The next move on the program, however, was to park in a shady lane of trees. Whereupon, the driver reached into a pocket and brought out a pint bottle of whiskey, and a little glass.

Thinking of all the stories we had heard or read of doped liquor, we pretended to take a drink. This was the signal for a greater show of geniality on the part of our escorts. Then, "You don't act as though you liked the stuff, so what do you say we have a cigaret? Did you ever smoke a Mary Warner?"

Have great Kick

That was the name of the cigarets as we understood them, never having heard of Mary Warner. When the cigarets were lit, a heavy, pungent odor, quite different from the smell of tobacco, filled the car. Since we had made no objection to smoking them, our escorts began to expatiate upon the virtues of the new weed.

"These cigarets have a great kick if you just draw it way down in your lungs…Hey, that ain't the way to smoke them—draw the smoke in. You're wasting it, kid. We were out on a party one night and the liquor was running low, and everybody smoked these. We had a great time. Say, that was some party, wasn't it?"

By this time we realized that we had pulled what the girls at the Arcadia would call blanks in the way of escorts, since no food or cabaret parties seemed to be forthcoming. As we pretended to sip the whiskey, we puffed at the cigarets, careful not to inhale, and trying to let the cigaret burn itself out as fast as it could. When ours was down to a stub, we put it out against the side of the car, and in an effort to save the "snipe" for evidence, if necessary, secreted it in the top of our stocking, which after the manner of young women was rolled.

---

[245] The Moulin Rouge at West End was a club located on Bourbon Street, near Bienville Street. In March of 1924, it was reported that the Moulin Rouge (along with the Little Club and the Tortorich Cafe) was one of three venues in New Orleans to be closed for a year, due to the illegal sale of alcohol. See "Judge Foster Signs Order Padlocking Cafes, Cabarets," *The Town Talk (Alexandria, LA)*, March 12, 1924.

The Thrills of 1924: Dorothy Day Encounters the "Underworld Denizens" of New Orleans

Too Many Cigarets

When it was noticed that we had ditched the Mary Warner, our escort showed what would seem to be undue anxiety about it. "Gosh, what did you do with it? Say, give me a match so I can see if I can find it? Threw it out the side of the car, did yuh? What did you do that for?"

It took several moments to divert his attention from the cigaret. He seemed for the moment to be irrationally anxious about it. Then, forgetting the cigaret he dropped his head over the wheel and began to murmur to himself. As far as we could make out, he was trying to recite the face on the bar room floor.[246] To all appearances, he was drunk, and since he had had not more than a sip of the whiskey, and there had not been the smell of liquor on his breath when we accepted the invitation to ride home, we came to the conclusion that he had been smoking too many of the cigarets which he recommended so strongly. Indeed, his further actions and remarks made this a certainty.

Auto Followed

Resisting importunate advances as long as we could—we took it for granted that all girls had to resist them enough to show that they were in earnest—we soon saw that it was no use. Our escorts were full of dope, and stubborn. Releasing ourselves from restraining arms, we slipped out of the car, and started to walk. Having an Indian's sense of direction, we fortunately aimed in the right direction, and with the automobile following us through the park, we gained the streets, and started in the right direction home.[247] For half a dozen blocks our would-be escorts followed us slowly along the curb, pleading with us to get back in and ride. But we had seen enough to know that they were indeed half crazy with the cigarets they had been smoking, and preferred walking if we couldn't get a street car or a cab.

Luckily it was a fine night, just before the cold spell, so we struck out briskly and made the thirty blocks home in some forty-five minutes. How many times was it we had heard the slang term, "Get out and walk!" Well, we had done it at last. If we had not been on an assignment, we would have been both mad and ashamed. As it was, it was all in the night's work.

(Continued Tomorrow)

---

[246] "The Face Upon the Barroom Floor," was a poem composed by John Henry Titus in 1872. The poem is also known as "The Face on the Floor," and "The Face on the Barroom Floor." Hugh Antoine d'Arcy later adapted Titus' poem in 1887 for publication in the *New York Dispatch*.

[247] An "Indian's sense of direction" is the uncanny ability of the Native American, whose "knowledge of direction is as true as the attraction of the magnetic needle to the pole." See John Madden, *The Wilderness and Its Tenants*, Volume 2 (London, England: Simpkin, Marshall, Hamilton, Kent and Co., 1897), 100-101.

Danceland Girls Make Only 4 Cents But Manager Explains That It "Isn't a Rough Joint"

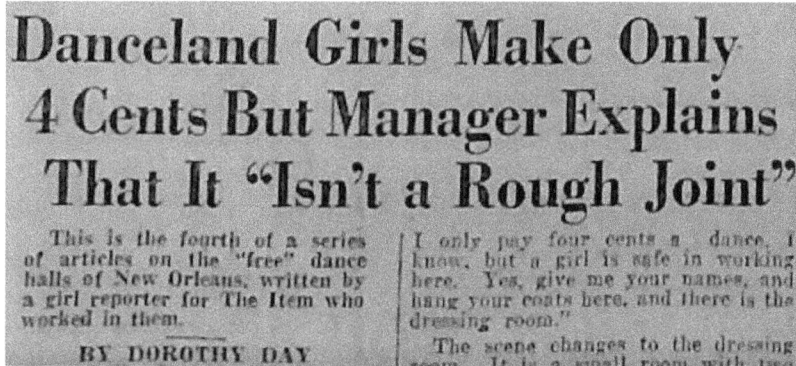

The New Orleans Item
Wednesday; February 6, 1924 (Pp. 1, 4)[248]

Danceland Girls Make Only 4 Cents But Manager Explains That It "Isn't a Rough Joint"

This is the fourth of a series of articles on the "free" dance halls of New Orleans, written by a girl reporter for The Item who worked in them.

BY DOROTHY DAY

Scene: The Danceland, corner of Canal and Burgundy, and just around the corner from the Arcadia.

Time: The third night of our employment in the free dance halls of New Orleans.

Dramatis Personae: Mr. Berg, manager of the Danceland, five members of a rather poor jazz band, twenty-five girls from the ages of sixteen to forty, three hundred or so men of all description, and us, reporters from The Item.[249]

Mr. Berg: "So you girls have been dancing over at the Arcadia. Well you can come on up here and dance if you want to. As for me, I wouldn't advise any girl to dance in a place like the Arcadia or the Roseland. They're rough joints. Lots of our girls are living at home with their families. Why, you wouldn't believe it, but sometimes their mothers come up here and watch 'em dance. Here, I only pay four cents a dance, I know, but a girl is safe in working here. Yes, give me your names, and hang your coats here, and there is the dressing room."

The scene changes to the dressing room. It is a small room with two small mirrors, two tables loaded with cosmetics. On one side of the room is a pile of shoes, worn out and stubbed as to toe and heel. Before the mirrors are three or four "nice" girls, painting and powdering and smoking cigarettes.

One, with a slick, straight hair cut and buck teeth. "How do you like my hair cut, kid?"

---

[248] The events of this evening occurred on January 5, 1924.
[249] Edward Berg was also the manager of the Danceland dance hall, which was located at 1005 Canal Street, in New Orleans. See "New Orleans Dance Hall Loses Case in Courts," *The Shreveport Times*, June 10, 1924.

169

The Thrills of 1924: Dorothy Day Encounters the "Underworld Denizens" of New Orleans

Another, little and plump and full of laughter and also obscenity: "Say you _____, if you got out on the floor and _____ you'd make some money instead of standing in here and talking like a _____. You poor _____, what the _____ do you think you're doing up here any way, _____." Etc.

Another with a business-like face and a straight line for lips. She is dressed in a simple, little-girl dress of old rose. She is flat chested and round shouldered and from the rear looks like fifteen, from the front like forty. When she smiles, her face is contorted but not with mirth. Says she, "Look at the dollar tip I just got. Gee, that was a swell guy. He's going to take me out afterward."

Another, glaring after the last one as she left the dressing room to continue earning an honest living: "Would you look at that _____. Sure she gets a dollar tip. If you _____ they'll give you a quarter, and if you _____," etc., increasing the amount by twenty-five cents with every vile remark.

Outside the dance hall is dimly lit and seems full of smoke as another girl opens the door of the well-lit dressing room and bursts in giggling shrilly. "Say, Gawd help me, every time they play "A Kiss in the Dark" that sailor gets me off in the corner and kisses the life outa me.[250] He's a cave man and gosh I'm stuck on 'im."

There is more talk of steadies, and fellahs and methods of love making, and emphasis is added by a plentiful use of profanity and obscenity, all in a friendly spirit. We wondered what they had left to say to each other when they started to get mad, as we had seen two girls do over in the Arcadia.

Business was not so good in the dance hall that night. The hall was crowded, jammed in fact, as usual, but the men were "pikers" and stood around and watched and talked to the girls instead of dancing.[251] Always there were ten or twelve girls standing around a pole in the middle of the floor, waiting for partners. The only bench in the room was next to the band, but when you got tired of standing, it was better to have the blare in your ears and be able to rest than to stand in the midst of the smoke and chatter.

The piano player is a chinless youth of tender years whose air of sophistication sits on him heavily. His thin hair is parted in the middle and fits straight and tight to his head like a mannikin's. He thumps heavily with both hands and feet, and occasionally stands up, with an air of boredom and plays while standing. The saxophone player almost reclines in his chair with his feet on the chair of the player next to him. He is a tall dark man, and when he takes his lips from his instrument, you notice that he has no teeth and that his mouth falls in like an old woman's. The other saxophone player is pop-eyed and looks as though with every spurt of melody, he were going to burst. His face is long and mournful and a feeling of the grotesque creeps over you as you watch him. The drummer has a million little tricks by which he charms the girls, who watch him when they are not dancing, and giggle at him and try to catch his eye. But he is very

[250] "A Kiss in the Dark" was composed by B. G. De Sylva and Victor Herbert.
[251] A piker, in this sense, is a person who does not want to spend any money.

insouciant and disregards them as he does the crowd of male admirers who hang over the railing of the coop which confines the band. With an air of great indifference, even of melancholy, he throws his drumsticks in the air, catches them lightly, sways h[i]ther and yo[n], lets his head fall forward and then catches it with a jerk. His shoulders are so broad and his face so impassive, that the diminutive figure of the banjo player by his side, has the appearance of a vivacious little gnome.

And every now and then some would-be dancer, stunted and cheaply dapper strides up with a ticket in his hand, which you grab before someone else gets it, get a strangle hold around his neck and with an assumption of pep and abandon which you do not feel, you dance. A hundred dances a night, if your heart is in your work and you want to make a living; 700 dances a week, 2,800 dances a month, 43,600 dances a year![252] Watta life, to quote the poor dancing girls.

(Continued Tomorrow)

---

[252] Day's math is slightly off, although this may have been a transposition error. Her handwriting is oftentimes difficult to read. 700 dances per week times fifty-two weeks would be 36,400 dances, an incredible amount in either scenario.

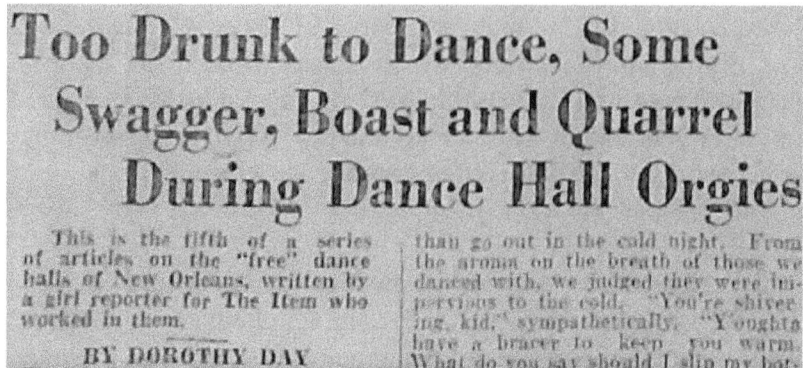

The New Orleans Item
Thursday; February 7, 1924 (Pp. 1, 4)[253]

Too Drunk to Dance, Some Swagger, Boast and Quarrel During Dance Hall Orgies

This is the fifth of a series of articles on the "free" dance halls of New Orleans, written by a girl reporter for The Item who worked in them.

────────

BY DOROTHY DAY

Everybody was drunk again. Or if they weren't drunk, they looked as though they were. The scene this third night of the writer's employment in the free dance halls of New Orleans, was the Roseland, a hall on the second floor of 318 St. Charles Ave. under the same management as the Arcadia.[254] It was a cold night, but nevertheless the hall was crowded with men who hung over the railing which extended the length of the dance floor. On the whole the men were better dressed and better looking than those who frequented the Arcadia and Danceland.

It was one of those bitter cold nights when there were no loiterers below the open windows to listen to the strains of jazz from the hall above. The hall was unheated and draughty but nevertheless those who were there preferred to stay rather than go out in the cold night.[255] From the aroma on the breath of those we danced with, we judged they were impervious to the cold. "You're shivering, kid," sympathetically. "Y'oughta have a bracer to keep you warm. What do you say should I slip my bottle under your cupe so you can take it out to the dressing room and have a little nip." Offers of this sort were many.

────────────

[253] The events of this evening occurred on January 6, 1924.

[254] Although Day stated that this was her third night of employment in the dance halls, it was actually her fourth.

[255] On Sunday, January 6, 1924 the temperature in New Orleans plummeted to nineteen degrees above zero (from a moderate forty to forty-six degrees two days before), resulting in numerous fires (e.g. due to burning rubbish to keep warm, an overheated furnace, a defective flue, and an overheated stove pipe), and damage to an estimated 3,000 pipes. See "The Weather," *The New Orleans Item*, January 4, 1924; "Cold Attended By Many Fires," *The New Orleans Item*, January 6, 1924; "N. O. Freezes," *The New Orleans Item*, January 7, 1924.

172

Enters With Lugger[256]

About ten o'clock a tall blond young man whose friends called him Mert, entered the hall with swagger and assurance and started to dance. "Feel this," he boasted, slapping his pockets one by one. "Pound se'sugar—And this. Bottle of milk. And this. Bottle of booze. And in this pocket I have a glass and a spoon. I'm my own bartender and I carry my toddies around with me. Only thing to do on a night like this."

With Mert was a little short fellow who seemed to have some difficulty navigating around the floor. When he lurched against the railing and dropped a ticket over it, he couldn't reach it, nor did it enter his mind to walk around the railing to get it. Being a direct actionist, he knocked the railing down, retrieved his ticket and went on with the dance, much to the amusement of the multitude, but not of the tall, gaunt, red-headed woman who stood like a sentinel at one end of the hall. She strode over to him fiercely, seized him by the shoulder and started to shake him.

The young man looked at her blankly, but Mert rushed to the rescue. "Tha's mah friend," he bellowed. "Do you know who I am? I'm the guy that supplies booze to the guy that owns this place. And do you know who mah friend is? He's the son of the man who owns the B_____ H_____ cafe. You jus' try getting fresh with mah frien' and I'll give yuh a sock in the toot,' you red headed _____."

Appeals to Policeman

Although Mert's friend wasn't known, Mert was, but nevertheless the red headed woman's dignity had to be assuaged by an appeal to the policeman. Other policemen, summoned from goodness knows where, entered the discussion, but Mert was triumphant, retiring from the scene of battle to the dance hall with greater assurance than before. His little friend swung with painstaking precision into a waltz.

Much cheered and refreshed by the disturbance, the girls danced with renewed vigor.

Mert and his friend were not the only uplifted guests of the dance hall. A crowd of young boys, none of whom looked to be over seventeen came in staggeringly and danced. When they weren't dancing with the girls on the floor, they danced with obscene posturing with one another, disregarded by the policeman, the manager or two women who acted as cashier and assistant managers. When the girls danced with them, they had to hold them to keep them from falling and ward off the objectionable advances towards intimacy which they fumblingly tried to make. Finally, late in the evening, assisting one another they staggered out giggling maudlinly.

"To Drink to Dance"

To dance or not to dance?[257] Dancing meant keeping warm, but it also meant submitting to the embrace of a staggering youth who took it for granted that his ten cent ticket entitled him to far greater intimacy than the dance demanded. To avoid this we stood behind the cashier's desk,

---

[256] A "lugger" is a conman or, in the instance of the following paragraphs, a person of dubious character.
[257] A play on William Shakespeare's *Hamlet* ("To be, or not to be…," Act III, Scene I).

behind a pole shiveringly most of the evening, content to be an observer rather than a participant of the so-called festivities. But finally we were confronted by a genial young drunkard who fumblingly poked a ticket at us, and clutching us around the waist, tried to dance.

He believed himself to be possessed of rare gifts in the way of dancing and painstakingly held us off at arm's length while he gazed at his feet and executed strange and complicated steps. Realizing finally that we were not gifted as he was, he contented himself with strolling rhythmically around the floor simpering inanely.

"Whereupon," he kept saying with a grin, "four hundred concupines uttered a very vulgar expression."

"Surely you mean porcupines," we told him. But no, he assured us gravely. "Four hundred, or was it five hundred concupines uttered a very vulgar expression. Whereupon—"

But the dance was over and our partner, forgetting that we hadn't heard the rest of the story, lurched against the railing and watched the other dancers with half-shut eyes.

"Drunk again," he kept murmuring sadly, as he watched the others. "All of 'em drunk. Too drunk to dance."

And most of them were.

(Continued Tomorrow)

Woman With Knife Chases Dance Hall Girl Through Streets After Cafe Clash

The New Orleans Item
Friday; February 8, 1924 (Pp. 1, 5)[258]

Woman With Knife Chases Dance Hall Girl Through Streets After Cafe Clash

This is the sixth of a series of articles on the free dance halls of New Orleans by a girl reporter for The Item who worked in them.

___

BY DOROTHY DAY

"You can't think what happened to me last night!"

This is the preface to many an amazing tale told in the dressing rooms of the Arcadia, Danceland or the Roseland free dance halls in which the writer was working for a week. Every night before the dancing begins, the girls who are employed in these halls sit around in the dressing rooms and chatter, and this chatter is most illuminating to the listener.

The speaker this time was a young woman whom the girls called Jimmie—a black-haired, black-eyed young woman who is so popular with the men who hang around the dance halls that she is correspondingly unpopular with the girls who are employed there to dance.

Has 2-Year-Old Baby

This youngster, who confesses to a brief married life of six months during her fifteenth year, and who has a two-year-old baby, and who is now nineteen years old, was formerly dancing at the Danceland, a rival hall to the other two. Upon meeting the manager of the Arcadia a Mr. Baring, she said that she was guaranteed five dollars a night by him, if she would change her place of employment. The generous manager stands to lose little by this however, for during all the nights the writer was dancing at the Arcadia and the Roseland, Jimmie had every dance, averaging more than the hundred a night which would bring her income up to five dollars.

"You see I got a steady bunch of customers," she explained her success. "These fellahs come in every night and dance about ten dances each with me and they wouldn't ever think of dancing

___

[258] The events of this evening occurred on January 7, 1924.

with any other girl. When there are only ten of them this brings my dances up to [a] hundred, but usually there are more.

Scads of Dates

"Did you see that little one what was dancing with me? My Gawd, the way he dances. When he got through doing his stuff, every guy on the floor was rushing to dance with me."

And dates! Every night Jimmie has scads of them. She accepts them all, and not keeping an engagement book, gets all mixed up, and every night there are near battles as to who will have the privilege of taking her out. It's on these dates that things happen.

"What didn't happen to me last night!" she chortled. "I went out with that big handsome fellah—his name is Oil"—she probably meant Earl—"and went cabareting. I can't think of all the places we went to, because I'm getting a habit of drawing a blank when I'm drinking. And I never could stand that apricot brandy, and Oil always has a bottle of that in his pocket. Now Sallie here gets a crying jag on. Three drinks and she just opens her mouth and howls. She was on a wailing jag last night, and down on the corner of Iberville and Royal, she just doubled her legs up underneath her and refused to move another inch, and we couldn't get a cab to save our lives. So we hailed a big truck, and piled her into it, and then we rode down to Canal street where we found a taxi.

Chased By Woman With Knife

"But anyway, what I started to tell you was this: I must have had a lucid moment or so, or I couldn't remember it. Anyway, we were all going into some dump on Royal street, where they have the rottenest orchestra I ever heard. We only go there when it's getting late and the liquor is running low, because they sell drinks there. It's a regular dive where sailors and loose women hang around and I always forget myself and josh the sailors and make the guy I'm with sore. Gee, last night, I was so far gone that every time one of them would look at me I'd yell.

"And then when I was dancing I bumped into one of the dames and I said, 'Get outa my way, you rough neck,' and she said, 'Who's a rough neck, you little _____,' and came after me. And Gawd, she had a knife strung around her neck on a string, and she started chasing me. Did I run? I'll say I run. I forgot my hat and coat and guy and Sallie here and just beat it out the door and down the street with her after me. And after her came a couple of guys and I didn't know whether they were trying to protect me or whether they were her friends. So I just kept on running. Sallie and the two guys we was with didn't catch up to me until the next morning when they found me at home after looking for me in every cabaret in New Orleans. Some night, I'll say, I'm offa apricot brandy for good!"[259]

(Continued Tomorrow)

---

[259] Day would later recall the potency of apricot brandy in her 1926 syndicated serial, "What Price Love." In the story, a minor character named Sadie relates the cause of her hangover: "Apricot brandy last night. I don't know where the guy got it, but it certainly was all there with the little old kick." See Dorothy Day, "What Price Love," *Chicago Herald Examiner*, June 16, 1926.

Girl Supplements Wages As Store Clerk by Work At Dance Hall at Night

This is the seventh of a series of articles on the free dance halls of New Orleans by a girl reporter for The Item who worked in them.

BY DOROTHY DAY

the dance hall, and the question assumes a more sinister aspect.

One of the women at the Roseland is a tall, handsome looking blonde. She was pointed out to us at the dance hall as being rather notorious

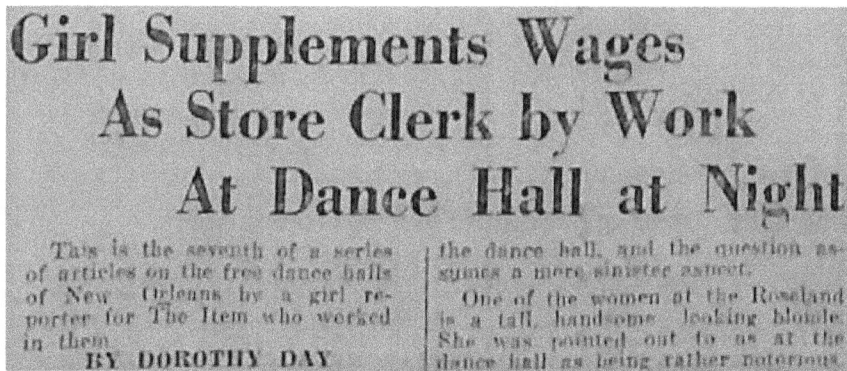

The New Orleans Item
Saturday; February 9, 1924 (P. 2)[260]
Evening Edition: Home Special Section (Pp. 1-2)

Girl Supplements Wages As Store Clerk by Work At Dance Hall at Night

This is the seventh of a series of articles on the free dance halls of New Orleans by a girl reporter for The Item who worked in them.

BY DOROTHY DAY

"Say kid, where do you live? What's your telephone number? Can I take you home tonight?" These are the questions asked dozens of times every hour of the girls who are employed to dance at the Arcadia, Roseland and Danceland, the three public dance halls of New Orleans in which the writer worked for a week.

Asked by the hundreds of men of all style and description, from the traveling salesmen just in New Orleans for a week and out for a good time, to the lowest riff raff of the streets, the girls pay little attention to such questions. Usually of course, they give the men their telephone number, make dates with them and recruit from their ranks their "steadies" without one of which they never seem to be.

But asked by a woman of a girl at the dance hall, and the question assumes a more sinister aspect.

One of the women at the Roseland is a tall, handsome looking blonde. She was pointed out to us at the dance hall as being rather notorious. In a way she is a beauty with her large blue eyes with drooping lids and thick lashes which curl up heavily. But her mouth is hard, and her voice has a peculiar hoarse quality.

Wants "Roommates"

"Where are you living, kid?" we heard her ask an attractive, eighteen-year-old girl who had been dancing at the Roseland for only a week. "Do you know, I'm looking for a room mate, or rather

---

[260] The events of this evening occurred on January 8, 1924.

not a room mate, but two of them. I got a friend with me already, but I know of a nice little flat that we could all get together."

This question, to our knowledge was repeated every night to the eighteen-year-old girl, who confided that she had left home some months before and whose mother did not know where she was living. She said that she already had a room mate, a girl who was a year younger than herself.

"But she may not be with me long," she said. "You see she's from the country, and every day she gets a letter from her mother asking her to come home, and she gets homesick. She's dancing over at Danceland now, though, and she's having so much fun, that she says she doesn't guess she'll go home. But if she does, why I'll let you know."

What is the basis of these overtures from a woman well over thirty, to this girl of eighteen, is the question which arises. It is not often that a woman of her age desires close companionship with a girl twelve years her junior. The contrast between the two reacts against the older. But she continues her questioning, "Why don't you come and live with me, girlie?"

"Crush" on Musician

As for the little country girl who was home sick before, but who isn't going home now because she is having so much fun at Danceland—"I'm not earning so much money," she confessed, "because I'm such a nut. I gotta an awful crush on the fellah that plays the saxophone, and he quits playing as often as he can and dances with me."

And Jenny doesn't get so many dances either, because she is still a little country girl and doesn't like to push her way to the front and swagger and sway at the fellahs like the other girls do. So she makes only about a dollar a night, which isn't enough to live on, of course, and continues her work at a store where she clerks in the day time.

Though she doesn't have so many dances as the others, she has quite as many offers of escort, and the reason she likes the dance hall is because there are parties every night.

Out of bed at seven in the morning in order to be at the store on time, on her feet all day, at the dance hall at seven thirty in the evening and on her feet again until twelve, then continuing the dizzy whirl until two or three in the morning, and up again at seven. She is no longer homesick. She hasn't the time to be.

(Continued Tomorrow)

The New Orleans Item
Sunday; February 10, 1924 (P. 1)[261]

Dance Hall Girl Wakes Up In Strange Room After Night Of Carousing in Cabarets

This is the last of a series of articles on the Free Dance Halls of New Orleans written by a girl reporter for The Item who worked in them.

_____

By DOROTHY DAY

Here is a story heard at the Roseland, one of the three public dance halls at which the writer was employed for a week. In telling the story, it is better not to give a description of the young girl who told it. For although she told the story herself, laughing the while, she was telling it to her associates, girls who were paid to dance every evening, and perhaps it will look different to her in print.

"Gee, I had some time last night!" This is the way most of these stories begin. "I had a date with His Nibs and I had a date with that little shrimp in the derby hat, who has such an adorable car, and I had a date with this guy I been going regular with who said that he would call for me at twelve o'clock.[262]

"And then when twelve o'clock came, I ditched them all. You didn't happen to see that tall blonde-haired man who came in around eleven o'clock last night, did you? Gosh, he certainly was a darling, and he danced every single dance with me after that. He kept asking me if I liked him a little bit, and I said no I hated him, you know, and he kept asking me to go out with him.

Waited at the Door

"When twelve o'clock came I just ditched all the others and there, sure enough, he was waiting for me outside the door, and we went to get something to eat. He wasn't no piker,[263] he wasn't, and we had a swell feed, lobsters and everything. He had a quart of likker with him and before I

_____

[261] The events of this evening occurred on January 9, 1924.

[262] The expression "His Nibs" is meant to denote a demanding, or tyrannical person.

[263] Day would use a similar expression, to describe two male characters, in her 1926 syndicated serial, "What Price Love." See Dorothy Day, "What Price Love," *Chicago Herald Examiner*, June 15, 1926.

knew it I was getting woozy. I shouldn't have been drinking any of it, because the guys had kept slipping me drinks all evening and by the time twelve o'clock came I didn't know whether I was going or coming.

"But I kept pouring it down me just the same, and this guy kept telling me, 'Gee, a little girl like you shouldn't drink so much. You're pouring it down like water.' But I kept right on drinking it.

"Then we went out to the Moulin Rouge, and there were only a few girls out there, but there were lots of fellahs and they were all stewed and every time my guy and I would dance, they'd keep jumping up and trying to cut in. There was one of them there who said that he was going to smash up the place unless I danced with him, so I went over to his table, only he was so drunk and he couldn't dance, so I sat down with him and kept telling him to calm down.

"Cusses Out Everybody"

"And of course the guy I was with kept coming after me and saying I was a cheap sort for jumping tables and all that sort of thing, and he'd drag me back to our table again, me swearing like mad. Every time I get drunk now, I swear all over the place, cussing out everybody.

"I couldn't see where we were going half the time, but I know we went to lots of places after that and then I don't know anything more at all until I woke up this morning.

"And gosh, what do you think. I wasn't home at all—I didn't know where I was. I was in a perfectly strange room, a great big room furnished with swell bird's eye maple furniture. I had all my clothes on except my dress and shoes and you can bet I got them on quick.

"When I got out in the hall, I ran into a woman who looked as though she worked around the place, and when I talked to her, she turned out to be the proprietor. I asked her where I was, and she said the _____ Hotel on Baronne street and when I asked her she laughed at me. [264]

Treated Her Swell

"She said, 'lots of girls come in here and then wake up the next morning and don't remember how they got here. It's the bum liquor that does it.' And she said that she had undressed me the night before and that I had been sick. Gee, she was nice.

"Believe me, I rushed home pretty quick and it's a good thing for me I'm not living at home, for I wouldn't know what to tell my mother. Anyway, I thought I'd seen the last of that fellah, but it turns out that I gave him my telephone number and he called me up this afternoon and wants to buy me a new dress because I spilt liquor all over the one I had on. He certainly did treat me swell, like a real gentleman, and I'm going out with him again tonight."

---

[264] This is not the Roosevelt Hotel, which Day had mentioned by name several times in her New Orleans articles.

Dempsey Scores Another Knockout When He Calls Dorothy Day "Little Girl"

By DOROBY DAY his head, and his nose might have

The New Orleans Item
Monday; February 11, 1924 (P. 10)

Dempsey Scores Another Knockout When He Calls Dorothy Day "Little Girl"[265]

By DOROTHY DAY

The main trouble with meeting celebrities at the station to get an interview is finding and recognizing them in the crowd of travelers. But there was no trouble in finding Jack Dempsey as he got off the train at the Union Station Sunday noon. The trouble was in getting at him. You could see him from one end of the platform to the other, plowing his way along through admiring throngs who collected from all sides at the sight of him and tagged along at his heels, beaming with enthusiasm. He overtopped them all.

There was any number of questions we'd planned on asking him, for instance: "Do you get many mash notes from women?" "Are you engaged to be married?"[266] "Do women ever propose to you?" "Do you think women ought to go to prize fights?"[267] "Whom do you like best, Ring Lardner or George Bernard Shaw, and isn't Charlie Chaplin a greater man than Nicolai Lenin?"[268]

About 6 1-2 Feet

And then we elbowed our way through the crowd and fell brazenly into step beside him, he knocked all the questions out of our head by calling us "little girly" (in spite of 5 feet 10 1-2

---

[265] Day had experience in interviewing boxers. In 1916, she interviewed Benny Leonard and Al McCoy for the *New York Call*. See Dorothy Day, "Can't Preach Sermon About Benny Leonard," *New York Call*, December 3, 1916.

[266] Dempsey had been married, in October of 1916, to a Maxine Cates. The couple separated in May of 1917, and were subsequently divorced a year later. See Roger Kahn, *A Flame of Pure Fire: Jack Dempsey and the Roaring '20s* (New York, NY: Harcourt Brace and Company, 1999), 19, 109.

[267] Although Dempsey did not answer the question, he later stated, in his 1940 autobiography, that there were thousands of women in attendance for his 1921 bout with Georges Carpentier. See Jack Dempsey and Myron Stearns, *Round by Round: An Autobiography* (New York, NY: Whittlesey House, 1940), 208.

[268] Leading up to the Dempsey-Carpentier fight, Ring Lardner had written a series of satirical articles for the Bell Syndicate of newspapers. See Ring W. Lardner, "Ring Lardner Compares Records of 2 Principles," *Pittsburgh Post-Gazette*, June 20, 1921; Ring W. Lardner, "Lardner Laughs What He Saw in a Ringside Seat," *El Paso Herald*, July 4, 1921.

inches) and helping us through the station by clutching our shoulder, the elbow being too far below him.[269]

For the benefit of those girls who do not read the sporting page or the Police Gazette and therefore have not kept up with the thousands of pictures of Dempsey therein, but have only caught occasional glimpses of him in the movies, a description follows.[270] There are no accurate figures to hand such as they publish before a big fight, as to the girth of his neck, waist and calf, height, reach and the size glove he wears. We can only say impressionistically that he is somewhere's about 6 1-2 feet high, has brown hair and brown eyes, white teeth and a mouth that isn't big enough for the size of his grin.

A "Gentleman Boxer"

He has an exquisitely tanned complexion which the French blue silk shirt he wore only emphasized. He wore a black suit, with a tiny stripe running this way and that way in it. His hands are huge, well shaped and well cared for, with never a bulge or twist at the joint to show that he used them for anything beside shaking the hands of admirers.

Surveying his face critically there is no sign that he has ever been battered in the ring. One ear stands out a little perhaps, accentuated by the fact that the other is so close to his head, and his nose might have been broken.[271]

We were about to ask him what was the secret of his beauty, but remembering whom we were speaking to, modified the question.

"Nobody gets hurt nowadays in a fight," he pooh-poohed.[272] "Once in a while a black eye or a bloody nose, but that does you good. Kids get those every day in the week. But fighting isn't what it used to be. And that reminds me, you wouldn't call me a prize fighter. I'm a gentleman boxer." And he laughed and everybody else laughed, but nevertheless we'll still think of him as a prize fighter.

---

[269] Dempsey's calling Day "little girly" is ironic, given that the heavyweight champion was born on June 24, 1896, barely a year-and-a-half earlier than his female interviewer. See Joe R. Carter, "Facts about Jack Dempsey, Champion Heavyweight Boxer," *The Shreveport Times*, February 3, 1924.

[270] Dempsey had appeared in a 1920 serial, entitled "Daredevil Jack." See "Farce and Melodrama on Photo Play Bills," *St. Louis Post-Dispatch*, February 16, 1920.

[271] Dempsey had nearly lost an ear after a blow from Bill Brennan, at Madison Square Garden on December 14, 1920. See Dempsey and Stearns, *Round by Round*, 198, 202.

[272] Dempsey was severely mistaken about the dangers of boxing. A cursory look at period newspaper articles shows at least nine deaths or horrendous injuries related to the sport, in both the amateur and professional ranks. The sport of boxing was almost banned in New York, after an investigation related to the death of Frankie Jerome. See "High School Boxer in Serious Condition," *The Morning Call (Allentown, PA)*, February 8, 1923; "Death After Boxing," *The Guardian (London, Greater London, England)*, March 6, 1923; "State Board Plans Action in Ring Death," *Minnesota Daily Star (Minneapolis, MN)*, September 21, 1923; "Marine Guard Meets Death in Boxing Match," *The Capital Times (Madison, WI)*, September 24, 1923; "Amateur Boxing Tragedy," *The Guardian*, November 5, 1923; "First Death from Boxing in Argentina," *Mount Carmel Item (Mount Carmel, PA)*, December 31, 1923; "Expect No Recoil in Boxing Status in Jerome Death," *The Brooklyn Daily Eagle*, January 14, 1924; "Fear Ban on Boxing," *The Los Angeles Times*, January 15, 1924.

Carpentier Decent Fellow

"Prize fighters used to fight without gloves," he instructed us. "And when they were fighting with gloves, the fights were really fights which lasted for 18 or 20 rounds. Nowadays they last three or four.

"Sure, I knew Carpentier. Met him a dozen times before we went into the ring and he was a real decent fellow. I didn't know Firpo, though. Didn't even see him until we got into the ring.[273]

"What do I think of George Bernard Shaw?" "All I can say, he doesn't know a thing about boxing. The other stuff he writes may be all right, but when it came to his surmises as to who was going to win the Carpentier fight, he was all wrong. Why, gosh, he said I had one chance in a thousand![274]

"Naw, I don't get many mash notes," and he became very bashful. "Hardly any.

Figure 19-"Doc" Kearns and Champion Jack Dempsey, photograph by William Sadlier, *The New Orleans Item*, February 11, 1924.

"If I did get any I wouldn't know anything about it, because my manager opens all my mail.[275] And as to whether I'm in love, I may be if I stay in New Orleans long enough. I understand the town is full of southern beauties. But I'm only going to be here three days. Otherwise I'd like to go out and make a speech at Newcomb as to how to keep physically fit."[276]

But in spite of his own physical fitness, we decided that his beauty hints to the girls at Newcomb wouldn't do them any good, because he confessed an overwhelming weakness for French pastry and pie.

"But gee, even a prize fighter—a gentleman boxer—

[273] Dempsey was perhaps too embarrassed to admit to Day that he had met Firpo, a year before their September 14, 1923 match. Firpo, a giant of a man, had actually kissed Dempsey's hand. Nicknamed "The Wild Bull of the Pampas," Luis Angel Firpo had entered the championship match with Dempsey with a record of twenty-five wins (twenty-one by knockout), two losses, no draws, and two no-decisions. The fight was considered controversial as Firpo, during the first round, knocked Dempsey out of the ring with a punch turned forearm. Dempsey was pushed back into the ring by a group of nearby reporters. He proceeded to knock out Firpo in the next round. See Dempsey and Stearns, *Round by Round*, 220, 223-227.

[274] Shaw actually had claimed that the odds were fifty-to-one in favor of Carpentier. See George Bernard Shaw, "Bernard Shaw Picks Georges," *The Shreveport Times*, June 30, 1921. On July 2, 1921, Dempsey met challenger Carpentier at Boyle's Thirty Acres in Jersey City, NJ. Carpentier had entered the fight with a record of eighty-four wins (fifty-three by knockout), five losses, five draws, and one no-decision. Dempsey had destroyed the challenger, knocking him out in the fourth round. See "No Change in Fistic Title," *The Nebraska State Journal (Lincoln, NE)*, July 3, 1921.

[275] Dempsey's manager, John "Doc" Kearns, also made the trip to New Orleans.

[276] H. Sophie Newcomb College was an all-female institution, located on Broadway, in New Orleans. See Lauren Dean, Newcomb College Institute, "An Overview of the Newcomb College Broadway Campus: 1918 to Present," *New Orleans Historical*, http://www.neworleanshistorical.org/items/show/168 (accessed December 19, 2017).

must have some vices," said he.

Boxers Seem Fine Fellows By Comparison After Sleek Sheiks Mincing at Cabarets

the enthusiasm of the opponents was

The New Orleans Item
Tuesday; February 12, 1924 (P. 10)[277]

Boxers Seem Fine Fellows By Comparison After Sleek Sheiks Mincing at Cabarets[278]

By DOROTHY DAY

What a noble and godlike sport boxing seems after a week in the dance halls, and what fellows the boxers seem after watching sleek sheiks mince around the cabarets.[279] Leaving it to the sporting editor[280] to write the story properly with the hero in the first paragraph and a gradual working back to the beginning—the first two contestants in the four preliminaries to the Dempsey exhibition Monday night were Freddie Brewer and Zack Blanchard.[281]

Finding our seats after the third round, we were able to identify the fighters by the color of their trunks, Brewer's being green and Blanchard's red. Our impression of this fight deciphered with difficulty from the notes taken with our eyes on the ring are that Brewer's back kept getting redder and redder and that he's the best looking of the two. Blanchard seemed to spend most of the fifth round resting his head on Brewer's shoulder, and then again from the way the former shoved the latter out of the clutch you'd think it was the other way around. We noticed especially the perfunctory and casual shake before the sixth round before they jump in at each other. Brewer's face had been pale up to this point, but Blanchard landed him one on the nose and his face was not so white. At the end of the sixth round the referee declared it a draw, and the contestants fell on each other's necks in friendly fashion.

---

[277] The Evening Edition of *The New Orleans Item* carried the alternate headline: "Boxers Seem Fine Fellows to Dorothy Day After Sleek Sheiks Mincing at Cabarets."

[278] Day's father, John I. Day, had reported on boxing matches for many years at *The Inter Ocean* (Chicago, IL). He had especially covered the fights of heavyweight champion, Jack Johnson. See John I. Day, "Johnson and M'Vey Will Fight Easter Monday at Sydney," *The Inter Ocean*, December 30, 1911; John I. Day, "Johnson Whips Flynn, Police Stopping Battle in the Ninth Round," *The Inter Ocean*, July 5, 1912.

[279] The boxing exhibitions were held on February 11, 1924 at the Coliseum Arena, which was located at 401 North Roman Street, in New Orleans. See "Dempsey Fights 3 Opponents 6 Rounds," *The Town Talk (Alexandria, LA)*, February 12, 1924.

[280] Fred Digby was the sporting editor for *The New Orleans Item*. His coverage of the Dempsey exhibition matches also appeared on February 12. See Fred Digby, "Champ Shows Old Skill in Coliseum Exhibition," *The New Orleans Item*, February 12, 1924.

[281] The Brewer-Blanchard bout was an officially sanctioned fight, which ended in a draw after six rounds. Freddie Brewer had entered the fight with a record of three wins (one by knockout), four losses, and one no-decision; Zack Blanchard with six wins (two by knockout), and one loss.

The Thrills of 1924: Dorothy Day Encounters the "Underworld Denizens" of New Orleans

Second Preliminary.

The second preliminary was between Joe Mandell and Sam Pizzitola.[282] Before the first round the seconds on both sides busied themselves with tying gloves on the pair and massaging their back muscles. In the first couple of rounds everything seemed to be against Mandell. Pizzitola kept landing blows on the back of his neck and in the very first round, knocked him to the floor. But he got to his feet on the third count. In the second round, Mandell picked up and the third round was all his except for one on the jaw that Pizzitola got in. In a tense silence you could hear the paper boys nonchalantly calling the morning papers and the cries, "Orange crush, who wants some ice cold lemon crush?" Then there'd be a roar that rose from floor to roof and everything would be drowned out. In the fourth round Pizzitola landed one but his arm slid along his opponent's ear and gave Mandell a chance. There was less clinching in this round and the enthusiasm of the opponents was such that they got in a few more wallops at each other after the gong. At the end of the fifth round, both were more anxious to fall on the stools hastily stuck between the ropes, but Pizzitola tried to disguise his eagerness by giving a vivacious little dance towards his seat. In the sixth round there was a rhythmical exchange of blows but they didn't resound as earlier ones did, and the two boxers seemed to be holding each other up. Pizzitola was pronounced the victor, and embraced Mandell as it seems the custom is and escorted him to his seat.

Doyle vs. Campau

The third fight was between Jack Doyle and Joe Campau.[283] In the first round everybody yelled for Jack, and in the second round the audience accused them of holding punches. Doyle had his head on Campau's chest most of the time. They couldn't seem to get each other disentangled to get in a single wallop. In the third round everybody jeered. "La, la," "Step on his toes," "On with the dance," and suddenly the excitement began. The roars shook the roof, falling and rising again and again, and pierced by shrill whistling. Doyle was knocked down, and turning over lightly three times, he got to his feet. Campau was on his knees at the end of the round which left the room in a turmoil. In the fourth Doyle kept staggering with a surprised and drunken air. Doyle kept falling against the rope and rebounded lightly, for a moment both seemed to be going blind because they punched aimlessly and kept missing each other. Through the fifth and sixth everybody kept shrieking, "put him out, Jack," but the fight ended in a draw.

The fourth fight, a ten-rounder between Charley Rodriguez and Delos Williams was interesting in the fact that everybody shouted for Charley all the way through and yet Williams won the decision.[284] There was so much infighting that the pale faced referee in the pongee shirt had to

---

[282] The Mandell-Pizzitola bout was an officially sanctioned fight, in which Pizzitola won the decision on points after six rounds. Joe Mandell had entered the fight with a record of seven wins (two by knockout), twelve losses, three draws, and one no-decision; Sam Pizzitola with fourteen wins (none by knockout), six losses, and one draw.

[283] The Doyle-Campau bout was an officially sanctioned fight, which ended in a draw after six rounds. "Irish" Jackie Doyle had entered the fight with a record of fourteen wins (three by knockout), thirteen losses, and four draws; Joe Campau with ten wins (four by knockout), ten losses, and one draw.

[284] The Rodriguez-Williams bout was an officially sanctioned fight, in which Williams won the decision on points. Charley Rodriguez had entered the fight with a record of fifteen wins (four by knockout), seven losses, and one draw; Delos "Kid" Williams with eight wins (three by knockout), seven losses, and four draws.

keep peering anxiously between the two. The crowd were demanding blood, but Williams had it all his own way, getting in six blows to Charley's one. The latter fought with his mouth wide open and we were afraid he'd bite his tongue. He began losing the sympathy of his supporters who baa-ed like sheep.

This seemed to infuriate the two into more action, and Williams was seen waving the mist out of his eyes. By the tenth round they were butting each other like a pair of goats and the crowd who thought that Charley would come to at the last minute were disappointed.

Magnificent Dempsey.

And here Dempsey appears upon the scene, the house rising to him as he walks into the arena magnificent in his purple tights with the red, white and blue rosette at his waist. After the 117-pounders or thereabouts who were appearing in the ring all evening, everybody gasped and roared their approval at the sight of Dempsey. It's no use talking in terms of polite fiction about bronzed shoulders or silkily moving muscles which are supposed to ripple. Dempsey was so lightning quick that you couldn't see if his muscles rippled or not.

Needless to say, no notes were taken during the three two-round bouts of the champion. You sat with your mouth open, as if that could assist you in following every move, and then you felt as though you were missing half of it.

Everybody kept shouting, "I'd hate to feel the way that Irishman feels," during the first bout with Martin Burke.[285] At the sounding of the gong, the opponents disdained to sit down, but restlessly permitted a few dabs of a towel from their seconds. In the second round Dempsey showed what he could do in the way of defending himself, holding off Burke with the utmost ease so that his lusty opponent couldn't get near him. Only at the end of his round, he held Burke lightly by the side of the head and delivered several cuffs with incredible swiftness.

Tommy Marvin and Dan O'Dowd were the other two opponents of the champion, and they weren't in it at all.[286] "Take 'em over your knee and spank 'em," the crowd yelled gleefully. Although Dempsey "pulled" his punches, he had to hold the last two contestants up from the floor as he delivered the blows which could only have been heavy from the weight of his arm and not from any force behind it. It was a great night!

---

[285] Martin Joseph Burke was a top-ranked light heavyweight contender, with a boxing record (at the time of the Dempsey exhibition) of thirty-three wins (eleven by knockout), seventeen losses, six draws, and one no-decision. Four days after losing his exhibition bout against Dempsey, Burke faced Gene Tunney for the light heavyweight championship. Burke fought fifteen rounds against Tunney, losing the decision on points.

[286] Tommy Marvin was a light heavyweight fighter, with a boxing record (at the time of the Dempsey exhibition) of four wins (three by knockout), five losses, and one draw. Dan O'Dowd was a heavyweight fighter, with a boxing record (at the time of the Dempsey exhibition) of fifteen wins (five by knockout), seventeen losses, and three draws.

The Thrills of 1924: Dorothy Day Encounters the "Underworld Denizens" of New Orleans

The Thrills of 1924

After interviewing celebrities, covering boxing matches, and going undercover as a dance hall flapper, Dorothy Day turned her attention toward the illegal gambling industry, which had a vast hold on New Orleans and its surrounding parishes. The impetus for this series of articles may have come from a vignette from one of Day's "All Around New Orleans" articles. In "The Lure of Lucre," published on January 10, Day had reported on women who placed bets on a regular basis, hopeful of attaining a life-changing windfall. However, very few people ever made a "killing," and Day rightfully stated that, "For every sportsman there [were] ten gamblers paying a heavy price for chances to get rich quick."

Based upon the attention garnered by Day's dance hall series, and her innate ability to blend into various communities and situations, it is easy to imagine her editor suggesting an exposé of women in the gambling industry. However, one may also wonder, what *was* the "heavy price" that women paid, and what games of chance did they partake of, in the Crescent City?

The "Thrills of 1924," consisted of seven articles, published each day from February 24 to March 1. Although only five of the seven articles were signed, all of the pieces unmistakably belonged to Day. As previously mentioned, two of the columns (February 26-27) were not about gambling, and seemed to be more in line with her former "All Around New Orleans" articles.

The "Thrills of 1924" (published on February 24), opened with Day encountering the mysterious Mrs. R., a reckless gambler who had claimed to be the grandniece of Aaron Burr. Shockingly, Mrs. R. also admitted that she had lost the astronomical sum of $5,000 while playing roulette. The two women then traveled to a roadhouse in Jefferson Parish, a suburb of New Orleans, where illegal gambling was tolerated to a point, and women were welcomed to try to make their "killing."

While traveling to the roadhouse, Day synthesized the history of gambling in New Orleans, paraphrasing from the 1885 *Historical Sketch Book and Guide to New Orleans and Environs*. After arriving at the gambling den, where there was no betting limit, Day used the 1907 *Hoyle's Games: Autograph Edition* to describe the dice game better known as "craps."

After reporting that there were only a few people winning at dice, Day stated that the pace of the game had moved too quickly, and that both she and Mrs. R. "were surprised at this because, never having been in a gambling house before, we expected that everybody would be drinking feverishly and smoking while they watched the play." This is yet another strange statement regarding personal pronoun usage (see "Going Undercover in New Orleans"). If Mrs. R. had lost $5,000 at roulette, how could Day claim that *they* had never been in a gambling house before?

Aside from violations of the state Prohibition laws, the women faced potential arrest and prosecution for illegal gambling. In September of 1923, police raided several local dens of iniquity wherein thirty-one men and women were arrested in New Orleans, for gambling with dice for money.[287]

---

[287] "Forty Arrested in Police Drive," *The Times-Picayune*, September 10, 1923.

The second article in the thrills series, published on February 25, presumably finds Day and Mrs. R. at the same roadhouse, with the focus upon the game of roulette. The article, written in mind to show the vast sums that women lost on gambling, also contained some humorous moments.

Day stated that a lone woman had "broken the bank," but her luck did not last long, and she wound up losing everything. At one point during the woman's winning streak, Day wondered whether the banker and his assistant would "retain their Buddhistic indifference." Day had also lost $5.00 at roulette, and realizing that there was no such thing as "beginner's luck" or a "lucky number" she left the roadhouse behind, swearing never to play the game again.

The "Thrills" columns published on February 26-27 were not about gambling, but were apparent leftovers from Day's work on "All Around New Orleans." However, the articles offered a fascinating look at life in the city. The first article contained vignettes about a jilted lover who had started a brawl at a local cafe, and a gathering of former soldiers, one of whom had survived an attack by headhunters in the Phillipines. The second article was about people whom authors Evangeline Booth and Thomas Burke would have defined as "denizens of the underworld." The article described such creatures as late-night coffee drinkers, underworld cats skulking around the fish market, a couple who had tried to stow away on a ship, and a woman, dressed in all black, who hosted a party dedicated to her faux passing.

The next "Thrill," published on February 28, concerned the rise of poker playing in "women only" clubs. Here, women paid annual dues of $15 to $25 to enter the "club," with the house garnering an additional commission of ten to twenty-five percent per hand.

Day had related the sadness of women so addicted to poker, that they were forced to sell their jewelry in order to continue gambling. Some women even went to the extremes of making paste replicas of their jewelry, in order to pawn their original pieces. Day also reported on the fraud that two women brazenly pulled off—one player pretended to be drunk, in order to distract the other gamblers, while her consort "cleaned" everyone out. It was later determined that the pair of women had pulled the same trickery in different cities.

The final "Thrill," published on February 29, concerned the ancient sport of horse racing. By far the article with the most depth in the series, the reader will notice that women gamblers were segregated in terms of facilities and hospitality. Day had reported that women were not allowed to bet, or sit with men, and they oftentimes had to slog through a muddied field in order to reach their isolated grandstand. Women were also cheated out of larger betting odds. Day had cited the case of a woman who bet on a horse named "Normal." The horse had won the race, and the men who bet on "Normal" had won twelve-to-one odds, while the woman only received a payout at six-to-one odds.

Toward the end of the horse racing article, there appeared three, seemingly cryptic statements, which were placed in the mouths of frustrated gamblers. Day had written, "I can't afford to come another day." "Thank the Lord I have my ticket back to New York." "I shan't come tomorrow, that's all there is to it." Perhaps these statements signified that Day knew that her time in New Orleans was almost at an end, or they were messages to someone back home. Day had learned that her semi-autobiographical novel, *The Eleventh Virgin*, was soon to be published by Albert and Charles Boni. She would shortly return to New York in anticipation of the novel's release.

There would be one more article published under Day's name, which seemed more like an afterthought, in that she had barely written forty-five original words. The article, published on March 1, concerned the heavy price that female gamblers paid. In addition to monetary losses, women suffered from a condition known as neurasthenia wherein they had experienced premature aging and the inability to relax. Day had interviewed Oscar Dowling, the President of the Board of Health, who stated that neurasthenia was a significant cause of heart and kidney disease.

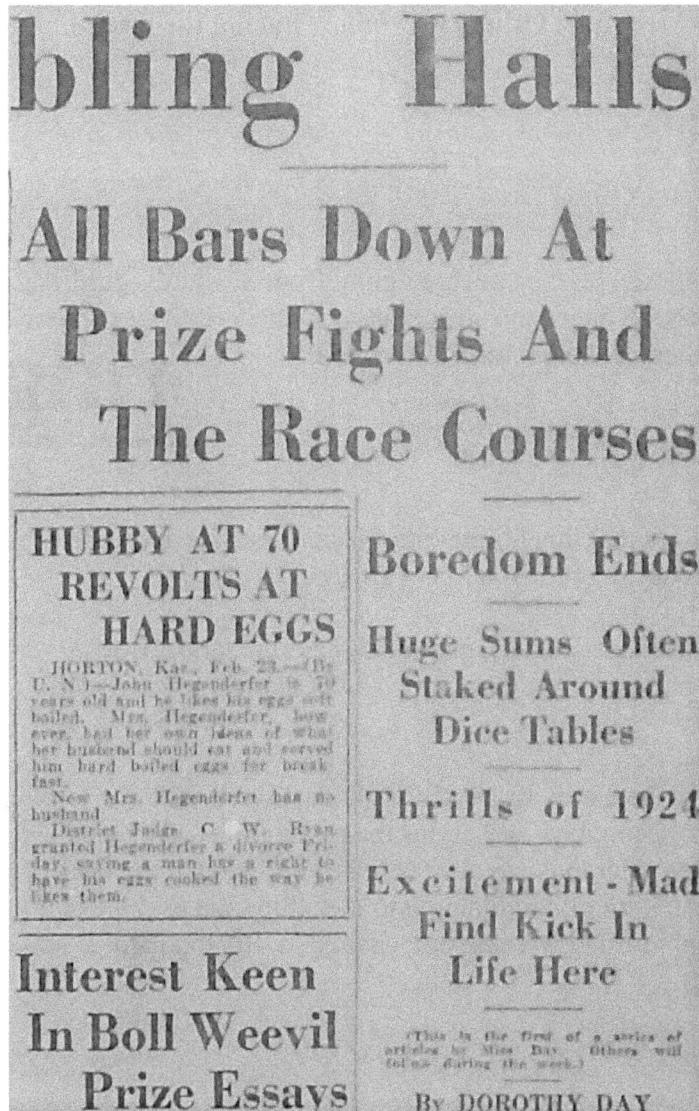

The New Orleans Item
Sunday; February 24, 1924 (Pp. 1, 4; Section 2)

Women Crowd Fashionable Gambling Halls

———————

All Bars Down At Prize Fights And The Race Courses

———————

Boredom Ends

———————

Huge Sums Often Staked Around Dice Tables

———————

Thrills of 1924

———————

Excitement - Mad Find Kick In Life Here

———————

The Thrills of 1924: Dorothy Day Encounters the "Underworld Denizens" of New Orleans

(This is the first of a series of articles by Miss Day. Others will follow during the week.)

By DOROTHY DAY

"Mamma goes where papa goes,
And sometimes papa stays home!"[288]

You hear it everywhere, from the lips of children on the street, jangling from the hurdy-gurdies, bawled out every night in the cabarets. It's good dance music and has a swing to it that sets your feet moving; the words have a chuckle in them and are a little bit wicked.

"Mamma loves squeezing,
Mamma loves teasing!"

The words go and nobody that sings it realizes that this idiotic bit of jazz is really a declaration of independence on the part of women of today, a proclamation of freedom.

No longer are prize-fights, wrestling matches, race courses, gaming tables and bars closed to women. Not only can they go wherever a man goes, but they can go alone, leaving their escorts at home.

The thrills of 1924! The vanities, the follies, the extravagances! For the last week we have indulged in them all and after surveying for seven days and nights the dissipations of women who are looking for a kick out of life, we are a nervous wreck. There is a dull pain at the back of our neck, editorially speaking, and we're thinking of complaining to the editor and asking for a nice quiet assignment covering murders and railroad wrecks for a change.[289] It's too hard keeping up with the women.

Hectic Pleasure-Seeking

It wouldn't have been so bad if we hadn't run into Mrs. R. over at the Roosevelt hotel.[290] We had intended to spend a few quiet afternoons at the race track, leaving most of our weekly pay check at home, visit the roulette rooms in those subdued roadhouses out in Jefferson parish, sit in at one or two poker games and see if for a change we couldn't win something.[291] But instead, Mrs. R.

---

[288] Day quoted the song, "Mama Goes Where Papa Goes," written by Milton Ager and Jack Yellen in 1923.

[289] Day's flippancy regarding "railroad wrecks" is surprising, given that she was a probationary nurse at the Kings County Hospital Center in Brooklyn, NY (from January 1918 until January of 1919). Day was on duty, on November 1, 1918, during one of the worst train disasters in New York history. Known as the Malbone Street Wreck, nearly 100 people were killed; scores more were injured. See Day, *The Eleventh Virgin*, 223-247; Day, *From Union Square to Rome*, 92-100; Day, *The Long Loneliness*, 88-93; Brian Cudahy, *The Malbone Street Wreck* (New York, NY: Fordham University Press, 1999).

[290] Mrs. R., who later identified herself as Aaron Burr's grandniece, was more than likely a descendent of the Reeve family. Her identity, however, could not be determined.

[291] Illegal gambling became such a problem in Jefferson Parish, that the former Mayor of Gretna, Dr. Charles Gelbke, proposed putting "a padlock on every gambling joint in the Free State." See "To Hang Padlocks on Gambling Joints," *The Town Talk (Alexandria, LA)*, July 12, 1924.

dragged us out on a round of hectic pleasure-seeking, which lasted afternoon and evening and way into the small but not still hours of the morning.

Mrs. R. is from Chicago, a fragile yet vital blonde who looks like the sister of her 17-year-old daughter. The daughter is an independent miss, who spends all her time at art and music and refuses to accompany her mother on her jaunts around the country. Mrs. R. spent her time nursing during the war, and her taste for excitement is hard to satisfy.[292]

"My dear, I'm so bored," she was complaining last week. "And besides I lost $5,000 on roulette and have to go slow for a while. Life seemed so dull yesterday afternoon that I called on Mr. Hegewisch, the Mexican consul, for the rebels and offered him my services in conducting his little old revolution.[293] Being the grand niece of Aaron Burr, who was so unjustly accused of wanting to set himself up as king in Mexico and who really had nothing but the welfare of the peons at heart, I feel that it's particularly fitting for me to become the Joan of Arc of Mexico.[294]

Escorts Not Needed

"The trouble is that both Mr. Hegewisch and Mr. Arce[295] have read so many E. Phillips Oppenheim mystery stories, all about beautiful Russian spies who are always duping people, that I'm afraid they're not going to accept my offer.[296] However, they're holding conferences about it and meanwhile I'm bored. What do you say we go out to Jefferson parish tonight and indulge my vicious taste for gambling some more? We don't need escorts, and if we did bring any along we wouldn't pay any attention to them after we got out there. We won't go out until after the theatre, so be prepared for a night of it."

Although practically every pool room and cigar store in town has a back room for games of chance operating under a club license, there are very few places where women can play, except in their own homes or the homes of their friends.

---

[292] As mentioned in Footnote no. 289, Day had also served as a probationary nurse toward the end of World War One.

[293] Adolfo E. Hegewisch, a noted New Orleans businessman, had also served as consul general for the Adolfo de la Huerta regime, which sought to overthrow the federal government in Mexico. See "Rebel Forces Seize Panuco, Capture 5,000," *The Shreveport Times*, February 23, 1924; "Businessman Found Slain in Orleans," *The Shreveport Times*, August 10, 1966.

[294] Mrs. R.'s view of Aaron Burr was obviously biased. In 1804, Aaron Burr hatched a treasonous plot to establish a separate country by annexing the western portion of the United States, including the Mississippi Territory and Florida. Using the city of New Orleans as a seat of power, Burr further proposed marching on Vera Cruz, and liberating Mexico from Spanish rule. See Buckner F. Melton, Jr., *Aaron Burr: Conspiracy to Treason* (New York, NY: John Wiley and Sons, Inc., 2002), 54, 57, 66, 76, 80-81, 122, 154.

[295] Jose Arce was a diplomatic agent, and former Deputy, under the command of Mexican rebel de la Huerta. Arce was, at one time, invited to become the Governor of Yucatan, Mexico, after the retirement of Ricardez Broca. See "Huerta, Rebel Leader, in U. S.?" *The Town Talk (Alexandria, LA)*, April 2, 1924; "Has Not Received Message," *The Town Talk*, April 2, 1924.

[296] Day was familiar with the work of E. Phillips Oppenheim, having reviewed his book, *The Way of These Women*, during her time as a student at the University of Illinois (Champaign-Urbana) in 1915. See D. D., "The Way of These Women," *Chicago Examiner*, October 2, 1915.

The Thrills of 1924: Dorothy Day Encounters the "Underworld Denizens" of New Orleans

Gone are the days when Hicks and Hewlett, Duval, Toussaint, St. Cyr, and many others ran their flourishing establishments day and night. Gone are the days of McGrath, Sherwood and Perritt, with their beautifully furnished houses where magnificent dinners and suppers were served to visitors and patrons.[297]

These three latter men have gone down in the history of the city for their distinctive personalities, enjoying a reputation for fair play, strict honesty and integrity not only in their business dealings, but in sporting circles.

Gambling Rooms Filled

McGrath was at No. 4 Carondelet street, afterward the "Boston Club," which he had purchased and fitted up at a cost of nearly $70,000. Prominent men from all over the country visited here and the rooms were filled with merchants, planters and lawyers and it looked more like a club than a gambling house.[298]

James Sherwood, who was famed as a raconteur, Charles Cassidy, the writer; "Count" Lorenzo Lewis, so-called on account of his urbane manners and faultless dressing; little Montiro, who wounded and captured the boldest and most daring burglar ever known to New Orleans; the notorious Charles Alexander Gordon. Fascinating men, known all over the city for their wit, their character and adventurous lives. Did they throw their houses open to the wives and daughters of New Orleans?[299]

The old stories of New Orleans don't say. What do the game keepers of today think of these jewelled, reckless women who throw away hundreds with one shake of the dice and who hang over the green cloth with set smiles? We wondered as we watched them that night.

To shoot dice successfully, you must be able to snap your fingers, hiss your point through your teeth, swing your arm with such a flourish that the dice go clicking across the green table.

We weren't able to do any of these things, so we lost $10 in as many minutes and decided to swear off and watch the others.

We had taken a taxi late that night after the theatre, and Mrs. R. had leaned forward and asked the driver: "Where's a good game?"[300]

---

[297] Day paraphrased from the *Historical Sketch Book and Guide to New Orleans and Environs*, 204.

[298] Ibid., 205.

[299] Ibid., 205-206.

[300] Four years after Day had left the Crescent City, Lyle Saxon claimed that the solicitation of taxi drivers was a common way of finding gaming establishments. He wrote, "For those seeking excitement, there are gambling houses beyond the city limits. Although prohibited by law, the demand for gambling houses is such that there are always many to be found. Any taxi driver will tell you about them, should your taste lie in that direction. Just ask." See Lyle Saxon, *Fabulous New Orleans* (1928; repr., New Orleans, LA: Robert L. Crager and Company, 1950), 267.

"Sky's the Limit"

The question was taken as a matter of course by the taxi driver, who mentioned half a dozen places for our consideration. "They're all out in Jefferson parish," he told us. "But there aren't any public ones in the city just now where women are allowed. They have a good straight game at all those places, though, and the sky's the limit."

It seemed that we had ridden a long while before we arrived at the nearest of the places that the driver had mentioned. Leaving the city limits, we were driven along bumpy roads, past cemeteries, and along well paved roads past charming residences whose porches gleamed in the moonlight. For the most part the road was dark although now and then we passed a filling station brightly lighted.

Finally turning down a long drive way, past a modest electric sign which you would have missed if you hadn't been looking for it, we arrived in a huge court yard at the rear of what looked to be a private residence rather than a road house. The only thing that looked strange was the large shell-strewn courtyard, and the long semicircle of sheds for the cars. One was reminded of race tracks, and the sheds gave a sporting look to the place.

Windows Curtained

The first floor was well lighted and although the shades were not drawn, the windows were so heavily curtained that it was impossible to see inside. Passing through a butler's pantry and dining room, we arrived at the scene of action, a long drawing room with two roulette tables and one table for dice. To the right as you went in was a comfortably furnished sitting room for women, with a soft spoken maid to relieve you of your wraps and supply you with powder and rouge, smelling salts, a cold towel and a couch if so desired.

The big room was very quiet considering the fact that all three tables were crowded, the roulette wheels were spinning, chips were being transferred from number to number and from hand to hand, and the dice were being coaxed and threatened alternately.

There were as many women as men and they all took an active part in the game. Everybody sat on high stools like those in front of a soda counter and stood up when their turn came to play. The table is deep like a pool table and no matter with what abandon and recklessness you fling your dice, they won't roll off.

Dice and Other Games

In back of the table stands the banker with the chips, blue ones for a dollar apiece, green ones $5, red ones $10, and then smaller stacks of $25, $50 and $100 chips in soft pastel shades. Most of the players were staking a dollar a throw, but there was one woman with a pile of $5 chips and one who was making money with a pile of $10 ones.

The Thrills of 1924: Dorothy Day Encounters the "Underworld Denizens" of New Orleans

But for the most part it seemed that the banker raked in most of the counters and few were winning. Facing the banker was a man with a little rake to capture your dice for you and to call your play.

Craps was the game that was being played, although there are other and more complicated games—ace in the pot, baseball, centennial, Newmarket or Yankee grab, Round the Spot, Passe Dix, poker dice, raffles, ten pins, and vingt-et-un[301].

For the benefit of those women who don't know how to play this game which seems to be more popular than roulette with the women of New Orleans, we will explain, according to Hoyle.[302] Two dice are thrown from the hand, without a box, and the caster is supposed to take all bets offered by any one else around the table. There are eleven possible throws from 2 to 12. If the first throw is seven or eleven, called a "natural," it wins for the caster at once. If the first throw is 2, 3, or 12, it is a crap, and wins for the players immediately.

Game Is Fast

If neither nick nor crap is thrown the first cast, whatever comes is called the point and the caster must try to throw this same point again before he throws seven. If he throws his point first, he wins, if he throws seven he loses and the dice are passed to the next in line.

Everybody plays with everybody else around the table whether he or she is known to each other or not. The game is a fast one, so swift that none has time to smoke even a cigaret. We were surprised at this because, never having been in a gambling house before, we expected that everybody would be drinking feverishly and smoking while they watched the play.

The game itself was enough of a stimulant to make cigarets and alcohol unnecessary and the fact that every players' senses were unblurred by anything but the mental stimulus of the game added to the intensity of the atmosphere.

(Miss Day on Monday will tell of the huge sums lost around the roulette tables.)

---

[301] Vingt-et-un is more commonly known as blackjack, or twenty-one.

[302] Edmond Hoyle, *Hoyle's Games: Autograph Edition* (1907; repr., New York, NY: A. L. Burt Company, 114), 202-203.

The Thrills of 1924

The rest, lost to all thoughts of home and family, regardless of many things of beauty and comfort money will buy were slowly, but steadily losing dollars by the hundreds.

BY DOROTHY DAY

The New Orleans Item
Monday; February 25, 1924 (P. 5)

The Thrills of 1924

The rest, lost to all thoughts of home and family, regardless of many things of beauty and comfort money will buy were slowly, but steadily losing dollars by the hundreds.

BY DOROTHY DAY

Hour after hour, the impersonal dialogue continues, the player's voice sibilant with anxiety, the gamekeepers' response, dull and colorless. There is the little chinkle of chips, the tiny sound of dice being raked across the board and the antiphony goes on and on till dawn.

At the next table, there is the soft whir of the roulette wheel and the knock-knocking of the ivory ball as it spins around the wheel seeking a resting place. The players are silent for the most part, speaking in murmurs for chips, only the banker or his companions calling the lucky number.

The chips are piled row upon row, ivory, red, green, blue, lavender pink and under the banker's hand is a pile of bills half a foot high. We noticed that when one of the men behind the table was called away, he did not move from the side of his partner until another had come to take his place. There is something sleepily sinister about these two men with their pleasantly impassive faces.

Tensity About Patrons

This room full of people, concentrating all their attention on objects which are animated only by a turn of a wheel or gesture of a wrist is uncanny. The players seek to preserve a bland expression but there is a tensity about them which is felt and a set look about their mouths.

The woman sitting next to us with sweet drooping eyebrows and a hard mouth, lost thirty one-dollar chips and turned to her purse hastily so that she shouldn't lose a minute of the play. She was beautifully gowned in jade green and her golden sandalled feet were tucked up on the rungs of her chair. The woman next to her played with an air of amused indifference, with five dollar chips and the movement of her arm as she reached out to place her bet, made the diamonds flash in the huge crucifix which she wore at her breast.

197

At the roulette table, the women were younger on the whole, although there was one woman who did not even make pretensions to youth or even middle age. She was almost shabbily dressed, and sat unashamed with a ragged handbag out of which she kept extracting bills for piles upon piles of chips.

Half Dozen Young Girls

A half dozen young girls, immaculately dressed, kept their wraps about them as though they had just dropped in for an hour's play although they were just as intent as the rest.

Nobody paid any attention to anybody else. Sex interest was so completely lacking in this room that when a new feminine arrival joined the group around the table, no one looked her way to size up either her clothes and her attractions. They abstractedly made way for her, their eyes upon the table.

This was a relief to us, for although our excitement craving companion had come well gowned, we wore street clothes. But nobody cares what you wear and nobody cares how you bet. Unless, of course, you're winning. That's human nature.

We'd like to tell how we took the $50,000 and staked it all on our lucky number (we were under the delusion that we have one, and that it's fifteen) and after waiting nonchalantly for the ivory ball to fall in the pocket, raked in $1,750,000. For that's what you'd win if you had $50,000 to stake and if they let you do it.

Bought Quarter Chips

But truth compels us to confess that we bought five dollars worth of quarter chips and kept them in front of us for a while in order that we could study the table, and also because we knew we wouldn't have them long and wanted to enjoy the sensation of having a stack whether they were won or paid for, while we could.

The banker's proficiency in raking in the chips, stacking them and passing them around again to winners and purchasers, engaged our attention for a while. Then we discovered when the chips had been swept off that we really knew nothing about roulette, either the layout or the methods of betting.

0-32-15-19-4-21-2—25-17-34 6 27 13 36-11-30-8-23-10, etc.

The above line is not a typographical error nor yet a secret code. It's the way the numbers run on the roulette wheel, every other letter being black or red until there are 36 numbers identifying the pockets. Just to make it harder, the zero pocket is green.

The Monte Carlo and the New Orleans wheels have 36 pockets and a zero, but many other American wheels have only 27, 30 or 33 numbers, giving a larger percentage.

The wheel spins slowly on its axis like a large flat top in a sort of hollow dish round the inner edge of which the little ball is thrown, always in the opposite direction to which the wheel is turning. The center of the green table is marked out in numbered squares and it's on these you place your bet.

Combinations Puzzling

It would take too long to enumerate all the ways of betting, by columns, by the first twelve, second twelve or third twelve numbers, odd or even, red or black being only a few of them. We didn't realize them ourselves until we got at home and drew diagrams and started figuring out.

The thing we couldn't understand was how anybody could evolve what are known as "systems" or "combinations," from the numbers listed above. Our only attempt at a combination was to place one chip on 15, one on each line between 15 and three other numbers. If the ivory ball landed in pocket fifteen, we stood to win $21.50 for the dollar we had staked. Unfortunately we kept losing until we had one chip left, staked it stubbornly on 15 and won $8.50 instead of the $21.50 we'd been working for. But we couldn't stop there. We had to go on, trying other fascinating combinations until we relinquished our seat, a ruined woman.

Woman Broke Bank

Haven't we heard that there is such a thing as beginner's luck? Another delusion shattered. What a moment it would have been to have continued winning and placing neat little stacks of chips on various numbers with that mysterious and assured air peculiar to one whose stacks of counters are increasing, until others followed our bets, as the custom is. Of course the situation wouldn't be complete unless you actually "broke the bank."

One woman had that enviable experience, lacking the climax of course which should have been ours. For this woman was not a beginner. She had the cold and glittering eye which all true gamblers should have but don't. Time after time she staked half a dozen chips or so and won. She did it seemingly without system and we wondered how she could remember on which numbers she had placed bets, and how many chips on each. But she remembered and the banker remembered and she kept right on winning. Gradually she had collected a following. Everybody watched what she did with breathless interest. She was beloved by the gods of chance just now, and everybody else wanted any crumbs which might fall from her table.[303] They surrounded her on all sides with their chips, and they won and she won, but the banker remained imperturbable.

Luck Didn't Last Long

We didn't see the bank busted, and we couldn't help wondering whether the banker and his companion would retain their expression of Buddhistic indifference.

But the little flurry of luck didn't last long, and pretty soon everybody was betting on their own again, and there was no longer the same place atmosphere as before.

---

[303] A reference to Mt 15:27. "She said, 'Yes, Lord, yet even the dogs eat the crumbs that fall from their masters' table'" [NRSV].

The Thrills of 1924: Dorothy Day Encounters the "Underworld Denizens" of New Orleans

It was two o'clock when we left the roadhouse, refusing the proprietor's hospitable invitation to wait for dinner. But afraid of the lure of the tables, and having lost between us all that my companion had said she was going to allow herself to lose, we strong-mindedly dragged ourselves away. In the two hours we were there, we had not been able to keep exact track of the losses of others. We only knew that of all the women who were there, only two were winning. The rest, lost to all thoughts of home or family, regardless of the many things of beauty and comfort that money will buy were slowly, but steadily losing dollars by the hundred. There may be a thrill in it, but the two delusions of "lucky number" and "beginner's luck" being shattered, we've decided we won't play roulette again.

————————

Tuesday's Item will continue this series of stories about women excitement seekers in New Orleans.

Thrills of 1924

Strangers talk together and no offense is taken and officers and seamen and men of doubtful trades dance with women of all classes loosely or courteously as the occasion required.

By DOROTHY DAY | Strangers talk together and no of-

The New Orleans Item
Tuesday; February 26, 1924 (P. 13)
Evening Edition: (P. 11)

Thrills of 1924

—Strangers talk together and no offense is taken and officers and seamen and men of
doubtful trades dance with women of all classes loosely or courteously as the occasion
required.

By DOROTHY DAY

"Ah laid in jail…
Mah face turned to the wall
Ah don' mind bein' in jail,
But ah don' like to stay there so long."[304]

———

It was the graveyard blues, the colored musicians were singing—a rhymeless thing sometime but
full of a strange rhythm as they sang it. Some of the words were unintelligible but you gathered
that the song was about a black girl that died, and a murder that was committed, and the
philosophical reflections of the unfortunate darkey in jail on life and women.

"Ah went out to the graveyard—and fell down on my knees
Said to that grave-digger, Oh send me back my good gal, please.
But the grave-digger sighed, and looked into mah eye—
'I'm sorry to tell yuh; Yo' gal has said her last goodbye.'"

It's a jagged melody with a monotonous plucking on the stringed instruments, and the darkeys
roll their eyes and heads and open their big mouths wide and wail.

———

[304] Day quoted the "Graveyard Dream Blues," a song written by Ida Cox, circa 1923. Day would later quote
the same song, and the first three paragraphs of this article, in her syndicated serial, "What Price Love." See Dorothy
Day, "What Price Love," *Chicago Herald Examiner*, June 14, 1926.

The Thrills of 1924: Dorothy Day Encounters the "Underworld Denizens" of New Orleans

This is the sort of thing that makes this Royal street restaurant popular with all classes—the men who come off the ships, street loungers, men and women coming from the theater and the more fashionable restaurants. There is a kick in this primitive music, of course, after the regular jazz of the more ordinary cabarets, but what gives the excitement seeker the real thrill, is sitting at the same table with women of doubtful or no reputation who fill the place every night, and with seamen who talk Spanish and Swedish, and strange jargons which you can't identify.

Strangers talk together and no offense is taken, and officers and seamen, and men of doubtful trades dance with women of all classes loosely or courteously as the situation requires.

Last night we sat there late at one of the corner tables, observing and fraternizing with our surroundings and it was a good night to be there because there was action and drama aplenty.

Not long after the dinner hour, through the glass paned door which leads into the kitchen you could see two uniformed policemen, comfortably munching sandwiches. They peered in the door, enjoying the music and the mad dancing, and the musicians more bold than we kept singing jovially, over and over again:

"Ah don mind bein' in jail, but I don't like to stay there long."

Probably it's the musicians themselves who dramatize the place. They sit and watch the room, and are filled with the spirit that permeates it, and they reflect that spirit.

Girls Share in Profits

For instance, there are the girls, who sit there night after night and make their living not only from the men they meet, but from the number of drinks they can induce the customers to buy. They are served ginger ale and they profit fifty-fifty on the liquor which they can induce others to consume. One of these girls is very handsome, of rather ample proportions, and marvelously waved, honey colored hair. She dimples when she smiles, but for some nights her eyes brooded over the room.

We were watching her late that night when a good-looking careless fellow entered the room, smiling at her casually as he did so. Panther-like, she leaped on him before anybody knew what was happening, and after hurling the water tumbler which was before her, picked up the carafe.

Everybody in the room stiffened except the musicians. Women wanted to flee, but feared the flying glasses. Then, too, they were getting the desired kick which led them to the place. The proprietor rushed to the scene, the cooks from the kitchen grinned as they peered out into the restaurant. The dancers stood back and waited for what would come next.

But the musicians! Imperturbably they struck up:

"Frankie went down to the hock shop.
She didn't go there for fun.
She went to pawn her Sunday clo'es

And get herself a forty-four gun,
To kill her man, what had done her wrong!"[305]

—and went on through the many verses. The room relaxed, everybody breathed more freely and in a moment people began to smile.

Girl Sits Quietly

Everybody was happy again, including the musicians who beamed at the impression they had made, except perhaps, the girl, who sat back quietly, her lip trembling, not hearing the scolding the Italian proprietor was giving her. The man, someone explained had been "going with" her for the last year, and the week before, had married a little girl from his town upstate.

"What she want to act like that for," he was blustering. "She don't gain nothing by it. I like to be with good feelings towards everybody." But no one listened to him; their sympathies were not with him.

At a long table on one side of the room, made by throwing three tables together, sat a dozen Spaniards talking together, and throwing back their heads with hearty laughs. They were none of them drinking, but they were filled with the joy of living, a spontaneous, pre-carnival hilarity that was infectious. Every now and then when the musicians stopped playing, the Spaniards sang together, Spanish tunes in which you could hear the rattle of the castanets and hear the swish of the dancer's skirts. The tallest of the men, the one with the most rollicking laugh, had only one eye. He was a bull fighter, someone said, and we gave him our admiration as every one else in the room seemed to do, for we had never seen a toreador before. But we wished that he had worn a wide sash about his waist.

All Ardent Americans

This is a restaurant, which at times can be sordid and maudlin and ugly in every way. But there are some excitement seekers who found a thrill in the sordid and ugly, there were beautiful women who bloom like orchids in an unhealthy and vicious setting. There are even those who find nothing but the morbid in such a place as this restaurant with it's chameleon changes of mood.

We have discovered the waiters in a patriotic mood, when Frenchmen, Spaniards and Italians alike, talk with Latin vivacity of the battles they've been in, the wounds they've received, how they've fought in the Phillipines, on the Mexican border, in France and in Italy. For French, Spanish or Italian, they are all ardent Americans, and any patron at the table who can show a soldier's button, especially the silver one of the disabled veteran, is immediately greeted as "Buddy" and reminiscences begin.

---

[305] Day quoted the song "Frankie and Johnny," written by Hughie Cannon in 1904. During her time in Greenwich Village with Eugene O'Neill (circa November, 1917 to January, 1918), Day had reportedly sung this song in various saloons, "matching the men drink for drink, and [she] knew ribald choruses…her companions had never heard of." See Sheaffer, *O'Neill*, 403; Boulton, *Part of a Long Story*, 40.

"The head hunters were after me, in the Phillipines," one was telling. "They'd gotten some of me buddies, and I swore they weren't going to get me. They'd cook and pass around the brains of a white man, and they claimed that the head of a white man made the heart of a lion."

Six Out of 175 Escape

"The stations were too far apart. They could surround us and cut us down."

"There were 175 of us and only six came out alive."

"It took six stretcher bearers to get me in. I lay there for twenty-four hours before they found me, and they'd only got me fifty yards, before one of them fell, then the other, and I got a shot in the hip. They needed six stretcher bearers then and finally they came out, and then two more got it."

Romance and thrill and high adventure! And with drink and music and revelry, in unpretentious surroundings in the old part of the city, where there is the atmosphere of Naples, and Paris and even of Shanghai—what more can women who crave excitement desire.

————

Tomorrow—The Thrills of Poker.[306]

---

[306] Day's exposé on poker actually appeared two days later. See "The Thrills of 1924," *The New Orleans Item*, February 28, 1924.

The Thrills of 1924

—Gossip has it, that one night, a month or so ago, an adventurous spirit seized one young woman who decided that she must stowaway on one of the huge freighters.

The New Orleans Item
Wednesday; February 27, 1924 (P. 5)

The Thrills of 1924[307]

—Gossip has it, that one night, a month or so ago, an adventurous spirit seized one young woman who decided that she must stowaway on one of the huge freighters.

Figure 20-Morning Call cafe, French Market, New Orleans. Interior view, 1930s. Unnamed WPA photographer-Works Project Administration photograph.

Everybody knows about the "Morning Call" that little coffee stand in the middle of the French Market.[308] There debutante and matron, working girl and blue stocking, sit elbow to elbow, cheek by jowl with what Evangeline Booth and Thomas Burke, both master stylists, would call denizens of the underworld, lost and abandoned creatures who slink in from the mist of the river front, evil faces from ill lit streets, murky shadows so impalpable as to be almost improbable.[309]

The "Morning Call" is to New Orleans what Child's Fifty-Ninth street restaurant is to New York. There is a harmless, though basically morbid (honesty compels us to say) thrill in sitting on the high stools at a late hour of the night and drinking the coffee which is really good and has a welcome warmth in this little circle of cold light hemmed in by the night

---

[307] This article represented the first of two unsigned "Thrills of 1924" columns written by Day, the other being "The Thrills of 1924" (February 28, 1924).

[308] The original Morning Call was founded in 1870 on Decatur Street, in the French Quarter. See "The Morning Call," http://old-new-orleans.com/NO_Morning_Call.html (accessed November 7, 2017).

[309] Both Evangeline Booth and Thomas Burke had written works devoted to "denizens of the underworld." See Evangeline Booth and Grace Livingston Hill, *The War Romance of the Salvation Army* (Philadelphia, PA: J. T. Lippincott, 1919); Thomas Burke, *Nights in London* (New York, NY: Henry Holt and Company, 1918). Day had previously written book reviews for Livingston Hill's *The Obsession of Victoria Gracen*, and Burke's *Limehouse Nights*. See D. D., "The Obsession of Victoria Gracen," *Chicago Examiner*, October 9, 1915; Dorothy Day, "Thousand and One Nights," *The Masses* 9, no. 12 (October, 1917): 30.

mists of the river. And there is an interesting waiter there with an Egyptian, or would you call it an Assyrian profile?[310]

Underworld for Cats

All around are the vegetable stalls, colorful and odorous, and far down the block, are the long dank alleys of the fish market, which we have decided is the underworld for cats. If you have ever noticed the fastidious grace which even the most bourgeoise of cats will avoid the wet and odorous, hastily scrubbing paws and jowl after any contamination, you will realize that only the most abandoned cats will sink to the horrid depths of the fish market. Why, we have even noticed kittens of tenderest age—however this is a story about humans.

It was this midnight or early morning coffee habit which led some of the younger set of New Orleans to discover that there is a watchman who will sometimes allow you to cross the tracks along the river front down in this section, go through the piers, and wander along the docks, a thrilling adventure even to the bravest on a misty night. Big freighters loom above the docks, so high when the river is up that they assume a wraithlike quality, and there is a swell on the river which you can hear rising and falling with a soft hiss against the piles. On a dry night there are spars to sit on, and the edge of the pier is raised so that it forms a convenient though terrifying seat. On some nights there is a moon.

Escort Registers Protest

Gossip has it, that one night, a month or so ago, an adventurous spirit seized one young woman who decided that she must stow away on one of the huge freighters. There was a convenient ladder—an escort (the thing simply isn't done without an escort, you know), and the night was clear enough so that she could see her way, and yet misty enough to cover her actions. She was an athletic young woman, and silent as a cat. Under protest, her escort followed and grumbled as he found a place by the side of her, on a pile of rope. It might have been the coffee they were drinking which made them overlook the fact that it might be well to find out when the boat was sailing before looking for the hold (if ships have holds nowadays) as all stowaways should.

After the two of them had wandered around the deck for a few minutes in search of someone who would give them the information, they had forgotten their purpose. Nevertheless, they found an affable and courteous young officer who took it for granted that it was perfectly all right for them to be where they were, and showed them around the ship, and tried to explain all about oil burners.

The young woman, however, had seen "The Hairy Ape" and wanted to find a ship with a stoke hold, so they took leave of the officer.[311] As to whether they found it or not, we don't know, because it was the young officer who told us of this escapade although to him it did not seem an escapade but a perfectly natural desire of a young woman to want to explore a ship in the dead of

---

[310] Day had fallen for a man (Lionel Moise) with an "Assyrian profile" in 1919. She later admitted that she was attracted to Moise because of his resemblance to Amenemhat III. See Day, *The Eleventh Virgin*, 251.

[311] Eugene O'Neill's *The Hairy Ape* was written in 1922. In the opening scene of the play, the lead character (Robert "Yank" Smith) stoked the engines of an ocean liner with coal.

the night. It is indeed hard to find a man who will be surprised at anything a woman will do nowadays. Anything may be expected of them.

In Black Draped Room

Then there is the gossip of the woman who had a studio down in "the quarter," that thrilling section of town, who was tired of the ordinary run of parties. This is truly gossip, because we heard it from someone who had heard it from someone else. And we don't know whether the someone else was at the party he mentioned, or not.

At any rate, the story goes that a large assembly gathered at the invitation of this woman who was widely known about town as an eccentric and an exotic, and sat in a black draped room with lowered lights while an orchestra with muted strings played Chopin's funeral march. It is not mentioned in the story we heard, whether any of the guests made any remarks about their hostess during this enforced wait for her appearance. If they had, like as not she would have appreciated these impromptu obituaries for her studied funeral party. When the black curtain which was suspended from one end of the room was finally drawn aside, the hostess was discovered to be lying on a black draped bier, clad in a long black gown, with her eyes closed and a lily on her breast. When she had appreciated the gasp of astonishment to its fullest, she languidly opened her eyes, rose from her couch, and joined her guests.

The story does not tell whether, like Des Esseintes, the French decadent, a dinner was served consistent with the opening of the party. [312] Russian rye bread, turtle soup, black ripe olives, smoked black pudding, game with sauces the color of licorice and truffle gravy, black heart cherries and rich dark wines.

Anything is Possible

But in New Orleans, the only city in the United States where cooking is a fine art not confined alone to the best restaurants, anything is possible. Nor was it stated the reason for this party. Everyone took it for a whim of a notoriously eccentric woman.

But here we find ourselves wandering from the "Morning Call," to the docks, to the decks of ships, to studio parties when what we were aiming at are the poker parties which add to the tensity of existence for the women of New Orleans.

However, have you ever noticed the hectic, fevered, wandering and irrelevant conversation of the present day woman who indulges in a continual and frenzied search for thrills? Then let this day's story act as an illustration and an object of what even two weeks of a thrilling life will do to you.

---

[312] Day is referencing Jean Des Esseintes, an eccentric literary character from Joris-Karl Huysmans' *À rebours* (also known as *Against Nature* or *Against the Grain*). Day had read most of Huysmans' novels, and she later admitted that her conversion to Catholicism was partly inspired by Huysmans' own conversion, as written in his autobiographical trilogy (*Là-bas*, *En route*, and *La Cathédrale*). See Day, *The Long Loneliness*, 107.

Carried to such an extreme that it becomes a vice; indulged in only by those women who can afford to lose, and lose continually, huge sums in the hopes of some day making a clean up; a pleasure that can be indulged in at the home, at the club, while traveling—this is a game of chance more widespread among women than roulette, mah jongg, bridge, or any other game of chance.

(To Be Continued)

The Thrills of 1924

—Other society women have been asked to join this little group but most of them are afraid. The stakes are too high.

The New Orleans Item
Thursday; February 28, 1924 (P. 12)
Evening Edition: (P. 11)

The Thrills of 1924

—Other society women have been asked to join this little group but most of them are afraid. The stakes are too high.

Women may go to the races and bet with men, they may play around the roulette wheel and the dice table with them in amicable intercourse, but they may not play poker with them. Whether it is because men think that this is a game which requires special skill, rather than luck, and cannot sit at the same table with a woman without arguing the age-old argument of the sexes, we don't know. Of course bridge is a gambling game, often for high stakes. But it is also a social and parlor game whereas poker is a "he-man" game, associated with the Klondike, the gold fields and the great open spaces where men are men—and they want to keep women out of it. But women won't be kept out. There is an intensity about this form of gambling which other games lack, a "kick" and a feeling of suspense which they must have. So they've gone ahead and formed clubs of their own at which they play day after day, and often far into the night.

Hates to See Bonehead Plays

"A man doesn't mind standing by seeing his wife, or the women he is with losing money at roulette," one man summed it up. "That's a chance. But he hates to see her making bonehead plays in poker, raising on a pair of jacks, trying to bluff. He hates to have his money thrown away, and he hates to have his wife making a fool out of herself and incidently him by showing how little she knows about the game, and what bad judgment she has. A man and wife can never take part in a game, because if one throws down the hand, the other will always pick it up to see what was being discarded, and to see if he or she couldn't have played it better. More divorces have been caused over poker!"

Excluded from Clubs

Women are excluded from all the clubs where poker is played about the city, but the truth of the matter is, they don't mind. And that's because alone, among their own sex, they can play as recklessly and as intuitively as they like.

The Thrills of 1924: Dorothy Day Encounters the "Underworld Denizens" of New Orleans

To begin at the top and go down, there is in this town, at the present time, a little group of six or eight women, the elite, the creme de la creme, most exclusive of society women who meet day after day and night after night for poker. "The sky's the limit," would be the motto of this club, if they called it a club, but they don't. So lost are they to all else but poker, that they take their afternoon and evening game for granted and make few other engagements. Sometimes the games start early in the afternoon and last until early the next morning and when you consider the game is stud poker, and there is betting on every card, and no limit to the betting, you can realize how enormous are the stakes.

Changes in Group

Of course the little group changes. A woman will lose her allowance, even her household money. She will pawn her jewelry, or having paste made even go so far as to sell it. And eventually she will tear her self away from the glittering vice, and someone else will step in to take her place. Or her nerves will become ragged, her face will take on lines and she won't be able to sleep at night.[313] All through her troubled dozing, she will see the cards being dealt out and she will bet and bet, and then when she looks at the buried card, she will find that it wasn't the ace she thought it, but a deuce, and she'll realize again that she has lost everything.

Other society women have been invited to join this little group, but most of them are afraid. The stakes are too high.

Prefers Slower Game

"I'm something of a fiend at poker," one woman told us, "but I couldn't play with them. I content myself with the little club I belong to which meets Tuesday and Thursday afternoons. It's stud poker, of course. Draw poker is too slow for women nowadays, though sometimes I wish they'd stick to draw. You have more of a chance to break even, and I prefer a slower game so that I have time to enjoy myself. Our husbands all think that we play a nickel limit but we've made it a 15-cent limit game. But even so I've lost $50 in an afternoon, and when you figure out we play twice a week, you can see what a few weeks of steady losing will do to your allowance."

So much for society women—those who can afford to lose.

For those who haven't entree to these New Orleans homes—for those whom the upper 10 would consider the bourgeoise, the demi-monde, and the transient there are clubs, the dues of which are from $15 to $25 worth of chips with which to enter a game.[314]

---

[313] Day was describing the effects of neurasthenia, a condition discussed in more detail in "The Thrills of 1924," on March 1, 1924.

[314] The "upper ten" is a phrase used to signify wealth, which originated in New York in the 1840s. Attributed to author Nathaniel Parker Willis, the term later became synonymous with the wealthiest individuals of any major city.

Clubs for Women

The chips bought, you are given a card which informs you, that having paid your dues for the coming year, you are a member in good standing and are entitled to the privileges of the club. There are hundreds of these clubs for men and some half dozen for women, through the city—in back of pool rooms, cigar stores, billiard parlors, and nominally they are social or athletic clubs.[315] But the club consists of a bare room, with a few tables and chairs, and the privileges mentioned on the membership card consist in sitting in a game and paying the house a cut of 10 to 25 percent from every pot.

There are club rooms in Gretna, Southport, Jefferson parish and in the heart of the city where women who have never seen each other before sit in a game. It isn't the companionableness or desirability of the women you are playing with; the game's the thing.

The fact that you don't know from Adam whom you are playing with, sometimes leads to disastrous consequences.

Woman Intoxicated

There is the story one club tells, how a well-dressed, and apparently refined woman sitting in the game showed, little by little, that she was under the influence of liquor. Although it is true of women of New Orleans that they drink very little, fearing the ravages not only of the climate but of games of chance, they are not the ones to judge too harshly those transients and weaker sisters who drink too much. Others in the game pretended to pay little attention to the signs of her condition, although every now and then she returned from powdering her nose a little more unsteady. It was an unsteadiness which would be noticeable only to the others who had an opportunity to watch her closely as she played. Of course she was losing steadily, and betting recklessly.

It is the custom at these games to drop out when you feel like it. There are usually only three games going on, and the clubrooms are often full. Many times there are other women sitting around, or watching the game, waiting for a chance to sit in.

Player Without a Conscience

On this afternoon, one of the women dropped out and another entered and the party became more exciting. Up to this time, the other women in the game with consideration, refused to take advantage of the other's condition to clean her up. But the newcomer had no conscience. From the moment she started to play, the others could see that she had been observing the condition of the other and was thinking to profit by it. The result was that the others threw scruples to the wind, and every one was out for herself. The game ended with the newcomer cleaning out not only the woman who was drinking, but the others as well. There was good feeling on all sides, however, for all agreed it had been a good game.

---

[315] An article published in the same issue of *The New Orleans Item* detailed a series of police raids in New Orleans on similar, "back room," establishments. See "Police Again Wage Raids on Handbooks," *The New Orleans Item*, February 28, 1924.

But opinion differed the next day. Rumor had it that the weak sister and the unscrupulous one had been working together and they had left town the night before, and that it was their practice to travel from town to town making their living by their wits.

In any city where there are clubs like those of New Orleans, one of the pair deliberately got drunk and entered the game. With no sign of recognition, the other would play, taking advantage of the fact that the others in the game would pay little attention to the sober one, while they were attempting to win from the drunken one.

This incident led to a little flurry among the clubs, however. Gamblers, whether they are men or women, are a philosophical lot and women are more so than men. Although men occasionally shoot each other over the card table, there is no record in New Orleans of a woman having done so yet.

(To Be Continued)

The Thrills of 1924

—The fever of the track has gotten into their blood and the next day will find them swarming and wriggling through'·e betting ring, shout- ing and screaming with enthusiam or silent and tense with dispair.

By DOROTHY DAY   [room at home. Even if it is pouring

The New Orleans Item
Friday; February 29, 1924 (P. 3)[316]

The Thrills of 1924

—The fever of the track has gotten into their blood and the next day will find them swarming and wriggling through the betting ring, shouting and screaming with enthusiasm or silent and tense with despair.

By DOROTHY DAY

"No improper language used in this room under penalty of being excluded from the grounds."

"No drinking or smoking allowed."

These signs affront the eyes of thousands of women who throng the race track daily and enter the betting ring between races. Some look at them and laugh, others look disgusted. "Something of an insult, eh?" one Englishwoman who was visiting the Fair Grounds, remarked.[317]

The two exquisitely gowned and furred women from Philadelphia, whose guest she probably was, looked around uncomfortably and told of Havre de Gras and Saratoga.[318] The youngest diverted the guest's critical scrutiny by starting a discussion on her losses.

"I've been coming out here for two weeks now, and aside from the first bet I made, I haven't cashed a one, although I've placed them every race. I've studied dope sheets, staying up hours to look up the record of the horses. I've memorized the sporting page until my eyes are most popping out. I've paid for tips every day. I've bet on hunches when I decided I couldn't 'dope

---

[316] Based upon the race results concerning the horses, Normal and Telescope, the events of this article occurred on February 26, 1924.

[317] Established in 1852, the Fair Grounds Race Track is located at 1751 Gentilly Boulevard. The surrounding area became known as City Park in 1872. See Bob Fortus, "The Fair Grounds: The Times-Picayune covers 175 years of New Orleans history," http://www.nola.com/175years/index.ssf/2012/02/the_fair_grounds_the_times-pic.html (accessed November 7, 2017).

[318] Within a year of the publishing of this article, Day's father helped to establish the Hialeah Park Race Track in Florida. See "John I. Day, Writer and Sports Editor," *The New York Times*, May 18, 1939.

them out' and then my hunches were eskew. If I placed a bet on a horse because I liked his colors or his name, I'd bet on him to win when I should have bet on him for place. They owe me a lot of money around here!"

Everybody Loves Horses

"Yes," said the Englishwoman dryly, her attention not to be diverted. "It seems to me that they could well afford to devote more space and furnishing to a better ring for the women. Racing's a gloriously healthy and legitimate sport. Everybody loves the horses and nothing is more exhilarating and exciting than spending your afternoons at the track. Women enjoy it as well as men and they pay out their money to make racing possible, and yet look how we're treated."

Figure 21-City Park-New Orleans Race Track, circa 1913, *The Times-Picayune* archive.

She looked around the room disdainfully as she spoke.

Downstairs at the Fair Grounds track, there is a huge, paper-strewn room, which appears to be as large as Madison Square Garden. The fruit stands and lunch counters here and there are like little oases in a desert. The room is always thronged with men and filled with cigarette smoke, but there are barnlike doors every few feet so that the room is well ventilated. Women are not allowed in this room, and if they wish to place a bet, they must go up into the grandstand, through a cave-like entrance, and then into a room not as large as your living room at home. Even if it is pouring rain women cannot go through the men's betting room but must get muddy and besplattered and wet, going around the grand stand to the enclosure to look at the horses and their jockeys.

Thousands Crowd Room

The woman's betting room, as we said, is a small room, slanting on one side with the grandstand, with not a window in it. On every fine day there are thousands of women who must crowd into this room and fight and tear their way to the three or four bookies, not only to place a bet, but to get information as to the horses, jockeys and odds on each race. Long before the gong rings which means that the race is over, the women have crowded into the room to find out which are the jockeys and what are the odds on the next race. There are only three little tables and three or four benches at which they may sit to study their "dope" sheets and figure out how they wish to bet. There are half a dozen glaring electric lights which show strained, smothered looking faces, pushing and swarming circles surrounding white but placid bookmakers.

Next to the betting room is a room from which you can order a cup of coffee or a sandwich. The little waitress, who serves the women, takes care of their umbrellas and superfluous wraps, also provides them with slips of paper on which to bet. She is a very little girl with blonde bobbed hair, and childish eyes. The cold day we were there, she was rather pinched and blue and wore an imitation fur coat under her white apron. Though frozen, she was jubilant, for she had played a hunch and won.

Dressing Room Worse

"I just picked a piece of paper up off the floor and there was the word 'Normal' on it," she was telling the sympathetic women she served, "so I knew a horse by that name was going to run in the next race, and I just had time to place a bet 6 to 1 to win."[319]

"Fortunately there's only one more race today, so you won't have time to lose much," one woman sighed. "If I only knew when to stop."

If the betting room is considered a pen and a disgrace to the track, the women's dressing room is worse. Although there seems to be plenty of space under the grandstand, the room is smaller than any theatre ladies' room. There is a colored maid to see that the floor and fittings are kept clean, but the walls and woodwork are dingy. In one corner there is a battered old couch but there are no other conveniences for resting.

Although it was an ugly, cold day, and there were fewer women at the track than there had been for weeks, even on the wettest days, the little hole was crowded with about 25 women who could scarcely move in the crush, who came there to find solace for their jangled nerves in smoking. There were two windows high up on one side of the room, but they were closed and you could have cut the air with a knife. If one has ever been in a room where men were smoking furiously and come away with hair and clothes reeking with the smell of tobacco, one wonders how women who are so gorgeously clad can risk crushing and odorizing their clothes in this way.

Get Closer Odds

"They seem to have it in for women at this track," one bejeweled creature was grumbling. "Look at these quarters. You'd think we were cattle. And the odds! Where they get ten to one downstairs, we get five to one up here. That kid in the restaurant got six to one on that long shot and they were getting ten and twelve to one downstairs. Of course you can send your money down, but you never know whether you're going to get it back, so you lose both ways."

"I bet on Telescope to win and cleaned up $600," one woman jubilated.[320]

---

[319] Per the racing results for New Orleans on Tuesday, February 26, 1924, Normal won the sixth race (one mile and a furlong) at the Fair Grounds. Driven by a jockey named Corcoran, Normal paid twelve-to-one odds to win, five-to-one to place, and five-to-two to show. See "Racing Results, New Orleans," *The Shreveport Times*, February 27, 1924.

[320] Per the racing results for New Orleans on Tuesday, February 26, 1924, Telescope won the fourth race (one mile) at the Fair Grounds. Driven by a jockey named Chalmers, Telescope paid seven-to-one odds to win, two-to-one to place, and one-to-two to show. See "Racing Results, New Orleans," February 27, 1924. *The Times-Picayune* had reported that the odds for Telescope were actually eight-to-one. See Wm. McG. Keefe, "Many Upsets Mark Racing Over Course Deep in Mud," *The Times-Picayune*, February 27, 1924.

"Yes, and if you'd bet downstairs, you'd cleaned up a thousand," another tried to dampen her enthusiasm.

"Never mind. I've made up for my losses today."

All you hear, it seems, is that they've made up their losses, never that they've won. They tell of others who win, and win huge sums, but one woman sniffed, "If they talk about winning fifty thousand, they mean five." Still our delusions weren't shattered. Five thousand seems a lot of money.

Women With Gray Hair

It isn't only the young and brilliantly dressed women who go to the races day after day, never missing. There are old women with gray hair, clutching programs, form sheets, and little books which tell the history and past achievements of every horse.

"Now how in the world did I know that he was a mud horse," one grandmotherly woman with a capacious bosom, was grumbling. She looked as though she should be home playing patience or placidly knitting, and the race track terminology sounded strange and incongruous from her lips.[321]

There are young girls in shabby imitation caracul coats, who looked as though they were shop girls out on a holiday, chewing pencils and jotting down figures on their programs. There are mothers and daughters together, women who looked as though they taught Bible class and led the choir in singing, school teachers and painted women. But the majority are amazing and beautiful creatures, whose clothes bespeak the Strand and the Rue de la Paix.[322]

And over and over again you hear, "I can't afford to come another day," or "Thank the Lord I have my ticket back to New York." "I shan't come tomorrow, that's all there is to it." But none of them mean it. The fever of the track has gotten into their blood and the next day will find them swarming and wriggling through the betting ring, shouting and screaming with enthusiasm, or silent and tense with despair.

---

[321] Playing patience referred to simple card games, such as Solitaire.

[322] Saenger's Strand Theatre was an upscale 2,000-seat venue, located at 229 Baronne Street in New Orleans. See "Strand Theatre: New Orleans, Louisiana," http://www.saengeramusements.com/theatres/nawlins/strand/nostrand.htm (accessed November 10, 2017).

THE NEW ORLEANS ITEM

The Thrills of 1924

BY DOROTHY DAY | with eyes that were like burnt coals

The New Orleans Item
Saturday; March 1, 1924 (P. 3)[323]

The Thrills of 1924

BY DOROTHY DAY

"No, we don't drink," one sophisticated young debutante confessed frankly. "That is, we don't drink much. Or you might put it that we don't drink much often. I noticed in the first article of this series in which I suppose I'll be quoted, the comment on the fact that women don't drink or smoke while they're gambling.[324] Gracious no! Gambling is enough of a strain on the looks without that. I go to bed sometimes with my face just stiff, frozen into a horrid mask, after an evening at dice or poker. And I sleep with my teeth clenched and wake up with a pain at the back of my neck. I don't know what I'll look like by the time I'm thirty.

"The temptation to drink is after the excitement is over. There's a fearful let-down then. Sunday evening's a bad time and you can't imagine the number of young women who proceed to get pie-eyed, or blotto, to use a still more elegant expression. Why last Sunday afternoon after we'd come in from the country club, we found—but no, I'll talk generally but not specifically.

"For the most part though, we're too fearfully concerned with our appearance to dissipate in that way."

"The society girl is probably the one who suffers least," one doctor who has offices in the Maison Blanche building and looks after the physical welfare of the upper ten, said. "That's because she has a good physique to start out with and some supervision from her elders and a great deal from her own class. But even so, at the end of the season, she is such a physical wreck that she has to take to her bed to recover. She has danced herself into a state of absolute physical exhaustion and is so physically tired that her nerves are deadened."

"Racing gets me more than anything else," one middle aged woman with eyes that were like burnt coals, said. "I can't keep away from the track and every day when the seventh race comes

---

[323] Although Day historian William D. Miller claimed that her "last signed articles for *The New Orleans Item* appeared in mid-March of 1924," no other signed articles were found after March 1, 1924. See William D. Miller, *Dorothy Day: A Biography* (San Francisco, CA: Harper and Row Publishers, 1982), 161.

[324] See Dorothy Day, "Women Crowd Fashionable Gambling Halls," *The New Orleans Item*, February 24, 1924.

around, I have all the symptoms you read of in patent medicine advertisements.[325] Every day I swear is going to be my last, but I've no strength of character left."

Dr. Oscar Dowling, president of the board of health, contributed his statement on the subject. "The effect of such diversions as horse racing, roulette or poker on the health of women who indulge, is hard to determine," he said. "Much depends on the individual, her temperament and physical inheritance.

"There are women, who season after season keep up a round of social engagements without visible effect. These fortunate women are endowed with a nervous system which correlates activities with the least amount of worry or annoyance. They are the women probably who can order their lives as they please and in whose minds there is no conflict. But the others are in constant conflict with the environment, its pleasures as well as responsibilities. These belong in the category of neuropaths and they often develop 'nervous breakdown,' technically, neurasthenia.

"Neurasthenia has been called by Europeans, 'the American disease' mainly because the life of the American people has been conducive to its development.[326] The worry and care of the modern woman, the inability to relax, in fact the almost total absence of any knowledge of how to relax is responsible for premature aging with all its attendant evils. The arteries harden, the heart dilates, the kidneys contract and in the years when she should be able to sit peacefully and watch life satisfactorily from the back row, she is stricken with disease. The social butterfly wears out her arteries and loses her looks if she leads a life that is too strenuous in the pursuit of pleasure."

---

[325] One period "patent medicine advertisement" claimed to cure symptoms of "nerve weakness, lost or depleted vigor, neurasthenia, premature age, impaired glandular activity and lack of animation and vital force." See "Man 74 Years Old is 'Rejuvenated' in 3 Weeks without Gland Operation," *The Shreveport Times*, August 12, 1923.

[326] Claude L. Wheeler, *"The American Disease" Neurasthenia: What are the Causes? What is the Remedy?* (New York, NY: The Bauer Chemical Company, 1909).

Conclusion

Although Day's time in New Orleans would be brief, her experiences in the Crescent City would bring her closer to conversion in the Catholic faith. Her exposure to the "underworld denizens" of the city would also aid her in her later dealings with people afflicted by vice: alcoholics, drug addicts, and those prone to theft or physical conflict.

For roughly three months, Day had lived in an apartment on St. Peter Street, overlooking the St. Louis Cathedral. She could not help but be fascinated by the large towers of the church, which dominated the horizon. Day later affirmed that she "…heard the Cathedral bells ringing for evening devotions," and attended Benediction services, which had a profound impact upon her.[327]

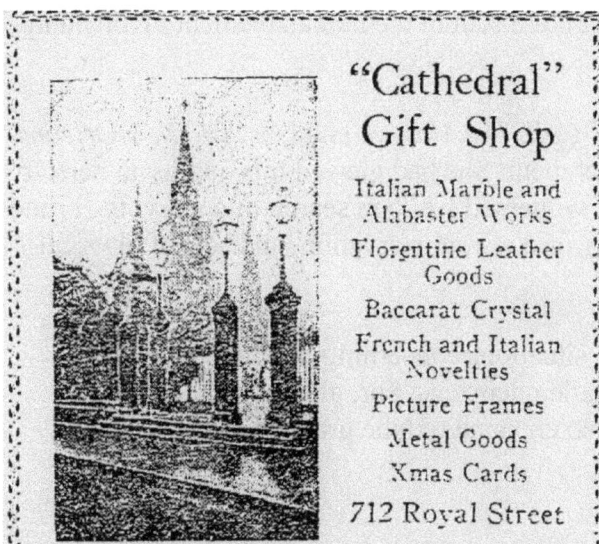

Figure 22-"Religious goods store," where Day possibly purchased her manual of prayers. *The Times-Picayune*, December 16, 1923.

In order to learn more about the Benediction hymns, Day had purchased a prayer manual from a nearby religious goods store. She recalled that she had read the Mass, and that:

I had to be at the office by seven in the morning and Sunday mornings I was too lazy to get up. But I learned a great deal from that little book. I did not know a single Catholic in New Orleans. If any of my associates were nominally Catholic, they did not let me know of it. There was no one for me to talk to. But my devotion was sincere and I continued to make "visits."[328]

Although there were many factors involved in Day's conversion—the birth of her daughter, certain authors (e.g. Fyodor Dostoyevsky, J. K. Huysmans, and William James), and hymns (e.g. *Te Deum* and *Benedicite*), she was equally moved by a rosary given to her as a Christmas present from her roommate, Mary Gordon.[329]

Day had recalled that she learned to say the Rosary at the evening services at the Cathedral, affirming that, "The very physical attitude of devotion of those about me made me bow my head."[330] A few years after Day had left New Orleans, she admitted in her diary that she kept using the rosary that Gordon had given her because it made her happy.[331]

Day converted to Catholicism in December of 1927. In December of 1932, Day co-founded the Catholic Worker movement; she would minister to the poor and marginalized unceasingly, for

---

[327] Day, *From Union Square to Rome*, 112.

[328] Ibid., 113.

[329] For an examination of the forces involved in Day's conversion, see Robert P. Russo, "The Saintly Chain of Causality in the Conversion of Dorothy Day," in *Dorothy Day and the Church: Past, Present and Future*, edited by Lance Richey and Adam DeVille (Valparaiso, IN: Solidarity Hall Press, 2016), 23-36.

[330] Day, *From Union Square to Rome*, 112.

[331] Ibid., 125-126.

the remainder of her life. Day also encountered many people addicted to vice. She well understood the aspects of our fallen human nature, as she had experienced much of the vice that afflicted those whom she had served. Day acutely understood her own brokenness, and she used this understanding to become closer to Christ in serving His poor.

It is highly ironic that two out of Day's last three articles for *The New Orleans Item* touched upon themes of neurasthenia. The condition, which affected both men and women, caused a lack of sleep, premature aging, and heart and arterial diseases. Also symptomatic of people suffering from addiction to vice, one has to wonder how Day—in the midst of a constant throng of "underworld denizens" was able to escape the Crescent City with little more than a black eye?

There are several reasons for Day's seemingly uncanny ability concerning her dealings with the broken masses. One must first allow that Day willingly accepted God's grace, which built upon her nature in a myriad of ways. However, one must not discount the human element involved in her growth toward greater sanctification.

Early in her career as a journalist for the *New York Call*, *The Masses*, and later *The New Orleans Item*, Day had developed the innate ability of detachment. She had viewed this quality in herself as a necessary response to the horrors that she had witnessed while in search of a story: the brutal victimization of the poor, mass riots concerning a world at war, starvation, and acts of physical violence during labor disputes.

Day's detachment had aided her in defusing many situations concerning potential violence, allowing her to deal more effectively with God's fallen denizens. For, although she may have encountered thrills in New Orleans in 1924, she also encountered the grace of God.

Coming in 2021…from Epiphany Press:

Not Contrary to Her Beliefs: The Probationary Nursing Career of Dorothy Day

By Robert P. Russo

An in-depth look at Day's nursing career, during the harrowing year of 1918 (The Spanish Influenza pandemic, the Malbone Street wreck, etc.).

GROUP OF STUDENT NURSES

Dorothy Day, fellow students, and staff, outside of the nurses' residence of Kings County Hospital in Brooklyn, New York (*The Outlook*, October 2, 1918, p. 181). Day is pictured in the second row, leaning into the first, fifth from the left.